JOEL

Zondervan Exegetical Commentary on the Old Testament

Editorial Board

General Editor
Daniel I. Block
Gunther H. Knoedler Professor Emeritus of Old Testament, Wheaton College

Associate Editors
Hélène Dallaire
Professor of Old Testament and Director of Messianic Judaism Programs, Denver Seminary

Stephen Dempster
Associate Professor of Religious Studies, Crandall University

Jason S. DeRouchie
Associate Professor of Old Testament, Bethlehem College and Seminary

Miles V. Van Pelt
Alan Belcher Professor of Old Testament and Biblical Languages, Reformed Theological Seminary

Zondervan Editors
Katya Covrett, editorial advisor
Nancy Erickson, executive editor

JOEL
Despair and Deliverance in the Day of the Lord

ZONDERVAN Exegetical Commentary ON THE Old Testament

A DISCOURSE ANALYSIS OF THE HEBREW BIBLE

JOEL BARKER

DANIEL I. BLOCK
General Editor

> The Hebrew text is from Deuteronomy 31:11–13, which highlights the importance of "hearing" the voice of Scripture:
>
> When all Israel comes to appear before יהוה your God at the place he will choose, you shall read this Torah before them in their hearing. Assemble the people—men, women and children, and the foreigners residing in your towns—so they can *listen* and learn to fear יהוה your God and follow carefully all the words of this Torah. Their children, who do not know this Torah, must *hear* it and learn to fear יהוה your God as long as you live in the land you are crossing the Jordan to possess. (NIV, modified)

ZONDERVAN ACADEMIC

Joel
Copyright © 2020 by Joel Barker

Published in Grand Rapids, Michigan, by Zondervan. Zondervan is a registered trademark of The Zondervan Corporation, L.L.C., a wholly owned subsidiary of HarperCollins Christian Publishing, Inc.

Requests for information should be addressed to customercare@harpercollins.com.

Zondervan titles may be purchased in bulk for educational, business, fundraising, or sales promotional use. For information, please email SpecialMarkets@Zondervan.com.

ISBN 978-0-310-94238-2 (hardcover)

Unless otherwise noted, Scripture quotations are the author's own translations. Scripture quotations noted as NIV are taken from The Holy Bible, New International Version®, NIV®. Copyright © 1973, 1978, 1984, 2011 by Biblica, Inc.® Used by permission of Zondervan. All rights reserved worldwide. www.Zondervan.com. The "NIV" and "New International Version" are trademarks registered in the United States Patent and Trademark Office by Biblica, Inc.®

Any internet addresses (websites, blogs, etc.) and telephone numbers in this book are offered as a resource. They are not intended in any way to be or imply an endorsement by Zondervan, nor does Zondervan vouch for the content of these sites and numbers for the life of this book.

No part of this publication may be reproduced, stored in a retrieval system, or transmitted in any form or by any means—electronic, mechanical, photocopy, recording, or any other—except for brief quotations in printed reviews, without the prior permission of the publisher.

Cover design: Tammy Johnson
Interior design: Beth Shagene

Printed in the United States of America

*To Abigail, Hannah, and Isaac. May you always live in the hope
and blessing that God lavished on your namesakes*

Contents

Series Introduction 9
Author's Preface and Acknowledgments 13
Abbreviations 15
Select Bibliography 17

Translation of Joel 21
Introduction to Joel 27
Commentary on Joel 45

Scripture Index 171
Subject Index 181
Author Index 185

Series Introduction

Prospectus

Modern audiences are often taken in by the oratorical skill and creativity of preachers and teachers. However, they tend to forget that the authority of proclamation is directly related to the correspondence of the key points of the sermon to the message the biblical authors were trying to communicate. Since we confess that "all Scripture [including the entirety of the OT] is God-breathed and is useful for teaching, rebuking, correcting and training in righteousness, so that [all God's people] may be thoroughly equipped for every good work" (2 Tim 3:16–17 NIV), it seems essential that those who proclaim its message should pay close attention to the rhetorical agendas of biblical authors. Too often modern readers, including preachers, are either baffled by OT texts, or they simply get out of them that for which they are looking. Many commentaries available to pastors and teachers try to resolve the dilemma either through word-by-word and verse-by-verse analysis or synthetic theological reflections on the text without careful attention to the flow and argument of that text.

The commentators in this series recognize that too little attention has been paid to biblical authors as rhetoricians, to their larger rhetorical and theological agendas, and especially to the means by which they tried to achieve their goals. Like effective communicators in every age, biblical authors were driven by a passion to communicate a message. So we must inquire not only what that message was, but also what strategies they used to impress their message on their hearers' ears. This reference to "hearers" rather than to readers is intentional, since the biblical texts were written to be heard. Not only were the Hebrew and Christian Scriptures composed to be heard in the public gathering of God's people but also before the invention of moveable type, and few would have had access to their own copies of the Scriptures. While the contributors to this series acknowledge with Paul that every Scripture—that is, every passage in the Hebrew Bible—is God-breathed, we also recognize that the inspired authors possessed a vast repertoire of rhetorical and literary strategies. These included not only the special use of words and figures of speech, but also the deliberate selection, arrangement, and shaping of ideas.

The primary goal of this commentary series is to help serious students of Scripture, as well as those charged with preaching and teaching the Word of God, to hear the messages of Scripture as biblical authors intended them to be heard. While we recognize the timelessness of the biblical message, the validity of our interpretation and the authority with which we teach the Scriptures are related directly to the extent to which we have grasped the message intended by the author in the first place. Accordingly, when dealing with specific texts, the authors of the commentaries in this series are concerned with three principal questions: (1) What are the principal theological points the biblical writers are making? (2) How do biblical writers make those points? (3) What significance does the message of the present text have for understanding the message of the biblical book within which it is embedded and the message of the Scriptures as a whole? The achievement of these goals requires careful attention to the way ideas are expressed in the OT, including the selection and arrangement of materials and the syntactical shaping of the text.

To most readers syntax operates primarily at the sentence level. But recent developments in biblical study, particularly advances in rhetorical and discourse analysis, have alerted us to the fact that syntax operates also at the levels of the paragraph, the literary unit being analyzed, and the composition as a whole. Discourse analysis, also called macro syntax, studies the text beyond the level of the sentence (sentence syntax), where the paragraph serves as the basic unit of thought. Those contributing to this series recognize that this type of study may be pursued in a variety of ways. Some will prefer a more bottom-up approach, where clause connectors and transitional features play a dominant role in analysis. Others will pursue a more top-down approach, where genre or literary form begins the discussion. However, we all understand that both approaches are required to understand fully the method and the message of the text. For this reason, the ultimate value of discourse analysis is that it allows the text to set the agenda in biblical interpretation.

One of the distinctive goals for this series is to engage the biblical text using some form of discourse analysis to understand not only what the text says, but also how it says it. While attention to words or phrases is still essential, contributors to this commentary series will concentrate on the flow of thought in the biblical writings, both at the macroscopic level of entire compositions and at the microscopic level of individual text units. In so doing we hope to help other readers of Scripture grasp both the message and the rhetorical force of OT texts. When we hear the message of Scripture, we gain access to the mind of God.

Format of the Commentary

The format of this series is designed to achieve the goals summarized above. Accordingly, each volume in the series will begin with an introduction to the book being explored. In addition to answering the usual questions of date, authorship, and provenance of the composition, commentators will highlight what they consider to be the main theological themes of the book and then discuss broadly how the style and structure of the book develop those themes. This discussion will include a coherent outline of the contents of the book, demonstrating the contribution each part makes to the development of the principal themes.

The commentaries on individual text units that follow will repeat this process in greater detail. Although complex literary units will be broken down further, the commentators will address the following issues.

1. **The Main Idea of the Passage:** A one- or two-sentence summary of the key ideas the biblical author seeks to communicate.
2. **Literary Context:** A brief discussion of the relationship of the specific text to the book as a whole and to its place within the broader arguments.
3. **Translation and Exegetical Outline:** Commentators will provide their own translations of each text, formatted to highlight the discourse structure of the text and accompanied by a coherent outline that reflects the flow and argument of the text.
4. **Structure and Literary Form:** An introductory survey of the literary structure and rhetorical style adopted by the biblical author, highlighting how these features contribute to the communication of the main idea of the passage.
5. **Explanation of the Text:** A detailed commentary on the passage, paying particular attention to how the biblical authors select and arrange their materials and how they work with words, phrases, and syntax to communicate their messages. This will take up the bulk of most commentaries.
6. **Canonical and Practical Significance:** The commentary on each unit will conclude by building bridges between the world of the biblical author and other biblical authors and with reflections on the contribution made by this unit to the development of broader issues in biblical theology—particularly on how later OT and NT authors have adapted and reused the motifs in question. The discussion will also include brief reflections on the significance of the message of the passage for readers today.

The way this series treats biblical books will be uneven. Commentators on smaller books will have sufficient scope to answer fully each of the issues listed above on each unit of text. However, limitations of space preclude full treatment of every text for the larger books. Instead, commentators will guide readers through #1–4 and 6 for every literary unit, but Full Explanation of the Text (#5) will be selective, generally limited to twelve to fifteen literary units deemed most critical for hearing the message of the book.

In addition to these general introductory comments, we should alert readers of this series to several conventions that we follow. First, the divine name in the OT is presented as YHWH. The form of the name–represented by the Tetragrammaton,

יהוה–is a particular problem for scholars. The practice of rendering the divine name in Greek as κύριος (=Heb. אֲדֹנָי, "Adonay") is carried over into English translations as "Lord," which represents Hebrew יהוה and distinguishes it from "Lord," which represents Hebrew אֲדֹנָי. But this creates interpretive problems, for the connotations and implications of referring to someone by name or by title are quite different. When rendered as a name, English translations have traditionally vocalized יהוה as "Jehovah," which seems to combine the consonants of יהוה with the vowels of אֲדֹנָי. However, today non-Jewish scholars often render the name as "Yahweh," recognizing that "Jehovah" is an artificial construct.

Second, frequently the verse numbers in the Hebrew Bible differ from those in our English translations. Since the commentaries in this series are based on the Hebrew text, the Hebrew numbers will be the default numbers. Where the English numbers differ, they will be provided in square brackets (e.g., Joel 4:12[3:12]).

Third, when discussing specific biblical words or phrases, these will be represented in Hebrew font and in translation, except where the transliterated form is used in place of an English term, either because no single English expression captures the Hebrew word's wide range meaning (e.g., *ḥesed* for חֶסֶד, rather than "lovingkindness"), or when it functions as a title or technical expression not readily captured in English (e.g., *gōʾēl* for גֹּאֵל, rather than "kinsman redeemer").

Daniel I. Block, general editor

Author's Preface and Acknowledgments

The book of Joel captures the imagination with vivid images of locusts, invasion, and cosmos-rending signs in the heavens. It also pictures abundant fertility for the land, an outpouring of God's spirit, and signs of God's authority over all nations. Joel uses these images to reflect on the nature of the day of the Lord and its implications for God's people. My study of Joel began with my doctoral thesis in which I examined it through a rhetorical-critical lens.[1] Those insights undergird this commentary and I have supplemented them with study of the text's discourse structure in order to show how Joel guides his audience from despair to deliverance in the day of the Lord, rooted in his understanding of the character of God. This commentary also has allowed me to explore how Joel's understanding of God, his people, and his creation find theological resonance throughout the canon.

I am very grateful for the support I have received throughout this project. I must first thank Stephen Dempster, who opened the door for this opportunity after a dinner conversation at a national meeting of the Evangelical Theological Society. Miles Van Pelt and Daniel Block have offered numerous helpful comments and corrections throughout this process. The editorial team at Zondervan do an excellent job of supporting authors and guiding our work to publication. I would also like to thank my colleagues and the administration of Heritage College and Seminary in Cambridge, Ontario who have been steadfastly encouraging and supportive. It is a privilege to teach at an institution that is deeply committed to the faithful proclamation of the Scriptures and to shaping our students by its truth. My hope is that this work contributes to our mission of serving God with passion and excellence.

Finally, I am deeply grateful to my wife Karen, whose love and support makes it possible to meet the many demands of an academic career. Our three children, Abigail, Hannah, and Isaac bring plenty of love, joy, and chaos into our lives. I am also thankful for my parents, who instilled in me a love for Christ and his kingdom, little knowing how well the name they gave me would fit.

---

1. Joel Barker, *From the Depths of Despair to the Promise of Presence: A Rhetorical Reading of the Book of Joel* (Siphrut 11; Winona Lake, IN: Eisenbrauns, 2014).

Abbreviations

Abbreviations for books of the Bible, pseudepigrapha, rabbinic works, papyri, classical works, and the like are readily available in sources such as the *SBL Handbook of Style* and are not included here.

AB	Anchor Bible
AJSL	*American Journal of Semitic Languages and Literatures*
ANEM	Ancient Near East Monographs
ANETS	Ancient Near Eastern Texts and Studies
AOAT	Alter Orient und Altes Testament
BASOR	*Bulletin of the American Schools of Oriental Research*
BBR	*Bulletin for Biblical Research*
BCE	before the Common Era
BHRG	*Biblical Hebrew Reference Grammar*
BibInt	Biblical Interpretation Series
BZAW	Beiheft zur Zeitschrift für die alttestamentliche Wissenschaft
CBQ	*Catholic Bible Quarterly*
CSHB	Critical Studies in the Hebrew Bible
CTM	*Concordia Theological Monthly*
GKC	*Gesenius' Hebrew Grammar*. Edited by E. Kautzch. Translated by Arthur E. Cowley. 2nd ed. Oxford: Clarendon, 1910
HSM	Harvard Semitic Monographs
HUCA	*Hebrew Union College Annual*
IEJ	*Israel Exploration Journal*
IHBS	*An Introduction to Biblical Hebrew Syntax*. Bruce K. Waltke and Michael O'Connor. Winona Lake, IN: Eisenbrauns, 1990
ITC	International Theological Commentary
JANES	*Journal of the Ancient Near Eastern Society*
JBL	*Journal of Biblical Literature*
JBS	Jerusalem Biblical Studies
JETS	*Journal of the Evangelical Theological Society*
JHS	*Journal of Hebrew Scriptures*

JNES	*Journal of Near Eastern Studies*
JNSL	*Journal of Northwest Semitic Languages*
Joüon	*A Grammar of Biblical Hebrew*. Paul Joüon. Translated and revised by T. Muraoka. 2 vols. Rome: Pontifical Biblical Institute, 1991
JSOT	*Journal for the Study of the Old Testament*
JSOTSup	Journal for the Study of the Old Testament Supplement Series
JSS	*Journal of Semitic Studies*
KAT	Kommentar zum Alten Testamentum
LHBOTS	Library of Hebrew Bible/Old Testament Studies
LXX	Septuagint
MBPS	Mellen Biblical Press Series
NAC	New American Commentary
NCBC	New Century Bible Commentary
NETS	*A New English Translation of the Septuagint*. Edited by Albert Pietersma and Benjamin G. Wright. New York: Oxford University Press, 2007
NICOT	New International Commentary on the Old Testament
NIGTC	New International Greek Testament Commentary
NIVAC	New International Version Application Commentary
OTL	Old Testament Library
OtSt	*Oudtestamentische Studiën*
RB	*Revue Biblique*
RSR	*Revue des sciences religieuses*
SBLAB	Society of Biblical Literature Academia Biblica
SBLEJL	Society of Biblical Literature Early Judaism and its Literature
SBLHB	Society of Biblical Literature Hebrew Bible/Old Testament
SBLMS	Society of Biblical Literature Monograph Series
SBLSS	Society of Biblical Literature Symposium Series
SHBC	Smyth & Helwys Bible Commentary
SSN	Studia Semitica Neerlandica
TDOT	*Theological Dictionary of the Old Testament*. Edited by G. Johannes Botterweck and Helmer Ringgren. Translated by John T. Willis et al. Grand Rapids: Eerdmans, 1964–1976
UUÅ	Uppsala Universitets Årsskrift
VT	*Vetus Testamentum*
VTSup	Supplements to Vetus Testamentum
WBC	Word Biblical Commentary
WMANT	Wissenschaftliche Monographien zum Alten und Neuen Testament
WEC	Wycliffe Exegetical Commentary
WTJ	*Westminster Theological Journal*
ZAW	*Zeitschrift für die alttestamentliche Wissenschaft*
ZECOT	Zondervan Exegetical Commentary on the Old Testament

Select Bibliography

Ahlström, G. W. *Joel and the Temple Cult of Jerusalem*. VTSup XXI. Leiden: E. J. Brill, 1971.

Allen, Leslie C. *The Books of Joel, Obadiah, Jonah and Micah*. NICOT. Grand Rapids: Eerdmans, 1976.

Andiñach, Pablo R. "The Locusts in the Message of Joel." *VT* 42 (1992): 433–41.

Assis, Elie. *The Book of Joel: A Prophet Between Calamity and Hope*. LHBOTS 581. New York: Bloomsbury, 2013.

Barker, Joel. *From the Depths of Despair to the Promise of Presence: A Rhetorical Reading of the Book of Joel*. Siphrut 11. Winona Lake, IN: Eisenbrauns, 2014.

Barton, John. "History and Rhetoric in the Prophets." Pages 51–64 in *The Bible as Rhetoric: Studies in Biblical Persuasion and Credibility*. Edited by Martin Warner. Warwick Studies in Philosophy and Literature. London: Routledge, 1990.

———. *Joel and Obadiah: A Commentary*. OTL. Louisville: Westminster John Knox, 2001.

Bechtel, Lyn M. "The Perception of Shame within the Divine-Human Relationship in Biblical Israel." Pages 79–92 in *Uncovering Ancient Stones: Essays in Memory of H. Neil Richardson*. Edited by Lewis M. Hopfe. Winona Lake, IN: Eisenbrauns, 1994.

Ben Zvi, Ehud and James Nogalski. *Two Sides of a Coin: Juxtaposing Views on Interpreting the Book of the Twelve / the Twelve Prophetic Books*. Analecta Gorgiana 201. Piscataway: Gorgias, 2009.

Bergler, Siegried. *Joel als Schriftinterpret*. Frankfurt am Main: Peter Lang, 1988.

Boda, Mark J. "From Complaint to Contrition: Peering Through the Liturgical Window of Jer 14,1–15,4." *Zeitschrift für die alttestamentliche Wissenschaft* 113 (2001): 186–97.

Bolin, Thomas W. *Freedom beyond Forgiveness: The Book of Jonah Re-Examined*. JSOTSup 236. Sheffield: Sheffield Academic, 1997.

Chance, John K. "The Anthropology of Honor and Shame: Culture, Values and Practice." *Semeia* 68 (1996): 139–51.

Chisholm, Robert. "When Prophecy Appears to Fail, Check Your Hermeneutic." *JETS* 53 (2010): 561–78.

Coggins, Richard J. *Joel and Amos*. NCBC. Sheffield: Sheffield Academic, 2000.

Crenshaw, James L. "Freeing the Imagination: The Conclusion of the Book of Joel." Pages 129–48 in *Prophecy and Prophets: The Diversity of Contemporary Issues in Scholarship*. Edited by Yehoshua Gitay. Atlanta: Scholars, 1997.

———. "The Expression MÎ YÔDĒA in the Hebrew Bible." *VT* 36 (1986): 274–88.

———. *Joel*. AB 24c. New York: Doubleday, 1995.

———. "Who Knows What YHWH Will Do? The Character of God in the Book of Joel." Pages 185–96 in *Fortunate the Eyes That See: Essays in Honor of David Noel Freedman in Celebration of His Seventieth Birthday*. Edited by Astrid B.

Beck, Andrew H. Bartelt, Paul R. Raabe, and Chris A. Franke. Grand Rapids: Eerdmans, 1995.

Deist, Ferdinand E. "Parallels and Reinterpretation in the Book of Joel: A Theology of Yom Yahweh?" Pages 63–80 in *Text and Context: Old Testament and Semitic Studies for F. C. Fensham*. Edited by W. Claasen. JSOTSup 48. Sheffield: Sheffield Academic, 1988.

Dillard, Raymond B. "Joel." Pages 239–314 in *The Minor Prophets: An Exegetical and Expository Commentary*. Edited by Thomas Edward McComiskey. Grand Rapids: Baker, 1992.

Dozeman, Thomas B. "Inner-Biblical Interpretation of Yahweh's Gracious and Compassionate Character." *JBL* 108 (1989): 207–23.

Everson, Joseph A. "The Days of Yahweh." *JBL* 93 (1974): 329–37.

Fensham, F. C. "A Possible Origin of the Concept of the Day of the Lord." Pages 90–97 in *Biblical Essays: Proceedings of the Ninth Meeting of die Ou-Testamentiese Werkgemeenskap in Sud-Afrika*. Bepeck: Potchefstroom Herald, 1966.

Finley, Thomas J. *Joel, Amos, Obadiah*. WEC. Chicago: Moody Press, 1990.

Fishbane, Michael. *Biblical Interpretation in Ancient Israel*. New York: Clarendon, 1985.

Futato, Mark D. "Sense Relations in the 'Rain' Domain of the Old Testament." Pages 81–94 in *Imagery and Imagination in Biblical Literature: Essays in Honor of Aloysius Fitzgerald, F. S. C.* Edited by Lawrence Boadt and Mark S. Smith. Washington: Catholic Biblical Association of America, 2001.

Garrett, Duane A. *Hosea, Joel*. NAC 19A. Nashville: Broadman & Holman, 1997.

Hayes, Katherine M. *The Earth Mourns: Prophetic Metaphor and Oral Aesthetic*. SBLAB 8. Leiden: Brill, 2002.

------. "When None Repents, Earth Laments: The Chorus of Lament in Jeremiah and Joel." Pages 119–44 in *Seeking the Favor of God—Volume 1: The Origins of Penitential Prayer in Second Temple Judaism*. Edited by Mark J. Boda, Daniel K. Falk, and Rodney A. Werline. Atlanta: Society of Biblical Literature, 2006.

Houston, Walter. "What Did the Prophets Think They Were Doing? Speech Acts and Prophetic Discourse in the Old Testament." *Biblical Interpretation* 1 (1993): 167–88.

Howard Jr., David M. "Rhetorical Criticism in Old Testament Studies." *BBR* 4 (1994): 87–104.

Hurowitz, Victor. "Joel's Locust Plague in Light of Sargon II's Hymn to Nanaya." *JBL* 112 (1993): 597–603.

Joosten, Jan. *The Verbal System of Biblical Hebrew: A New Synthesis Elaborated on the Basis of Classical Prose*. Jerusalem Biblical Studies 10. Jerusalem: Simor, 2012.

Kapelrud, Arvid S. *Joel Studies*. UUÅ 4. Uppsala: A. B. Lundequist, 1948.

Kelly, Joseph. "Joel, Jonah, and the YHWH Creed." *JBL* 132 (2013): 805–26.

Kennedy, George A. *New Testament Interpretation through Rhetorical Criticism*. Chapel Hill: University of North Carolina Press, 1984.

Kessler, John A. "The Shaking of the Nations: An Eschatological View." *JETS* 30 (1987): 159–66.

Klein, Ralph W. "The Day of the Lord." *CTM* 39 (1968): 517–25.

Landy, Francis. "Three Sides of a Coin: In Conversation with Ben Zvi and Nogalski, *Two Sides of a Coin*." *JHS* 10 (2010). No Pages. Online: http://www.jhsonline.org/Articles/article_139.pdf.

Linville, James R. "The Day of Yahweh and the Mourning of the Priests in Joel." Pages 98–114 in *The Priests in the Prophets: The Portrayal of Priests, Prophets and Other Religious Specialists in the Latter Prophets*. Edited by Lester L. Grabbe and Alice Ogden Bellis. JSOTSup 408. London: T&T Clark, 2004.

Loewenstamm, S. E. "The Trembling of Nature During Theophany." Pages 173–89 in *Comparative Studies in Biblical and Ancient Oriental Literature*. AOAT 24. Neukirchen-Vluyn: Neukirchener, 1980.

Luria, Ben Zion. "And a Fountain Shall Spring Forth from the House of the Lord." *Dor le Dor* 10 (1981): 48–58.

Magonet, Jonathan. *Form and Meaning: Studies in Literary Technique in the Book of Jonah*. Frankfurt: Peter Lang, 1976.

Möller, Karl. *A Prophet in Debate: The Rhetoric of Persuasion in the Book of Amos*. JSOTSup 372. Sheffield: Sheffield Academic, 2003.

Moshavi, Adina. "Can a Positive Rhetorical Question Have a Positive Answer in the Bible?" *JSS* 56 (2011): 253–73.

———. "Interrogative: Biblical Hebrew." Pages 306–16 in vol. 2 of *Encyclopedia of Hebrew Language and Linguistics*. Edited by Geoffrey Khan. Leiden: Brill, 2013.

———. "Rhetorical Question or Assertion? The Pragmatics of הֲלוֹא in Biblical Hebrew. *JANES* 32 (2011): 91–105.

Nash, Kathleen S. "The Palestinian Agricultural Year and the Book of Joel." PhD diss., Catholic University of America, 1989.

Nogalski, James. *The Book of the Twelve: Hosea—Jonah*. SHBC. Macon: Smyth & Helwys, 2011.

———. "Joel as 'Literary Anchor' for the Book of the Twelve." Pages 91–109 in *Reading and Hearing the Book of the Twelve*. Edited by James Nogalski and Marvin A. Sweeney. SBLSS 15. Atlanta: Society of Biblical Literature, 2000.

Ogden, Graham S. and Richard R. Deutsch. *Joel & Malachi: A Promise of Hope—A Call to Obedience*. ITC. Grand Rapids: Eerdmans, 1987.

Prinsloo, Willem S. *The Theology of the Book of Joel*. BZAW 163. Berlin: Walter de Gruyter, 1985.

Raabe, Paul R. "Why Prophetic Oracles Against the Nations?" Pages 236–57 in *Fortunate the Eyes that See: Essays in Honor of David Noel Freedman in Celebration of His Seventieth Birthday*. Edited by Astrid A. Beck, Andrew H. Bartelt, Paul R. Raabe, and Chris A. Franke. Grand Rapids: Eerdmans, 1995.

Redditt, Paul L. "The Book of Joel and Peripheral Prophecy." *CBQ* 48 (1986): 225–40.

Rendtorff, Rolf. "'Alas for the Day!' The 'Day of the Lord' in the Book of the Twelve." Pages 186–97 in *God in the Fray: A Tribute to Walter Brueggemann*. Edited by Todd Linafelt and Timothy K. Beal. Minneapolis: Fortress, 1998.

Schart, Aaron. "Deathly Silence and Apocalyptic Noise: Observations on the Soundscape of the Book of the Twelve." *Verbum et Ecclesia* 31 (2010): No Pages.

Seitz, Christopher R. *Joel*. ITC. London: Bloomsbury, 2016.

Simkins, Ronald A. "God, History, and the Natural World in the Book of Joel." *CBQ* 55 (1993): 435–52.

———. "'Return to Yahweh': Honor and Shame in Joel." *Semeia* 68 (1994): 41–54.

———. *Yahweh's Activity in History and Nature in the Book of Joel*. Ancient Near Eastern Texts and Studies 10. Lewiston: Edwin Mellen, 1991.

Stiebert, Johanna. *The Construction of Shame in the Hebrew Bible: The Prophetic Contribution*. JSOTSup 346. London: Sheffield Academic, 2002.

Strazicich, John. *Joel's Use of Scripture and the Scripture's Use of Joel: Appropriation and Resignification in Second Temple Judaism and Early Christianity*. BibInt 82. Leiden: Brill, 2007.

Stuart, Douglas. *Hosea-Jonah*. WBC 31. Waco: Word Books, 1987.

Sweeney, Marvin A. *The Twelve Prophets: Vol. 1.* Berit Olam. Collegeville, Minn.: Liturgical, 2000.

Toffelmire, Colin. *A Discourse and Register Analysis of the Book of Joel.* SSN 66. Leiden: Brill, 2016.

Troxel, Ronald L. "Confirming Coherence in Joel 3 with Cognitive Grammar." *ZAW* 125 (2013): 578–92.

_____. *Joel: Scope, Genre(s) and Meaning.* CSHB 6. Winona Lake, IN: Eisenbrauns, 2015.

_____. "The Problem of Time in Joel." *JBL* 132 (2013): 77–95.

Tucker, Gene M. "Prophetic Superscriptions and the Growth of a Canon." Pages 56–70 in *Canon and Authority.* Edited by Burke O. Long and George W. Coats. Philadelphia: Fortress, 1977.

van der Merwe, C. J. H. "Another Look at the Biblical Hebrew Focus Particle גַּם." *JSS* 54 (2009): 313–32.

van der Merwe, C. J. H. and Ernst Wendland. "Marked Word Order in the Book of Joel," *JNSL* 36 (2010): 109–30.

Watts, John D. W. "Superscriptions and Incipits in the Book of the Twelve." Pages 110–24 in *Reading and Hearing the Book of the Twelve.* Edited by James Nogalski and Marvin A. Sweeney. SBLSS 15. Atlanta: Society of Biblical Literature, 2000.

Wendland, Ernst R. *The Discourse Analysis of Hebrew Prophetic Literature.* Mellen Biblical Press Series 40. Lewiston, NY: Edwin Mellen, 1995.

_____. *Prophetic Rhetoric: Case Studies in Text Analysis and Translation.* 2nd ed. Dallas: SIL International, 2014.

Wolff, Hans Walter. *Joel and Amos.* Hermeneia. Philadelphia: Fortress, 1977.

Yates, Gary E. "The Problem of Repentance and Relapse as a Unifying Theme in the Book of the Twelve." *Themelios* 41 (2016): 248–62.

Translation of Joel

Joel 1

Superscription

¹The word of YHWH that came to Joel, son of Pethuel.

Despair on Account of the Locusts

²Hear this, o elders! Give ear, o inhabitants of the land! Has this been in your day? Or even in the days of your fathers? ³Proclaim concerning this to your sons, and your sons to their sons, and their sons to the generation after. ⁴The remainder from the gnawing locust, the swarming locust ate, and the remainder from the swarming locust, the creeping locust ate, and the remainder from the creeping locust, the stripping locust ate.

⁵Awake, o drunkards! And weep! Wail, all drinkers of wine, on account of the sweet wine, for it is cut off from your mouths. ⁶Now a nation has come up upon my land, many, and there is no counting [them]. Its teeth are the teeth of a lion, and the fangs of a lioness are to it. ⁷It has made my vine a desolation, and my fig tree, a splinter. It has completely stripped it bare, and made white its tendrils.

⁸Wail like a virgin clothed in sackcloth, concerning the lord of her youth! ⁹Cut off are the grain-offering and drink-offering from the house of YHWH. The priests, the ministers of YHWH, mourn. ¹⁰The field is destroyed. The earth mourns, for the grain is destroyed, the new wine dries up, the fresh oil fails.

¹¹Be ashamed, o farmers! Wail, o vine-grower, on account of the wheat and barley, for destroyed is the harvest of the field! ¹²The vine dries up, and the fig tree withers. The pomegranate tree, even the fig tree and the apple tree, all the trees of the field have dried up. Even joy is dried up from the sons of man.

¹³Gird up and mourn, o priests! Wail, o ministers of the altar! Enter, spend the night in sackcloth, o ministers of my God! The grain-offering and drink-offering are withheld from the house of your God. ¹⁴Consecrate a fast! Call a solemn assembly! Gather the elders! All those living in the land [to] the house of YHWH your God. Then, cry out to YHWH!

Despair in the Day of YHWH—The Drought

¹⁵Alas for the day! For near is the day of YHWH. And like destruction from the Almighty it will come. ¹⁶Has not the food been cut off from before our eyes? From the house of our God, joy and mirth?

¹⁷Grains of seed are withered under their furrows. The storehouses are desolated; the granaries are destroyed, for the corn is dried up. ¹⁸How the beasts groan! Herds of cattle wander, because there is no pasture for them. Even the flocks of sheep suffer.

¹⁹To you, o YHWH, I call, for fire consumes the pastures of the wilderness and flame sets afire all the trees of the field. ²⁰Even the beasts of the field are panting for you, for the streams of water are dried up, and fire consumes the pastures of the wilderness.

Joel 2

Despair in the Day of YHWH—The Invasion

¹Blow a trumpet in Zion! Sound an alarm on my holy mountain! Let tremble all the inhabitants of the land! For the day of YHWH is coming, for it is near. ²A day of darkness and gloom, a day of cloud and heavy darkness.

Like dawn being spread upon the mountains, a people great and numerous. There has not been anything like it from before, and after it there will not be again from generation to generation. ³Before it a fire devours, after it a flame blazes. Like the garden of Eden is the earth before it, but after it a desolate wasteland. There is no escape from it. ⁴Like the appearance of horses is their appearance, and like mighty steeds they run. ⁵Like the sound of chariots upon the tops of the mountains they leap, and like the sound of a consuming fire they devour chaff, like a numerous people, being arrayed for battle.

⁶From before it, peoples tremble. All faces turn pale.

⁷Like mighty warriors they run. Like men of battle they ascend the wall. Each goes in his own path. They do not change their way. ⁸Each does not crowd his brother. Each man goes in his position. Through the defenses they come. They do not break ranks. ⁹In the city they rush about. Upon the walls they run. Upon the houses they climb. Through windows they enter like a thief.

¹⁰Before them the earth trembles, the heavens quake. The sun and moon grow dark, and the stars gather their brightness. ¹¹Now YHWH utters his voice before his army, for very great is his host, and mighty is the one who does his word. Indeed, great is the day of YHWH, and very terrifying. Who can withstand it?

Hinge: The Call to Return to YHWH

¹²"Yet even now," declares YHWH, "Return to me with all your heart, with fasting, weeping, and mourning." ¹³Rend your hearts and not your garments. Return to YHWH your God for gracious and compassionate is he, slow to anger, and great in steadfast love, and he relents from evil. ¹⁴Who knows? He may turn and relent, and leave after him a blessing, a grain-offering and a drink-offering for YHWH your God.

¹⁵Blow a trumpet in Zion! Sanctify a fast! Call a sacred assembly! ¹⁶Gather the people! Sanctify the congregation! Collect the elders! Gather the children and the nursing infants! Let the bridegroom come out from his room, the bride from her chamber. ¹⁷Between the porch and the altar, let the priests, the ministers of YHWH, weep. Let them say,

"Have compassion, o YHWH, upon your people! Do not give your inheritance into reproach, as a byword among the nations. Why should they say among the peoples 'Where is their God?'"

Divine Deliverance from the Locusts and Drought

¹⁸YHWH was jealous for his land. He had compassion upon his people. ¹⁹YHWH answered and he said to his people,

"Listen! I am sending to you the grain, the new wine, and the oil, and you will be satisfied by them. I will not again make you a reproach for the nations. ²⁰The northerner I will remove from among you. I will drive it into a parched and desolate land, its head to the sea of the east, its tail to the sea of the west. Its stench will arise, and its foul smell will go up, for it has done great things."

²¹Do not fear, o land! Shout and rejoice for YHWH has done great things! ²²Do not fear, o beasts of the field, for the pastures of the desert have sprouted, for the tree has borne its fruit, and the fig tree and the vine have given their wealth. ²³Children of Zion, shout! Rejoice in YHWH your God! For he has given you the early rain for righteousness. He has brought showers down upon you, the early and later rains as before. ²⁴The threshing flood will be full of grain. The wine-vats will overflow with new wine and oil.

²⁵"I will restore to you the years which the locusts have devoured—the creeping locust, the stripping locust, and the gnawing locust. My great army that I sent among you. ²⁶You will surely eat and be satisfied. Then you will praise the name of YHWH your God, who has done astounding things with you. My people will never again be put to shame.

²⁷Then you will know, that I am in the midst of Israel. I am YHWH your God, there is no other. My people will never again be put to shame."

Joel 3[2:28–32]

Deliverance through the Spirit of YHWH

¹⁽²⁸⁾It will happen after this: "I will pour out my spirit upon all flesh, and your sons and your daughters will prophesy. Your elders will dream dreams, your young men will see visions. ²⁽²⁹⁾Even upon male and female servants in those days, I will pour out my spirit.

³⁽³⁰⁾I will give signs in the heavens and the earth—blood, fire, and pillars of smoke. ⁴⁽³¹⁾The sun will be turned to darkness and the moon to blood before the coming of the great and terrible day of YHWH."

⁵⁽³²⁾And it will happen, [that] all who call upon the name of YHWH will escape. For upon Mount Zion and in Jerusalem there will be an escaped group, just as YHWH said, including the survivors, whom YHWH is calling.

Joel 4[3]

Deliverance through Divine Judgment on the Day of YHWH

¹"For behold, in those days and at that time, when I restore the fortunes of Judah and Jerusalem, I will gather all nations and I will bring them to the Valley of Jehoshaphat. ²I will judge them there on behalf of my people and my inheritance, Israel, whom they scattered among the nations. My land they divided. ³For my people they cast lots. They exchanged the young men for prostitutes. The young women they sold for wine, and they drank it.

⁴"Now, what are you to me, Tyre, Sidon, and all the regions of Philistia? Are you seeking a recompense against me? If you are paying me back, swiftly and speedily I will return your recompense upon your head. ⁵For my silver and my gold you have taken, my good precious items you have brought into your temples. ⁶The children of Judah and Jerusalem you sold to the children of Javan, in order to send them away from their borders.

⁷"Look, I am rousing them from the place where you sold them. I am returning your retribution upon your head. ⁸I will sell your sons and daughters into the hands of the children of Judah, and they will sell them to the Sabeans, to a nation far off."

YHWH has spoken.

⁹Proclaim this among the nations! Sanctify a battle! Rouse the warriors! Let draw near and go up all the men of battle! ¹⁰Beat your plowshares into swords, and your pruning hooks into spears! Let the weak say, "I am strong." ¹¹Hasten and come, all nations from all around! Gather yourself there.

Bring down your warriors, o YHWH!

¹²"Let [them] be roused! Let the nations ascend to the valley of Jehoshaphat, for there I will sit to judge all the nations from all around. ¹³Send in the sickle for the harvest is ripe. Come, tread, for the winepress is full. The wine-vats overflow, for great is their wickedness."

¹⁴Multitudes, multitudes in the Valley of Decision, for the day of YHWH is near in the Valley of Decision. ¹⁵The sun and moon darken, the stars gather in their light.

¹⁶YHWH roars from Zion and from Jerusalem he utters his voice. The heavens and the earth quake. But YHWH is a shelter for his people, a refuge for the children of Israel. ¹⁷"You will know that I am YHWH your God, dwelling in Zion, my holy mountain. Jerusalem will be holy, nations will no longer pass through her."

¹⁸It will be on that day, the mountains will drip sweet wine. The hills will flow with milk. All the streams of Judah will flow with water. And a stream will flow from the house of YHWH, which will water the wadi of Shittim.

¹⁹Egypt will become a desolation. Edom will become a desert of desolation, because of the violence against the children of Judah whose innocent blood they poured out upon their land.

²⁰But Judah will be inhabited forever, and Jerusalem from generation to generation. ²¹"I will avenge their blood [that] I have not avenged."

YHWH dwells in Zion!

Introduction to Joel
Despair and Deliverance in the Day of the Lord

The book of Joel bears witness to the rhetorical power of prophetic literature. Through its vivid imagery, this book guides its audience through visions of devastation and terror that lead to promises of restoration and hope. This journey also provides Joel with the opportunity to articulate elements of YHWH's relationship with his people. Joel evokes a sense of threat through the imagery of a destructive locust plague, a drought, and an invading army led by none other than YHWH. He also urgently reminds his audience of the character of YHWH, expressing his belief that judgment is not the final word. He then offers his audience hope, promising relief from all of these crises. At the heart of this prophecy lies the specter of the day of the Lord (day of YHWH), which the prophet invokes explicitly on five occasions (Joel 1:15, 2:1, 11; 3:4[2:31]; 4:14[3:14]).[1] Joel repeatedly returns to this climactic signal of divine intervention into human affairs, attributing both chaos and comfort to his agency. Joel uses the day of YHWH as a symbol of both despair and hope, depending on the state of the divine-human relationship. He reveals that the same power that causes cities, nations, and heavenly bodies to tremble also offers security and the promise of enduring peace.

The present work explores the meaning and significance of this prophetic book. It draws upon insights from current research on *Joel* and on the rhetorical structure and strategies of Hebrew prophetic literature used to communicate its message with persuasive power.[2] At the heart of prophetic literature is a desire to convince its audience to adopt its perspective on God and the world. Michael Fox notes, "by any definition prophecy is rhetoric. The prophets were concerned with persuasion and they are indeed persuasive."[3] This commentary examines the means by which

---

1. The different versification of the Hebrew text and English translations complicates the study of *Joel*. This dates back to 1526 and the second Rabbinic Bible, which divided *Joel* into four chapters and is the standard layout for the Hebrew text, including that given in the *Biblia Hebraica Stuttgartensia*. The Vulgate and Greek text are divided into three chapters, which is the arrangement that most English translations follow. Joel 1:1–2:27 are identical in both traditions, but 3:1–5 in the Hebrew tradition is 2:28–32 in most English Bibles. Joel 4:1–21 in the Hebrew text thus corresponds to 3:1–21 in English Bibles. Following the guidelines for this series, I will refer to the Hebrew versification with the corresponding English verses in square brackets.

2. I italicize *Joel* when I am referring to the book in order to distinguish it from the eponymous prophet. When chapter and verse numbers are included, this italicization is unnecessary (i.e., Joel 1:1).

3. Michael V. Fox, "The Rhetoric of Ezekiel's Vision of the Valley of the Bones," *HUCA* 51 (1980): 4.

Joel engages his audience and takes them through doubt and despair in order to bring them to a place where they can celebrate promises of divine deliverance. Joel emphasizes the agency of YHWH, whose actions are rooted in his commitment to restore his people and judge the nations on the day of YHWH. Before engaging in this process, we must first address some preliminary considerations. These include the date of the book, its literary integrity, its place within the Minor Prophets, and its status as rhetorical discourse.

The Historical Context

The historical background for *Joel* is contested. This is due to the lack of information within the book that can be used to identify its time of composition. There is no mention of regnal year in the superscription and no identifiable person or event mentioned within the text. Further, very little can be said about the prophet himself. He is identified only as "the son of Pethuel" in 1:1b, which is an otherwise unattested name. Consequently, opinions concerning *Joel's* date of composition vary widely. Six theories can be mentioned from the era of modern critical scholarship. I have listed them in chronological order and will then evaluate their relative merits.

1. Ninth century BCE. Some older scholarship argues that *Joel* is one of the earliest prophetic books, dating to the time of Joash (835–796 BCE). This is suggested in part due to *Joel's* position in the Hebrew order of the Minor Prophets, where it is the second book of the collection, found between Hosea and Amos. Adherents to this position attribute *Joel's* lack of reference to a regnal year to Joash's youth when he ascended the throne, suggesting that the prophet had no reason to mention a king during the time of Jehoida's regency.[4]

2. Late seventh–early sixth centuries BCE. Another possibility is that Joel prophesies about the coming Babylonian invasion and exile. In this reading, the locusts of Joel 1–2 are metaphors for human soldiers who will lay waste to the land.[5] The argument for this date also builds on possible allusions between Joel 4:4–8[3:4–8], Zeph 1:14–18, and Jer 47:4, which suggest that the three works come from the same historical period. The failure to mention the king comes about because Joel addresses his audience by age (i.e., elders, young men, children) rather than social position.[6]

---

4. K. Credner, *Der Prophet Joel: Übersetz und eklärt* (Halle: Buchhandlung des Waisenhauses, 1831), 40; Gleason Archer, *A Survey of Old Testament Introduction* (Chicago: Moody, 1974), 304.

5. Douglas Stuart, *Hosea—Jonah*. WBC 31 (Waco: Word Books, 1987), 225–26. I will address the issue of possible referents for the locusts in the following chapters.

6. Arvid S. Kapelrud, *Joel Studies*. UUÅ 4 (Uppsala: A. B. Lundequist, 1948), 191.

3. Mid-sixth century BCE. Recent scholarship suggests the exilic period for the date of *Joel*. This has long been considered unlikely due to the prophet's repeated references to the community gathering under priestly leadership in the temple (Joel 1:9, 13–14; 2:17), which would make it implausible that Joel prophesied while the temple was in ruins. However, one proposal suggests that *Joel* reflects a time during the fifteen year window when the altar was again functioning but before the temple had been fully reconstructed (cf. Ezra 3:1–7).[7] An exilic date might also explain the prophet's failure to mention specific sins for which the people are guilty and his concern to reassure them of God's presence in the midst.[8]

4. Late sixth–early fifth centuries BCE. The majority position is that *Joel* stems from a time relatively early in the postexilic period. This is the easiest solution to the lack of a regnal year in the superscription, the absence of reference to a "major" enemy like Assyria or Babylon, and the focus on priestly leadership.[9] This date also makes sense of *Joel's* numerous allusions to other prophetic works.[10] Another piece of evidence is the reference to the Sabeans in 4:8[3:8] who lost their control of trade routes through the region toward the end of the fifth century, which suggests that *Joel* best fits a time that precedes their demise.[11]

5. Late fifth–early fourth century BCE. Some commentators push the date of *Joel* further into the postexilic period. This proposal suggests that the imagery of an invader scaling Jerusalem's walls implies a time after 445 BCE when the walls were rebuilt during Nehemiah's governorship. The apparent waning of Sabean influence during this time is not considered a major handicap since the purpose of the reference is to create a sense of poetic justice as the nations receive their just rewards for selling the Judahites as slaves to the Greeks (4:6[3:6]).[12] Other evidence for this period includes an attempt to calculate the date of solar eclipses that could reflect *Joel's* references to the darkening of the heavenly bodies.[13]

6. Third–second centuries BCE. Some have argued that *Joel* derives from the Ptolemaic or Maccabean periods. This comes from the reference to Egypt in Joel 4:19[3:19] and suggests that this reflects a time it governed Judea.[14] The latest proposed date for *Joel* is in the Maccabean period, which is based on an argument concerning the literary unity of the book that is addressed below.[15]

In evaluating these six theories, the first and the sixth are the least plausible. As will be shown throughout the commentary, *Joel's* allusions to other books suggest that

---

7. Tova Ganzel, "The Shattered Dream. The Prophecies of Joel: A Bridge Between Ezekiel and Haggai" *JHS* 11 (2011). Online at http://www.jhsonline.org/Articles/article_153.pdf.

8. Elie Assis, *The Book of Joel: A Prophet Between Calamity and Hope*. LHBOTS 581 (New York: Bloomsbury, 2013), 11–20.

9. Willem S. Prinsloo, *The Theology of the Book of Joel*. BZAW 163 (Berlin: Walter de Gruyter, 195), 6.

10. James L. Crenshaw, *Joel*. AB 24c (New York: Doubleday, 1995), 24–28. I will discuss the significance of many of these allusions throughout this commentary.

11. Jacob M. Myers, "Some Considerations Bearing on the Date of Joel," *ZAW* 74 (1962): 177–95.

12. James Nogalski, *The Book of the Twelve: Hosea—Jonah*. SHBC (Macon: Smyth & Helwys, 2011), 202.

13. F. R. Stephenson, "The Date of the Book of Joel," *VT* 19 (1969): 229.

14. Marco Treves, "The Date of Joel," *VT* 9 (1959): 154

15. Bernard Duhm, *Israels Propheten* (Tübingen: J. C. B. Mohr, 1922), 398.

a date early in the monarchic period is unlikely.[16] On the other end of the spectrum, pushing *Joel* into the Ptolemaic and Maccabean periods is a significant departure from the overall consensus. A singular reference to Egypt, without any further links to the situation of this late date, does not provide sufficient evidence.

The remaining four options all have elements that render them plausible. However, each depends on arguments from inference, using Joel's references and imagery to establish the underlying context. It is difficult to determine to what degree we can map the prophet's figurative language to concrete, historical situations.[17] For example, the image of an enemy breaching the walls of Zion in 2:7–9 does not require that the Jerusalem of Joel's day had functioning city walls. Joel could be invoking memories of a past invasion, or more simply creating a drama of a city under siege to convey the sense of threat. Likewise, Joel's references to astronomical phenomena do not require an actual eclipse when they fit into the prophetic lexicon of how nature responds to God's actions.

This gap between the use of imagery and its reference to a specific, identifiable reality means that any conclusion regarding *Joel's* date of composition can only be held lightly. While it is true that having a firm grasp of a prophet's historical situation is useful for understanding their message, it is also important not to demand too much of the evidence. Determining the message and intention of *Joel* must come from a study of the text itself, without locking it too firmly into a particular historical perspective.[18] This approach may even provide some benefits in allowing the interpreter to apply *Joel's* message to a variety of circumstances in the life of the people of God.

With the above caveats in mind, I argue that the fourth theory (late sixth–early fifth centuries BCE) is the most plausible. This locates *Joel* in a time early in the postexilic period. While the absence of a reference to a king is not conclusive, it still suggests a time without royal leadership. I also suggest that the appeal to elders in 1:2 evokes the leadership function of their office, rather than simply their age. This provides an alternative authority structure to compensate for the absence of a king. Moreover, the proposed remedy to the crises of 1:2–2:12 is to gather under priestly leadership, further specified as the temple grounds in 2:12–17, which does seem to presuppose a functioning religious system. Joel's concern that the locust invasion could cause a cessation of sacrifice (1:9, 13) also suggests a time when the cultic

---

16. John Strazicich, *Joel's Use of Scripture and the Scripture's Use of Joel: Appropriation and Resignification in Second Temple Judaism and Early Christianity*. BibInt 82 (Leiden: Brill, 2007), 27–30. Strazicich does excellent work noting how Joel appropriates and resignifies previous literature for his own communicative purposes, and then how *Joel* itself is used in other parts of the biblical literature.

17. For a provocative approach to this question, see James R. Linville, "Bugs Through the Looking Glass: The Infestation of Meaning in Joel," in *Reflection and Refraction: Studies in Biblical Historiography in Honour of A. Graeme Auld*, ed. Robert Rezetko, Timothy H. Lim, and W. Brian Aucker (Cambridge: Cambridge University Press, 2006), 283–98. Linville removes almost *every* trace of historicity from Joel's referents, which I think is unwarranted, but he does provide a useful corrective to those who try to find concrete reality behind every image.

18. Prinsloo, *Theology*, 92. Prinsloo calls the task of establishing *Joel's* date of composition "virtually impossible."

system was facing an immediate rather than a systemic crisis, as would have been the case in the exilic period. The references to slave trading in 4:4–8[3:4–8] also seem to best fit a time after the fall of Jerusalem, when the circumstances would have left the remaining Judahites vulnerable for exploitation. This could also explain the references to Egypt and Edom in Joel 4:18[3:18], setting Joel in a context that recalls the probable situation of Obadiah.[19] An early postexilic date for *Joel* also explains the numerous allusions to other prophetic literature, including Isaiah, Ezekiel, Amos, Micah, and Obadiah.

Literary Integrity of Joel

Closely related to the issues of *Joel's* date of composition is the discussion of the book's unity. There are two points within the book where interpreters detect a dramatic shift: Joel 2:18 and 3:1[2:28].[20] This has led to theories that the book was composed in two parts at different times and then later combined. Joel 2:18 marks the first major shift where scenes of devastation and divine absence suddenly become announcements of restoration rooted in the promise of God's presence. This has led to the suggestion that 1:2–2:17 is a call to lament in response to a locust plague, to which 2:18–4:21[3:21] was added to in the Maccabean era to ascribe to it eschatological significance rooted in the development of the day of YHWH.[21] Joel 3:1[2:28] also seems to mark a major shift since it leaves behind the images of locusts, droughts, and agricultural disasters that dominate 1:2–2:27.[22] Consequently, some suggest that Joel 1:2–2:27 is "historical" in its outlook while 3:1–4:21[2:28–3:21] is "eschatological." The different ways in which Joel uses the day of YHWH are taken as further evidence of this bifurcation, since Joel uses it to prefigure a day of destruction for the Judahites in 1:15, 2:1, 11, while it marks God's presence and promises to restore in 3:5[2:28] and 4:14[3:14].

These claims of disjunction are exaggerated. Most commentators now recognize *Joel's* essential unity as it offers a coherent development of a response to crisis. There are numerous theories attempting to work out the details of the relationship between the two "halves" of *Joel*, but on a broader level it is possible to trace the progression of

---

19. For a mid-sixth century date for Obadiah, see Daniel I. Block, *Obadiah*. ZECOT 27 (Grand Rapids: Zondervan, 2013), 24–27.

20. A recent, unique proposal is that Joel 1:1–3:5 [2:32] is bound together through the "author's rhetorical use of genres," while Joel 4:1–21 [3:1–21] comprises "later expansions." See Ronald L. Troxel, *Joel: Scope, Genre(s) and Meaning*, CSHB 6 (Winona Lake, IN: Eisenbrauns, 2015), 29. I will reference his work on how Joel 3:1–5 [2:28–32] relates to 1:2–2:27 in my discussion of that passage but I also believe there are significant reasons to view the entire book as a unified composition.

21. See Bernard Duhm, "Anmerkungen zu den zwölf Propheten," *ZAW* 31 (1911): 184–88.

22. James Nogalski, *Redactional Processes in the Book of the Twelve*. BZAW 217 (Berlin: Walter de Gruyter, 1993), 2–3. Nogalski calls the approach that highlights the gap between Joel 1:2–2:27 and 3:1 [2:28]–4:21 [3:21] as a division by content, while the approach that sees a major gap between Joel 1:2–2:17 and 2:18–4:21 [3:21] is a division according to form.

Joel's argument.[23] In 1:2–2:17, Joel builds up the nature of the crisis through images of a locust plague, drought, and invasion before urging his audience to cry out to YHWH for restitution. Joel 2:18–4:21[3:21] then systematically reverses all of the crises found in the first half of the book, culminating in the guarantee of YHWH's presence among his people and punishment for those nations who thought to take advantage of their weakness.[24] Wolff helpfully notes a symmetrical relationship between Joel 1:2–2:17 and 2:18–4:21[3:21] where issues including agricultural scarcity, catastrophe for Jerusalem, and the call to return to YHWH become celebrations of agricultural bounty, rescue for Jerusalem, and guarantees of YHWH's presence among his people.[25]

Joel is also bound together by the use and repetition of key themes. Numerous themes from the first part of the book recur in the second part, including the idea of Zion as a sacred mountain (2:1; 4:7[3:7]), escape from an invader (2:3; 3:5[2:32]), and summons to gather (1:14; 2:16; 3:2[2:29]; 4:11[3:11]).[26] This is a sign of conscious literary artistry that demonstrates *Joel's* essential unity.[27] Additional examples of thematic repetition include *Joel's* return to the idea of "knowing" God on the basis of his salvific actions on Judah's behalf (2:27, 4:17[3:17]). *Joel* also makes use of the "nations" both on a metaphorical level to refer to locusts (1:6) and on a more literal level to refer to the judgment that God will pour out on Judah's enemies (4:12[3:12]). Similarly, God's actions cause the heavens and earth to quake and the heavenly luminaries to dim in both of the supposed halves of the book (2:10, 4:16[3:16]).[28]

The theme of the day of YHWH is also essential to the literary integrity of this book. Joel explicitly invokes it three times in his description of the crises facing his Judahite audience (1:15; 2:1, 11) and twice in his announcement of the resolution (3:4[2:31]; 4:14[3:14]). Joel also highlights the urgency of the day, describing it as "near" in 1:15, 2:1, and 4:14[3:14]. Older scholarship suggested that the shift in the meaning of the day of YHWH points to disunity in *Joel*, arguing that the same author would not use it in both positive and negative contexts in the same composition.[29] However, this does not take into account the creativity that prophets demonstrate when invoking the day of YHWH. This can be seen in the variety of situations in

---

23. For example, Prinsloo suggests that Joel follows a staircase model in which each subsequent unit develops and expands upon the one that preceded it (Willem S. Prinsloo, "The Unity of the Book of Joel," *ZAW* 104 [1992]: 66–81). Garrett suggests a pattern of dual interlocking chiasms, one of which covers Joel 1:2–2:27, while the other is found in 2:20–4:21 [3:21]. In doing so, Garrett picks up on how issues raised at the beginning of *Joel* are addressed in its later stages, even though the specifics of his proposed chiasms are debatable. See Duane A. Garrett, "The Structure of Joel," *JETS* 28 (1985): 289–97.

24. Nogalski, *Book of the Twelve*, 203. I will provide a more detailed explanation of the book's argument and structure below.

25. Hans W. Wolff, *Joel and Amos*. Hermeneia (Philadelphia: Fortress, 1977), 7.

26. Graham S. Ogden and Richard R. Deutsch. *Joel and Malachi: A Promise of Hope—A Call to Obedience*. ITC (Grand Rapids: Eerdmans, 1987), 54–55.

27. See John A. Thompson, "The Use of Repetition in the Prophecy of Joel," in *On Culture and Religion*, ed. Matthew Black and William A. Smalley (The Hague: Mouton, 1974), 108.

28. Ferdinand Deist, "Parallels and Reinterpretation in the Book of Joel: A Theology of Yom Yahweh?" in *Text and Context: Old Testament and Semitic Studies for F. C. Fensham*, ed. W. Claasen, JSOTSup 48 (Sheffield: Sheffield Academic, 1988), 72.

29. Maurice Vernes, *Le peuple d'Israel et ses espérances relative à son avenir depuis les origines jusqu' à l'époque persane Ve siècle avant J. C.* (Paris: Sandos et Fischbacher, 1872), 47.

which the prophets apply it. The exact expression יוֹם־יהוה occurs fifteen times in the OT, five of which appear in *Joel*, revealing its centrality to the message of the book (Isa 13:6, 9; Ezek 13:5; Joel 1:15; 2:1, 11; 3:4[2:31]; 4:14[3:14]; Amos 5:18, 20; Obad 15; Zeph 1:17, 14; Mal 3:23[4:5]). The day of YHWH texts expand significantly when we consider related expressions like "on that day" or "in those days" when they directly invoke YHWH's actions.[30]

At its core, the day of YHWH announces YHWH's direct and unmistakable engagement with human affairs. Its duration is not limited to a twenty-four-hour period, but rather to a moment or event where YHWH breaks through the normal course of events and asserts his authority in this world. It is frequently marked by cosmic signs and wonders. Throughout the prophetic literature, this has both positive and negative repercussions for Israel and Judah, as well as foreign nations, depending on the nature of their relationship with YHWH. When Israel is complacent, Amos 5:18–20 informs them that the day of YHWH will be a day of darkness, not light, and they should dread its coming. When Babylon becomes overly arrogant, Isaiah declares that the day of YHWH announces its doom, which provides hope for Israel's restoration (Isa 13:1–22).[31] Consequently, it is not surprising that Joel uses the day of YHWH to express both despair and hope, especially when there is a clear point of transition in 2:12–17 where he urges the people to cry out to YHWH. This provides the context for the shift in the expectations surrounding the day of YHWH, as Joel's audience appears to follow the course he suggests.

In summary, *Joel* constitutes a unified literary work. Its two halves are united by shared lexical and thematic links. Further, there is a logical development in the book's argument as the announced crises give way to resolution, rooted in YHWH's sovereignty over human affairs that is made evident through the announcements of the coming day of YHWH.

Joel and the Book of the Twelve

Joel has a significant place in discussions of how the Minor Prophets work as a collection, commonly called the Book of the Twelve. This title refers to the practice of transmitting these books on a single scroll and is frequently used in scholarly discussion of the corpus. The idea that these books function as a unified collection dates back into the intertestamental period when Jesus ben Sira celebrates "the bones

---

30. For the argument to expand the day of YHWH corpus in the Book of the Twelve see James Nogalski, "The Day(s) of YHWH in the Book of the Twelve," in *Thematic Threads in the Book of the Twelve*, ed. Paul Redditt and Aaron Schart, BZAW 325 (Berlin: de Gruyter, 2003), 192–213. I also favor including texts that do not have the exact phrase יום יהוה if they are clearly invoking motifs associated with the day of YHWH. See Joel Barker, "Day of the Lord" in *Dictionary of the Old Testament: Prophets*, ed. Mark J. Boda and J. Gordon McConville (Downers Grove, IL: IVP Academic, 2012), 133.

31. Ibid., 132–43. I will discuss further parallels between Joel's use of the day of YHWH and other prophetic literature in my study of the passages where it appears.

of the twelve prophets" (Sir 49:10). In the Hebrew Masoretic tradition, *Joel* is the second book of the collection, following Hosea. In the LXX tradition, it is fourth, following Hosea, Amos, and Micah and preceding Obadiah.[32] Scholars have expended significant effort to detail the interrelationships between the books of this collection, searching for unifying themes and the process of composition. Theories of redactional activity dominate the discussion, as scholars seek to understand the formation of this collection. *Joel's* importance is evident in the suggestion that it is the "literary anchor" for the Book of the Twelve.[33] *Joel* commences with what could be a response to Hosea's call to repentance and it ends with YHWH roaring in Zion, prefiguring Amos's condemnation of foreign nations. Its concern with agricultural fertility, especially through the use of "grain, wine, and oil" is echoed throughout the Book of the Twelve (Hos 2:23–25; Amos 4:9; Hag 1:10–11; 2:9). Additionally, *Joel's* appeal to turn to YHWH in the midst of crises sets the paradigm for appropriate responses in the rest of the collection.[34]

Joel's connections with the rest of the Book of the Twelve are worth considering. They compel us to consider a key hermeneutical question regarding the extent to which an adequate interpretation of *Joel* depends upon its placement in and connection to this corpus. Nogalski argues that this context is necessary for understanding its meaning, suggesting that this book is crafted to link up with themes presented in Hosea and Amos. This allows him to suggest that *Joel's* location after Hosea's calls to repentance explains why *Joel* does not specify the sin of which his audience is guilty.[35] He further suggests that the agrarian crises described in 1:2–20 are an actualization of the warnings of what would happen if Israel did not repent as presented in Hosea 2. However, others are less persuaded that it is necessary to interpret individual books against the backdrop of the larger collection. They prefer to focus on the distinct message of each of the twelve books, which describe a variety of times and circumstances from the divided monarchy to the postexilic community.[36]

It is possible to balance these perspectives. Interpreters can acknowledge shared themes and concerns while preserving the unique contribution of each book.[37] This is

---

32. The fact that the Masoretic and LXX traditions place the Minor Prophets in different sequences suggests that their organizing principle is not simply chronology, which allows us to consider *Joel* as postexilic. Sweeney suggests that the LXX sequence clusters judgment on the northern kingdom by beginning with Hosea, Amos, and Micah, while the Masoretic sequence focuses on Jerusalem and its relationship with Israel and the nations by placing *Joel* immediately after Hosea. See Marvin A. Sweeney, "Sequence and Interpretation in the Book of the Twelve," in *Reading and Hearing the Book of the Twelve*, ed. James Nogalski and Marvin A. Sweeney, SBLSS 15 (Atlanta: Society of Biblical Literature, 2000), 49–65.

33. James Nogalski, "Joel as 'Literary Anchor' for the Book of the Twelve" in *Reading and Hearing the Book of the Twelve*, ed. James Nogalski and Marvin A. Sweeney, SBLSS 15 (Atlanta: Society of Biblical Literature, 2000), 92.

34. Ibid., 107.

35. Nogalski, *Book of the Twelve*, 205–6. I will explore this question in more detail in my analysis of the call to return to YHWH in 2:12–17.

36. Block, *Obadiah*, 22.

37. David L. Petersen, "A Book of the Twelve?" in *Reading and Hearing the Book of the Twelve*, ed. James Nogalski and Marvin A. Sweeney, SBLSS 15 (Atlanta: Scholars, 2000), 3–10. Petersen helpfully describes the corpus as a "thematized anthology" with its focus on the day of YHWH.

especially true when many of the shared themes that connect this collection (the fertility of the land, the fate of God's people, the character of God) are found throughout other books in the OT.[38] Ben Zvi champions an approach focusing on the individual books, arguing that ancient readers of these texts would be much more likely to treat them as independent works. He focuses on introductory markers such as incipits, superscriptions, and the names of individual authors, as well as concluding markers such as orientations toward hope and the presence of unique expressions.[39] He notes that there is no similar introduction or conclusion to a literary work entitled the Book of Twelve. It is a construct of later interpreters, both ancient and modern.

As this relates specifically to interpreting *Joel*, Ben Zvi notes that Hosea ends not with a summons to repentance that informs the context of *Joel*, but rather a call to reflect on what has just been said.[40] Similarly, Joel 1:1 does not explicitly invoke Hosea, but rather introduces the reader to a new prophetic figure who is the recipient of the word of the Lord. These markers of introduction and conclusion create a "powerful internal coherence" for each book, suggesting their integrity as literary units.[41] This approach also permits interpreters to give proper attention to Joel's interactions with books outside the Minor Prophets, notably Isaiah (see Joel 1:10, 12 // Isa 24:7; Joel 1:15 // Isa 13:6; Joel 4:10[3:10] // Isa 2:4/Mic 4:3).[42] The themes that *Joel* shares and potential allusions to other biblical books can be understood as part of his rhetorical strategy rather than signals of shared redactional layering.[43] Consequently, I read *Joel* as an independent literary work, and I do not focus on how its composition influences the broader discussion of the formation of the Book of the Twelve. I will explore *Joel's* connections to other books within this corpus where appropriate. I will argue that *Joel* presents a coherent message concerning the relationship between God and his people that should be considered in its own light, while also considering the ways in which the prophet adapts other biblical texts for his own purposes.

Joel as Rhetorical Discourse

One of the core elements of prophetic communication is the necessity of persuasion. Prophets in the OT did not wield coercive power and could not compel obedience. However, as those who communicated God's messages to Israel and Judah, there was an underlying urgency to prophetic communication. They were heralds of YHWH's court entrusted with the responsibility to convey to Israel and Judah

---

38. Francis Landy, "Three Sides of a Coin: In Conversation with Ben Zvi and Nogalski, *Two Sides of a Coin*," *JHS* 10 (2010). Online at http://jhsonline.org/Articles/article_139.pdf.

39. Ehud Ben Zvi and James Nogalski, *Two Sides of a Coin: Juxtaposing Views on Interpreting the Book of the Twelve / the Twelve Prophetic Books*, Analecta Gorgiana 201 (Piscataway NJ: Gorgias, 2009), 72–80.

40. Ibid., 87.

41. Landy, "Three Sides."

42. Richard J. Coggins, "Interbiblical Quotations in Joel," in *After the Exile: Essays in Honour of Rex Mason*, ed. John Barton and David James Reimer (Macon: Mercer University Press, 1996), 77–78.

43. Landy, "Three Sides."

what was required of them in situations ranging from abundant prosperity to the devastation of exile. Consequently, prophetic books elevate their discourse through the creative use of language in order to sear their messages onto the hearts of their intended audience.[44] A compelling advantage of discourse and rhetorically oriented approaches to prophetic literature is the ability to look beyond individual passages and explore the development of the prophet's argument as a whole. To this end, there are four elements that need to be considered in undertaking this study of *Joel*.[45]

The first is to consider the constituent *units* or *passages* into which a discourse is divided. This permits the interpreter to trace the flow of *Joel's* argument, following the progression through the various topics addressed. Prophetic literature uses different signals within the text to establish the boundaries of a passage.[46] *Joel* marks boundaries by shifting its mode of address from directive to descriptive (1:14 // 1:15), repetition of key phrases to conclude a passage (1:19–20; 2:26–27), and literary devices like *inclusio* (2:1–11) and rhetorical questions (1:2; 2:17). This book also marks the beginning of new passages through the introduction of divine speech (2:12) and the use of formulaic phrases (3:1[2:28]; 4:1[3:1]). My discussion of how the text is divided into discourse units is found in the Structure and Literary Form sections of the commentary.

The second element is to monitor the development of the *situation* that each of these passages reflects. This helps the interpreter to consider the ways in which these individual passages interrelate and advance the prophet's argument. This step corresponds to the discussion of Literary Context in the layout of the commentary. The concept of rhetorical situation is well-developed in communications studies, focusing on the nature of the problem (exigence) that the speaker seeks to address, their relationship with the audience, and the constraints under which they are operating.[47] This typically requires an exploration into the background of the world of the audience. As mentioned above, this is incredibly challenging in the case of *Joel*, but it is possible to look at the situation that the text creates and consider the responses that it proposes.

When studying a complete prophetic book like *Joel*, it is also important to take note of the dynamism of the rhetorical situation. The situation does not remain static

---

44. For an excellent study of the broad scope of the techniques that prophets use to communicate, see D. Brent Sandy, *Plowshares and Pruning Hooks: Rethinking the Language of Biblical Prophecy and Apocalyptic* (Downers Grove, IL: InterVarsity Press, 2002).

45. This is a modification of the approach developed in Karl Möller, *A Prophet in Debate: The Rhetoric of Persuasion in the Book of Amos*, JSOTSup 372 (London: Sheffield Academic, 2003), 21–42. It also provided the foundation for my previous study of *Joel*. For a more detailed discussion of rhetorical methodology, see Barker, *Depths of Despair*, 37–65.

46. For a detailed examination of bounding structures in prophetic literature, see Ernst R. Wendland, *The Discourse Analysis of Hebrew Prophetic Literature*, MBPS 40 (Lewiston, NY: Edwin Mellen, 1995), 24–70.

47. Lloyd F. Bitzer, "Functional Communication: A Situational Perspective," in *Rhetoric in Transition: Studies in the Nature and Uses of Rhetoric*, ed. Eugene E. White (University Park: Pennsylvania State University Press, 1980), 23.

throughout the discourse, and the rhetorical strategies adapt to meet new situations as they arise.[48] Joel begins to prophesy against the backdrop of a devastating locust invasion, which then morphs into crises of drought and invasion. We see the situation worsening until it culminates with the announcement that YHWH leads an invading horde against his people in 2:11. Having developed the urgency of the situation, Joel can shift focus to the call to response in 2:12–17. His rhetorical situation then changes in 2:18–4:21[3:21] as he delves into YHWH's answer to the cries of the Judahite audience. The situation shifts from crisis to restoration, which means that the problem that the prophet faces is no longer one of motivating his audience to respond, but rather one of directing them to trust YHWH's promises. Consequently, the different passages in the latter half of the book go to great lengths to assure the audience that YHWH is in their midst and that divine action exemplified by the day of YHWH is a reason for celebration rather than consternation. The development of the rhetorical situation in *Joel* allows us to understand how the prophet can use similar images to convey dramatically different messages.

The third element is to examine the different rhetorical *strategies* of the text. In order to enhance the communicative power of their messages, prophets employ a wide variety of methods and literary devices, which I will discuss in the Explanation of the Text portions of the commentary. I offer detailed engagement with Joel's rhetorical strategies as they address the situation of each passage, but four overarching techniques deserve special mention.

1. *Inclusion*: Joel is very concerned with making sure that he establishes the widest possible audience for his prophetic communication. This begins as early as 1:2 when he calls on the "elders" and the "dwellers of the land" to hear his message. This is a *merismus*, intended to draw the entire Judahite community into his audience. His concern for inclusion reaches its peak when he calls on his audience to cry out to YHWH in response to the mounting crises. In 2:16, he summons elders and children (explicitly mentioning nursing infants), as well as brides and bridegrooms who should be exempt from cultic duty. When Joel announces a powerful outpouring of YHWH's spirit in 3:1–2[2:28–29], he lists sons, daughters, old men, young men, male servants, and female servants as its recipients. Joel thus emphasizes the inclusive nature of this gift from YHWH. Joel is also inclusive in his summons to the nations through the repeated use of the word כל ("all"). He summons *all* of the nations (4:2[3:2]), who will gather *all* of their soldiers (4:9–10[3:9–10]), and who will *all* meet him in the place of judgment (4:11–12[3:11–12]).

---

48. On the dynamism of rhetorical situations, see Lauri Thurén, *The Rhetorical Strategy of 1 Peter with a Special Regard to Ambiguous Expressions* (Turku: Abö Akad, 1990), 70. Thurén notes that "an argumentative text is seldom so static that the rhetorical situation would remain the same throughout the text."

2. *Recursion*: Essential to Joel's rhetorical strategy is his use of recursion, where he returns to a similar theme or image but infuses it with new meaning. As argued above, this is a sign of the book's essential unity, but it also reveals how the rhetorical situation of the book has developed. For example, 1:4 employs four synonyms for locusts, emphasizing the waves of devastation that they create. Joel 2:25 uses the same four synonyms in the context of celebrating YHWH's deliverance. Similarly, 1:10 mourns the loss of grain, wine, and oil, while their return in 2:19, 24 celebrates YHWH's restorative actions. In 1:14, the prophet calls the people to a cultic gathering to cry out to YHWH. He picks up the same cry in 2:15–16, adding further detail concerning the exact words that the audience should utter at this gathering.

   Joel's use of the day of YHWH also fits this rhetorical strategy. As mentioned above, the prophet directly invokes the day on five occasions, expressing both despair (1:15, 2:1, 11) and hope (3:4[2:31]; 4:14[3:14]). The day of YHWH is "near" in 1:15, 2:1, and 4:14[3:14], indicating that its immediacy remains, even as the situation shifts. Further, signs of the day of YHWH include the darkening of heavenly luminaries in 2:11, 3:4[2:31], and 4:14[3:14]. The first case inspires terror as it announces YHWH as the leader of the horde assaulting Jerusalem, while the second and third cases offer hope, rooted in YHWH's actions on behalf of his people. Joel invokes the same images, but they serve very different functions as we track the development of his argument.

3. *Delay*: Joel frequently employs delay to build suspense. Joel 1:2–3 calls the audience to consider "this" and to tell it to multiple generations, before finally revealing the exact nature of the threat in 1:4. Joel 2:1–11 goes through an extended description of an army assaulting Zion, before finally revealing that YHWH is the leader of this army in 2:11. This provides the finishing touch to the despair associated with the day of YHWH in 1:2–2:11. Finally, 4:9–12[3:9–12] presents an extended summons to the nations to come and face YHWH in battle, delaying the revelation that this is futile and that in fact they are facing divine judgment. On a broader level, Joel also delays YHWH's positive responses to the cries of his people, building suspense concerning whether the visions of devastation and destruction are the final word. Joel 1:14 urges the audience to cry out to YHWH, while 1:19–20 again implores YHWH to act in response to the devastated landscape. Joel 2:15–17 again calls the audience to cry out to YHWH, this time offering greater detail. It is not until this third direct appeal that YHWH begins his restorative response in 2:18.

4. *Divine Agency*: Integral to Joel's strategy is his presentation of YHWH as the primary actor in the drama. When facing disaster, the only recourse available to the Judahite audience is to cry out to YHWH. Once they have uttered their appeals, they become observers awaiting divine response. This is emphasized

in 2:18–4:21[3:21], where the first-person voice occurs frequently, referring to YHWH's actions. YHWH announces his intention to restore agricultural prosperity, pour out his spirit, and bring judgment against hostile nations, while the Judahite audience has no further active role to play. YHWH's agency accomplishes Joel's transition from despair to hope, and his audience awaits its manifestation.

The fourth element is to consider the *effectiveness* of prophetic discourse. If prophets were concerned with persuasion, it is important to reflect on the impact of their communication. However, we rarely have evidence of an immediate response to prophetic persuasion and in certain cases, such as Isaiah, the purpose of prophetic communication was to drive the audience away from the prophet's message (Isa 6:8–13). It is incredibly challenging to consider the impact of prophetic communication and this final stage is the least developed of the underlying rhetorical methodology. Without direct statements of how the audience responded to Joel's message, the interpreter must look to the progression of the text itself. *Joel* offers guidance for this process in its transition from despair to hope. The turnaround beginning in 2:18 implies a rhetorical situation in which his repeated appeals to cry out to YHWH in 1:2–2:17 were heeded. The progression throughout the book suggests that the audience took to heart his understanding of the situation and their appeals to YHWH evoked a positive response.

Effectiveness of prophetic rhetoric also extends beyond the horizon of the immediate audience. As readers and hearers who revere the text, we experience its persuasive communication in our own situations and settings. We must reflect on the continuing impact of *Joel* as it resonates with other biblical literature and in the life of the church. This concept of rhetorical effectiveness is the foundation for the discussions of Canonical and Practical Significance found in the commentary.

The Structure of Joel

There are many proposals for the overall structure of *Joel* related to the discussion of the book's date and unity discussed above. Even though the majority position is that *Joel* is a unified composition, most interpreters still divide the book into two halves, usually emphasizing the shift in tone between 2:17 // 2:18.[49] Beyond this larger point of disjunction, discourse markers within the text delimit its constituent passages and signal the progress of its argument. On a macrostructural level, 1:1 provides the introductory superscription before Joel draws his audience down into despair in 1:2–2:11. This downward trajectory pivots in 2:12–17 when the prophet shifts from crisis to a call for the audience to cry out to YHWH. Joel 2:18–4:21[3:21]

---

49. Examples include Crenshaw, *Joel*, ix–x; Nogalski, *The Book of the Twelve*, 214; Stuart, *Hosea—Jonah*, 226; Leslie Allen, *The Books of Joel, Obadiah, Jonah, and Micah*, NICOT (Grand Rapids: Eerdmans, 1976), 42–43.

then envisions YHWH's positive response to the people's cries, providing deliverance from despair as YHWH reverses all of the preceding crises.

The downward trajectory of 1:2–2:11 can be further divided into three passages that draw the Judahite audience into increasing despair. Joel 1:2–14 introduces the threat of an overwhelming locust invasion that systemically devastates Judah's agriculture and by extension the operations of the sacrificial system. This passage is structured by the repetition of the pattern command + vocative + reason that Joel uses to address the entire community (1:2, 14) and its constituent elements (1:5, 8, 11, 13).[50] The *merismus* of "elders" and "inhabitants of the land" frames this passage, calling the community to face the magnitude of the disaster and to seek YHWH in response.

The mode of communication changes in 1:15–20 as the imperatives cease and the text begins with an exclamatory utterance אֲהָהּ לַיּוֹם ("alas for the day"), before providing the first mention of the day of YHWH. Joel also shifts to the first person, linking himself to the situation facing his audience in 1:16 and offering a direct appeal to YHWH in 1:19–20. The image-world also shifts from waves of locusts to a devastating drought, marking a development in the nature of the crisis. The end of this passage is signaled through *epistrophe*, a literary device that uses the repetition of key words or phrases to signal the end of a textual unit. In this instance the phrase אֵשׁ אָכְלָה נְאוֹת מִדְבָּר ("fire consumes the pastures of the wilderness") is found in both vv. 19 and 20.

Joel 2:1–11 is the third passage in the trajectory toward despair. It begins with an initial command to sound an alarm in Zion. It is bounded by an *inclusio* centered upon the day of YHWH and its effects on Zion. Joel blends locust imagery with military imagery to create a picture of an unstoppable invasion force. The prophecy reaches its lowest point with the revelation that this is YHWH's army, and he is directing its assault against his own city.

Joel 2:12–17 provides the hinge from despair to deliverance by urging the audience to cry out to YHWH in response to these crises. YHWH's own speech to the Judahite audience marks the beginning of this unit in 2:12 as he urges the people to "return to me." The rest of the passage explores YHWH's character and details how the audience should answer his directive. Joel 2:17 concludes with Joel providing speech with which the Judahite audience should directly address YHWH, neatly reversing the direction of communication from 2:12. Their appeal to YHWH ends as they conceive of the nations asking the climatic rhetorical question, "where is their God?"

---

50. Ernst R. Wendland, *Prophetic Rhetoric: Case Studies in Text Analysis and Translation*, 2nd ed (Dallas: SIL International, 2014), 3.

Joel 2:18–4:21[3:21] provides YHWH's responses to the crises that place the book on an upward trajectory. It also divides into three passages that offer deliverance from despair. Joel 2:18–27 begins with a *waw*-consecutive + prefix conjugation verb that grounds YHWH's turn toward zeal and compassion for his people. Lexical recursion from the aforementioned crises further marks YHWH's commitment to deliver the Judahite audience from the threat of locusts, drought, and invasion by turning agricultural scarcity into abundance. This passage again culminates with *epistrophe* as 2:26 and 27 both conclude with the same declaration from YHWH: וְלֹא־יֵבֹשׁוּ עַמִּי לְעוֹלָם ("My people will never again be put to shame").

Joel 3:1–5[2:28–32] provides the next step in YHWH's deliverance, as YHWH provides spiritual restoration to mirror physical restoration. Its beginning is marked by the temporal phrase וְהָיָה אַחֲרֵי־כֵן ("it will happen after this"), which introduces an overwhelming outpouring of the divine spirit upon the entire community. This provides a hopeful context for Joel's use of the day of YHWH (3:4[2:31]), which takes the same signs as in 2:10–11 but turns them into promises of restoration. The end of 3:1–5[2:28–32] is marked by repetition of the divine name, highlighting YHWH as the agent of deliverance.

Joel 4:1–21[3:1–21] concludes the journey toward deliverance by shifting its focus from the internal relationship between YHWH and the Judahite audience to the threat posed by foreign nations. Joel 4:1–21[3:1–21] confirms YHWH's presence among his people and his intention to bring judgment on the nations. This passage begins with an introductory temporal phrase בַּיָּמִים הָהֵמָּה וּבָעֵת הַהִיא ("in those days and at that time"), before promising judgment. Various subunits of this passage actualize the judgment announced in 4:1–3[3:1–3], condemning specific nations (4:4–8[3:4–8]), presenting the day of YHWH as a day of judgment on the nations and a day of rescue for Zion (4:9–17[3:9–17]), and offering hope of paradise-like blessing rooted in YHWH's presence in Zion (4:18–21[3:18–21]). Whereas Joel 2:17 concludes with the nations putting Judah to shame, asking "where is their God?", 4:21[3:21] marks the end of this final passage with the ringing affirmation "YHWH dwells in Zion."

This structural outline points to the cohesive nature of the book. Following the superscription, the book embarks on a trajectory toward despair for three passages in 1:2–2:11 that call into question the relationship between YHWH and his people. This trajectory is reversed by three passages in 2:18–4:21[3:21] that provide deliverance from despair and affirm YHWH's commitment to the Judahite audience. Joel 2:12–17 is the fulcrum of the book as it urges the audience to directly appeal to YHWH on the basis of its understanding of the divine character. The analysis that follows will explore the rhetorical strategies through which this book draws its audience from despair to deliverance, rooted in the nature and actions of YHWH.

		Outline of the Book of Joel: Despair and Deliverance in the Day of the Lord	
1			A. Superscription (1:1)
2		1. The Crisis Revealed (1:2–4)	B. Despair on Account of the Locusts (1:2–14)
3			
4			
5		2. The Calls to Lament (1:5–14)	
6			
7			
8			
9			
10			
11			
12			
13			
14			
15		1. The Announcement of the Day of YHWH (1:15–16)	C. Despair in the Day of YHWH —The Drought (1:15–20)
16			
17		2. The Effects of the Day of YHWH (1:17–18)	
18			
19		3. The Appeal to YHWH (1:19–20)	
20			
1		1. The Announcement of the Day of YHWH (2:1–2b)	D. Despair in the Day of YHWH —The Invasion (2:1–11)
2			
3		2. The Advance of the Locust Army (2:2c–5c)	
4			
5			
6		3. The View of the Victims (2:6)	
7		4. The Locust Army Attacks (2:7–9)	
8			
9			
10		5. The Advent of the Day of YHWH (2:10–11)	
11			
12		1. The Call to Return (2:12–14)	E. Hinge: The Call to Return to YHWH (2:12–17)
13			
14			
15		2. The Plan of Return (2:15–17)	
16			
17			

Introduction to Joel

Verses	Subsection	Section
18–20	1. YHWH's Restoration (2:18–20)	**F. Divine Deliverance from the Locusts and Drought (2:18–27)**
21–24	2. Calls to Rejoice (2:21–24)	
25–27	3. YHWH's Promises (2:25–27)	
1–2	1. YHWH's Gift of the Spirit (3:1–2)	**G. Deliverance through the Spirit of YHWH (3:1–5[2:28–32])**
3–4	2. The Signs of the Day of YHWH (3:3–4)	
5	3. Security in Zion (3:5)	
1–3	1. The Introduction of YHWH's Judgment on the Nations (4:1–3)	**H. Deliverance through Divine Judgment on the Day of YHWH (4:1–21[3:1–21])**
4–8	2. YHWH's Judgment on Tyre, Sidon, and Philistia (4:4–8)	
9–17	3. YHWH's Judgment on the Nations (4:9–17)	
18–21	4. YHWH's Restoration of Judah and Jerusalem (4:18–21)	

Joel 1:1

A. Superscription

Main Idea of the Passage

Joel 1:1 identifies YHWH as the source of the prophetic message and Joel as the vehicle through whom it will be communicated.

Literary Context

Joel follows the pattern of the prophetic books of the OT by beginning with a superscription that claims divine authorization for the words that follow. A superscription in a prophetic book identifies the material that follows with the figure whom it names.[1] Consequently, all of the ensuing material, including challenges to YHWH's character and his relationship with his people, remains under the initial assertion that the entire book has divine authorization. Whenever the text uses Joel's voice to call on the audience to cry out to YHWH (1:2–14; 2:15–17), warns it of the impending day of YHWH (2:1–11), or promises deliverance and restoration (2:21–28), the declaration in the superscription that all of this is the word of YHWH remains in effect.

→ A. Superscription (1:1)
  B. Despair on Account of the Locusts (1:2–14)
  C. Despair in the Day of YHWH—The Drought (1:15–20)
  D. Despair in the Day of YHWH—The Invasion (2:1–11)
  E. Hinge: The Call to Return to YHWH (2:12–17)
  F. Divine Deliverance from the Locusts and Drought (2:18–27)
  G. Deliverance through the Spirit of YHWH (3:1–5 [2:28–32])
  H. Deliverance through Divine Judgment on the Day of YHWH (4:1–21 [3:1–21])

---

1. John D. W. Watts, "Superscriptions and Incipits in the Book of the Twelve," in *Reading and Hearing the Book of the Twelve*, SBLSS 15, ed. James D. Nogalski and Marvin A. Sweeney (Atlanta; Society of Biblical Literature, 2000), 111.

Translation and Outline[2]

Joel 1:1

A. Superscription (1:1)

1a	דְּבַר־יהוה	The word of YHWH
1b	אֲשֶׁר הָיָה אֶל־יוֹאֵל בֶּן־פְּתוּאֵל׃	that came to Joel, son of Pethuel

Structure and Literary Form

Superscriptions in prophetic books are structurally independent and likely added during the course of transmission.[3] They assert that the following text is divinely sanctioned.[4] The superscription in 1:1 is terse. It consists only of an introductory verbless clause identifying the following utterances as divinely sourced speech and a relative clause revealing the name of the one to proclaim this message. It fits into one of the broader patterns of superscriptions in prophetic books. Tucker identifies three categories: (1) those beginning with either דְּבַר ("word") or חֲזוֹן ("vision") plus the name of the prophet (cf. Isa 1:1; Jer 1:1; Amos 1:1; Obad 1); (2) those beginning with the expression דְּבַר יהוה ("word of YHWH") followed by identifying the recipient of the divine word (Hos 1:1; Joel 1:1; Mic 1:1; Zeph 1:1); (3) and those beginning with the word מַשָּׂא ("oracle") followed by clarifying information about the prophet or the audience of the oracle (Nah 1:1; Hab 1:1).[5] Joel 1:1 fits into the second category, although it is unique in that it adds no explanatory information after the name of the prophet.

Explanation of the Text

The most notable element of *Joel's* superscription is its brevity, conveying only the most basic information. It asserts that what follows is the דְּבַר יהוה ("word of YHWH"), asserting its authoritative status.[6] The recipient of the divine word is Joel ben Pethuel. This form of the prophet's name provides one generation of his family lineage. However, the name Pethuel is otherwise unattested in the OT so it does not provide any clarity about the time period or social location of the

---

2. The backbone of each of these Translation and Outline sections comes from the excellent work of van der Merwe and Wendland. I have modified their breakdown of the text to fit my understanding of its discourse shape. The translation is my own. See Christo H. J. van der Merwe and Ernst R. Wendland, "Marked Word Order in the Book of Joel," *JNSL* 36 (2010): 109–30.

3. Gene M. Tucker, "Prophetic Superscriptions and the Growth of a Canon," in *Canon and Authority*, ed. Burke O. Long and George W. Coats (Philadelphia: Fortress, 1977), 56–70. Watts has an extended conversation about the role of superscriptions in the formation of the Book of the Twelve. Watts, "Superscriptions," 111–24.

4. Marvin A. Sweeney, *The Twelve Prophets: Vol. 1*, Berit Olam (Collegeville, MN: Liturgical, 2000), 152.

5. Tucker, "Prophetic Superscriptions," 62. Tucker's categories do not cover every prophetic book in the OT. Those not mentioned above have a narrative shape to their opening lines, commonly called an "incipit." This category covers Jonah, Haggai, and Zechariah. See Watts, "Superscriptions," 114–15.

6. Tucker, "Prophetic Superscriptions," 63–64.

prophet.[7] It is also worth noting the lack of regnal formulae in this superscription. All three of the Major Prophets and six prophets within the Book of the Twelve (Hosea, Amos, Micah, Zephaniah, Haggai, and Zechariah) provide some reference to reigning monarchs in order to identify the historical context of the prophecy. The absence of such a formula in *Joel* contributes to the debate about its time of composition.

The terseness of this superscription leaves readers with gaps in their understanding that cannot be filled. However, its minimalism serves the rhetorical purpose of amplifying the fact that this discourse is divine communication. The biography of the prophet is insignificant in comparison to the revelation that what follows is the word of YHWH. It is also possible that the lack of identifying detail accords a certain timelessness to the message of *Joel* since there is no particular circumstance to which it conclusively belongs. One commentator suggests that this ambiguity would make *Joel* easier to use in liturgical contexts as a means of response to different crises.[8] Although there is no evidence for this claim, it does invite the reader to consider how God's word to Joel might resonate wherever it is heard and read.

---

7. The LXX identifies the name of Joel's father as Bethuel, a name which occurs at Gen 22:22–23; 24:15, 24, 47, 50. That Bethuel is the father of Rebekah and the nephew of Abraham. There is no connection between that Bethuel and the father of the prophet Joel. Strazicich suggests that the compliers of the LXX may have adapted the name to avoid a potential embarrassment in that the name Pethuel could mean "seduced by YHWH." See Strazicich, *Joel's Use of Scripture*, 62.

8. Raymond B. Dillard, "Joel," in *The Minor Prophets: An Exegetical and Expository Commentary*, 3 vols.; ed. Thomas E. McComiskey (Grand Rapids: Baker, 1993), 243.

CHAPTER 2

Joel 1:2–14

B. Despair on Account of the Locusts

Main Idea of the Passage

The Judahite audience faces a crisis described as an overwhelming invasion of locusts. Joel directs the entire community to become fully aware of the gravity of the situation and appeal to YHWH for restoration. He urges the priests to lead the people's outcry from the temple grounds.

Literary Context

Joel 1:2–14 begins the downward trajectory of the prophecy with a vivid description of the initial crisis and an appeal to the audience to engage in communal lament.[1] He intertwines images of rampaging locusts and the damage that they cause with the ruin of the Judahite community's agricultural bounty, and even more alarmingly, the cessation of the sacrificial system. This passage creates a sense of urgency, indicating that the only response to the unfolding disaster is to cry out to YHWH. Joel 1:2–14 also establishes the foundation for 1:15–20, which transitions away from a call to a communal gathering and begins to offer the words for appeal.[2] The urgency that underlies this initial passage invites the audience to reflect upon the gravity of the unfolding crisis. This permits Joel to propose what he suggests is an appropriate solution in forthcoming passages.

---

1. Dillard, "Joel," 243; Wendland, *Prophetic Rhetoric*, 7. Wendland follows Dillard in assuming that *Joel* is oriented toward lament, although it does not perfectly fit any established genre.

2. Prinsloo, *Theology*, 28.

A. Superscription (1:1)
→ **B. Despair on Account of the Locusts (1:2–14)**
   1. The Crisis Revealed (1:2–4)
   2. The Calls to Lament (1:5-14)
C. Despair in the Day of YHWH—The Drought (1:15–20)
D. Despair in the Day of YHWH—The Invasion (2:1–11)
E. Hinge: The Call to Return to YHWH (2:12–17)
F. Divine Deliverance from the Locusts and Drought (2:18–27)
G. Deliverance through the Spirit of YHWH (3:1–5 [2:28–32])
H. Deliverance through Divine Judgment on the Day of YHWH (4:1–21 [3:1–21])

Translation and Outline

(See pages 50–51.)

Structure and Literary Form

Joel 1:2–14 is bounded by an *inclusio* in 1:2 and 14. Joel 1:2 announces the impending crisis by appealing to the זְקֵנִים ("elders") and יוֹשְׁבֵי הָאָרֶץ ("inhabitants of the land"), effectively drawing in the entire Judahite community. The following verses then appeal to specific sub-groups within these larger categories. Joel 1:14 widens the perspective again, summarizing the situation with a command directed once again to the "elders" and "inhabitants of the land." The prophet commands them to gather and cry out to YHWH, now that Joel has detailed the full gravity of the situation. By returning to the "elders" and the "inhabitants of the land" in 1:14, the text signals the completion of its series of appeals. Joel 1:14 also signals that it concludes this first literary unit by means of a climactic imperative וְזַעֲקוּ אֶל־יהוה ("then, cry out to YHWH"), which encapsulates all of the commands that the prophet has given throughout this passage.[3] The appeals to the sub-groups, including drunkards, agricultural laborers, and priests build toward this all-encompassing declaration.

Another key to the structural cohesion of 1:2–14 is its use of imperative verbs. Joel employs eighteen imperative forms in this passage, imploring the audience to hear and respond (1:2, 3, 5, 8, 11, 13, 14) and revealing his claim to the authority to compel a response. The frequent use of imperatives makes the urgency of the situation abundantly clear. Joel does not linger on a lengthy description of the crisis. Instead, once he identifies its shape, he focuses on calling the audience to respond appropriately.

---

3. van der Merwe and Wendland, "Word Order," 120.

Joel 1:2–14

			B. Despair on the Account of the Locusts (1:2–14)
			1. The Crisis Revealed (1:2–4)
			a. The Call to Hear (1:2a–b)
2a	שִׁמְעוּ־זֹאת הַזְּקֵנִים	Hear this, o elders!	
2b	וְהַאֲזִינוּ כֹּל יוֹשְׁבֵי הָאָרֶץ	Give ear, all inhabitants of the land!	
2c	הֶהָיְתָה זֹּאת בִּימֵיכֶם	Has this been in your day?	b. Assertions of Incomparability (1:2c–3c)
2d	וְאִם בִּימֵי אֲבֹתֵיכֶם׃	Or even in the days of your fathers?	
3a	עָלֶיהָ לִבְנֵיכֶם סַפֵּרוּ	Proclaim concerning this to your children,	
3b	וּבְנֵיכֶם לִבְנֵיהֶם	and your children to their children,	
3c	וּבְנֵיהֶם לְדוֹר אַחֵר׃	and their children to the generation after.	
4a	יֶתֶר הַגָּזָם אָכַל הָאַרְבֶּה	The remainder from the gnawing locust, the swarming locust ate,	c. The Locusts' Assault (1:4)
4b	וְיֶתֶר הָאַרְבֶּה אָכַל הַיָּלֶק	and the remainder from the swarming locust, the creeping locust ate,	
4c	וְיֶתֶר הַיֶּלֶק אָכַל הֶחָסִיל׃	and the remainder from the creeping locust, the stripping locust ate.	
			2. The Calls to Lament (1:5–14)
			a. A Call to the Drunkards (1:5–7)
			(1) A Command to Lament (1:5)
5a	הָקִיצוּ שִׁכּוֹרִים	Awake, o drunkards!	
5b	וּבְכוּ	And weep!	
5c	וְהֵילִלוּ כָּל שֹׁתֵי יָיִן	Wail, all drinkers of wine, on account of the sweet wine,	
5d	עַל עָסִיס כִּי נִכְרַת מִפִּיכֶם׃	for it is cut off from you.	
			(2) The Effect of the Locusts (1:6–7)
6a	כִּי גוֹי עָלָה עַל אַרְצִי	Now a nation has come up upon my land,	
6b	עָצוּם וְאֵין מִסְפָּר	many, and there is no counting [them].	
6c	שִׁנָּיו שִׁנֵּי אַרְיֵה	Its teeth are the teeth of a lion,	
6d	וּמְתַלְּעוֹת לָבִיא לוֹ׃	and the fangs of a lioness are to it.	
7a	שָׂם גַּפְנִי לְשַׁמָּה	It has made my vine a desolation,	
7b	וּתְאֵנָתִי לִקְצָפָה	and my fig tree, a splinter.	
7c	חָשֹׂף חֲשָׂפָהּ וְהִשְׁלִיךְ	It has completely stripped it bare,	
7d	הִלְבִּינוּ שָׂרִיגֶיהָ׃	and made white its tendrils.	
			b. A Call to Wail (1:8–10)
			(1) A Picture of Wailing (1:8a)
8a	אֱלִי כִבְתוּלָה חֲגֻרַת שַׂק עַל בַּעַל נְעוּרֶיהָ׃	Wail like a virgin clothed in sackcloth, concerning the lord of her youth!	
9a	הָכְרַת מִנְחָה וָנֶסֶךְ מִבֵּית יְהוָה	Cut off are the grain-offering and drink-offering from the house of YHWH.	(2) Reason for Wailing (1:9a)
9b	אָבְלוּ הַכֹּהֲנִים מְשָׁרְתֵי יְהוָה׃	The priests, the ministers of YHWH, mourn.	(3) The Mourning of the Priests (1:9b)

10a	שָׁדַד שָׂדֶה	The field is destroyed.	(4) Agricultural Destruction (1:10)
10b	אָבְלָה אֲדָמָה	The earth mourns,	
10c	כִּי שֻׁדַּד דָּגָן	for the grain is destroyed,	
10d	הוֹבִישׁ תִּירוֹשׁ	the new wine dries up,	
10e	אֻמְלַל יִצְהָר׃	the fresh oil fails.	
11a	הֹבִישׁוּ אִכָּרִים	Be ashamed, o farmers!	c. A Call to the Farmers (1:11–12)
11b	הֵילִילוּ כֹּרְמִים עַל־חִטָּה וְעַל־שְׂעֹרָה	Wail, o vine-grower, on account of the wheat and barley,	(1) A Command to be Ashamed (1:11a–b)
11c	כִּי אָבַד קְצִיר שָׂדֶה׃	for destroyed is the harvest of the field!	(2) Further Agricultural Destruction (1:11c–12d)
12a	הַגֶּפֶן הוֹבִישָׁה	The vine dries up,	
12b	וְהַתְּאֵנָה אֻמְלָלָה	and the fig tree withers.	
12c	רִמּוֹן גַּם־תָּמָר וְתַפּוּחַ כָּל־עֲצֵי הַשָּׂדֶה יָבֵשׁוּ	The pomegranate tree, even the fig tree and the apple tree, all the trees of the field have dried up.	
12d	כִּי־הֹבִישׁ שָׂשׂוֹן מִן־בְּנֵי אָדָם׃	Even joy is dried up from the sons of man.	
13a	חִגְרוּ	Gird up	d. A Call to the Priests (1:13–14)
13b	וְסִפְדוּ הַכֹּהֲנִים	and mourn, o priests!	(1) The Commands to the Priests (1:13a–e)
13c	הֵילִילוּ מְשָׁרְתֵי מִזְבֵּחַ	Wail, o ministers of the altar!	
13d	בֹּאוּ	Enter,	
13e	לִינוּ בַשַּׂקִּים מְשָׁרְתֵי אֱלֹהָי	spend the night in sackcloth, o ministers of my God!	
13f	כִּי נִמְנַע מִבֵּית אֱלֹהֵיכֶם מִנְחָה וָנָסֶךְ׃	The grain-offering and drink-offering are withheld from the house of your God.	(2) The Reasons for the Priests' Cries (1:13f)
14a	קַדְּשׁוּ־צוֹם	Consecrate a fast!	(3) The Call to Address YHWH (1:14)
14b	קִרְאוּ עֲצָרָה	Call a solemn assembly!	
14c	אִסְפוּ זְקֵנִים	Gather the elders!	
14d	כֹּל יֹשְׁבֵי הָאָרֶץ בֵּית יְהוָה אֱלֹהֵיכֶם	All those living in the land [to] the house of YHWH your God.	
14e	וְזַעֲקוּ אֶל־יְהוָה׃	Then, cry out to YHWH!	

The use of imperatives ceases in 1:15–20, suggesting that a new literary unit has commenced, which interacts with the Judahite audience in a different manner.

The frequent use of imperatives also helps to shape the literary structure of this unit. It divides into two parts: 1:2–4 announces the crisis and 1:5–14 issues a series of calls for segments of the Judahite audience to respond by crying out to YHWH. Joel 1:2 begins its section with synonymous imperatives שִׁמְעוּ ("Hear!") and וְהַאֲזִינוּ ("Give ear!"), before announcing the nature of the crisis in 1:3–4. Joel 1:5–14 consists of a series of calls to cry out to YHWH that follow a particular pattern. Each separate cry contains an imperative, a vocative identification of the addressee, and a reason for wailing (1:5, 8, 11, 13). These subunits combine to provide a comprehensive response to the crisis. They indicate that each element of the Judahite audience must do its part in crying out to YHWH.

Explanation of the Text

1. The Crisis Revealed (vv. 2–4)

Joel's first task is to emphasize the gravity of the situation. Joel 1:2–3 accomplishes this goal by first introducing the unique nature of the current crisis, suggesting that its magnitude requires the audience's full attention. Joel 1:2a–b sets the tone for the broader persuasive strategy of this unit, commencing with two parallel imperatives: שִׁמְעוּ־זֹאת הַזְּקֵנִים ("Hear this, o elders!") and וְהַאֲזִינוּ כֹּל יוֹשְׁבֵי הָאָרֶץ ("Give ear, all inhabitants of the land!"). This use of a parallel command to specify the nature of the intended audience is a common rhetorical technique found in wisdom instruction (Prov 4:1; 7:24), diplomatic discourse (2 Kgs 18:28–29), and other prophetic oracles (Hos 4:1; Amos 3:1; Mic 6:1; Isa 1:10; Ezek 6:3).[4]

These commands identify the intended audience as the הַזְּקֵנִים ("elders") and the יוֹשְׁבֵי הָאָרֶץ ("inhabitants of the land"). Elders are part of the traditional tribal leadership structure and they performed numerous functions, including acting as counselors (Num 11:16–30; 1 Kgs 12:6, 13), serving in legal capacities (Deut 21:2–20; Ruth 4:9–11), and representing the people in religious service (Lev 4:15; 9:1–2; Josh 7:33; 1 Kgs 8:3).[5] The specific parameters of their authority are not Joel's concern. Rather, he is appealing to them as a body that shapes the audience's answer to his commands. On account of the nature of their authority, elders maintain the connection to traditional knowledge. Their affirmation of the uniqueness of the current crisis, and their commitment to retelling it would carry great weight.[6] The phrase "inhabitants of the

---

4. Sweeney, *Twelve*, 155. Wolff highlights the connection to wisdom literature, referring to the commands in Joel 1:2 as a literary form identified as the "call to receive instruction." However, the wide variety of literary contexts in which this approach is used suggests that it is unlikely that one can isolate the origin of this form. See Wolff, *Joel and Amos*, 84.

5. Sweeney, *Twelve*, 155. Some focus instead on "elders" as a term indicating advanced age, suggesting that these people can bring to bear a longer view that points to the uniqueness of the current situation. See for example Duane A. Garrett, *Hosea,*

Joel, NAC 19A (Nashville: Broadman & Holman, 1997), 313. However, understanding "elders" as reference to the people's leaders makes more sense given that it is placed in parallel with the phrase "inhabitants of the land." Consequently, Joel targets the entire people, from its leaders to its constituent members, with the power of the prophetic word.

6. The phrase "counsel of the elders" occurs alongside the vision of the prophets and the teaching of the priests as a form of instruction for the broader people of Israel (Jer 18:18; Ezek 7:26). See Cornelius van Dam, *The Elder*, Explorations in

land" encompasses the rest of the nation, signifying the totality of the audience that the prophet intends to address (cf. Jer 10:18; Hos 4:1).

Joel then employs a rhetorical strategy of delay to heighten the tension. Before identifying the nature of the crisis, he pauses to stress its incomparability. He asks two rhetorical questions in 1:2c–d, הֶהָיְתָה זֹּאת בִּימֵיכֶם ("Has this been in your day?") and וְאִם בִּימֵי אֲבֹתֵיכֶם ("Or even in the days of your fathers?"). The implied answers to these questions are negative, in keeping with the principle of "reversed polarity" that governs rhetorical questions.[7] A rhetorical question is a useful strategy for engaging an audience since it "establishes a consensus, or common ground between the speaker and addressee, which is then used to advance the argument."[8] The prophet essentially invites the "elders" from 1:2a to draw upon their knowledge and life experience to confirm that they are facing an unmatched threat.[9] This verse thus establishes the exceptionality of the current situation and calls the audience to listen to the forthcoming prophetic word.

Joel continues this strategy of delay in 1:3 by stressing the incomparability of the situation, again without revealing its nature. He orders the audience to communicate this message to successive generations through the repetition of בָּנִים ("children"), which occurs four times in the three clauses in this verse. Essentially, four generations are in view: 1:3a points to the generation witnessing the crisis and וּבְנֵיכֶם ("your children") whom the witnessing generation will tell. Joel 1:3b refers to the third generation as וּבְנֵיהֶם ("and their children") who will hear the message from the second generation, while 1:3c introduces the fourth generation as לְדוֹר אַחֵר ("the generation after") who will hear about this crisis from the third generation. Joel's attention to detail in commanding the telling and retelling of this crisis stresses that it should become a matter of continual remembrance. Further, the reference to future generations in 1:3c works in tandem with the reference to prior generations in 1:2d. If previous generations have not witnessed anything like this and successive generations are to hear about it continuously, then it is undoubtedly a noteworthy event.

Following this delay in 1:2–3, 1:4 finally reveals the precise nature of the catastrophe. This verse describes the crisis as a locust invasion that completely devastates the land and its produce. The interpretation of this locust invasion is debated, with some arguing that the locusts are a metaphor for an attacking army, while others view them as a literal locust plague. Locust imagery dominates 1:2–2:11, again recurring in 2:25. Those who argue that the locusts are metaphorical point to the use of locust imagery in other biblical contexts (cf. Judg 6:3–5; 7:12; Jer 46:23; Nah 3:15–16).[10] They also note the highly hyperbolic language employed in Joel 1, suggesting that a cyclical appearance of a known phenomenon like a locust invasion would not occasion such heightened rhetoric.[11] Instead,

---

Biblical Theology (Phillipsburg, NJ: Presbyterian & Reformed, 2009), 60.

7. Adina Moshavi, "Can a Positive Rhetorical Question Have a Positive Answer in the Bible?" *JSS* 56 (2011): 253–54. Moshavi notes that the principle of "reversed polarity" governs rhetorical questions across multiple languages. Here, the positive question "has this happened before?" implies a negative answer, whereas a negative question such as "has this *not* happened before?" would imply a positive answer.

8. Adina Moshavi, "Interrogative: Biblical Hebrew," in vol. 2 of *Encyclopedia of Hebrew Language and Linguistics*, ed. Geoffrey Khan (Leiden: Brill, 2013), 310.

9. Crenshaw, *Joel*, 86. Crenshaw notes broader evidence of the use of an "appeal to the unprecedented." He cites Sumerian texts that employ incomparability as a strategy to gain an audience. Of course, establishing the novelty of the situation in order to compel a desired response is far from being only an ancient phenomenon.

10. Pablo R. Andiñach, "The Locusts in the Message of Joel," *VT* 42 (1992): 433–44.

11. Stuart, *Hosea—Jonah*, 242.

the invasion of Judah by the Babylonian army would be a much more likely reason to employ the language of devastation and destruction.[12] Further, the fact that Joel 1:6 explicitly mentions that a גוֹי ("nation") has invaded has been taken as evidence suggesting the presence of human invaders.[13]

However, these arguments are not conclusive. The use of hyperbolic language does not necessarily indicate that the crisis is metaphorically represented. Instead, one can argue that Joel seized upon the occurrence of a known threat and used it to call the community to a greater awareness of the spiritual reality of the day of YHWH unfolding around them. An actual locust invasion could certainly function as a harbinger of that day, much like the plagues functioned in Israel's exodus from Egypt.[14] Second, Joel's description of the locusts' behavior corresponds with reports of actual locust infestations. Joel describes how they destroyed two of Israel's most important agricultural resources: vines and fig trees (1:7). He creates an image of the locusts stripping off the bark so the bare branches become bleached, which accurately describes what happens when locusts ravage these trees.[15] The detail of Joel's description suggests that he is using imagery drawn from an actual invasion of locusts.

This invasion creates a striking backdrop for his prophetic message. The destruction caused by the locusts creates a threat that Joel uses to guide his audience to the response that he desires. Further, an invasion of locusts in 1:2–14 fits with the nature of the hope found in 2:18–27 when YHWH restores all that the locusts have destroyed.[16]

The rhetoric of 1:4 is connected to 1:2–3 since again it uses three clauses to describe four generations, or waves, of locusts. Joel refers to each wave with a synonym, probably reflecting different stages of development of the desert locust. However the exact meaning of each synonym is unknown.[17] Joel is not focusing on temporal succession as in 1:3, but on the severity of the event.[18] The use of synonyms for each wave of locusts is essential to Joel's rhetorical strategy along with syntactical repetition. Each of the three clauses in 1:4a–c commences with the construct noun יֶתֶר ("remainder"), followed by one of the four words for locust. The verb אָכַל ("it ate") occurs next, followed by the subsequent locust synonym. Consequently, there is symmetry here since the four generations of locusts equal the four generations of the audience who will witness and retell the account of this crisis.

The effect of this repetition is to highlight the land's total destruction, since what remains after each wave of locusts is devoured by the successive wave. The combination of the rhetoric of delay in 1:2–3, the stylized use of successive generations of both audience and locusts, and the revelation of the locusts' complete devastation in 1:4 are the key rhe-

---

12. Ibid., 240. Stuart does not distinguish between the invasions of 597 BCE and 586 BCE. Presumably, either would be traumatic enough to trigger the images of devastation that Joel employs. Of course, Stuart's commitment to the preexilic date for *Joel* renders a metaphorical reading more suitable.

13. Ogden and Deutsch, *Joel & Malachi*, 11.

14. Ronald A. Simkins, "God, History, and the Natural World in the Book of Joel," *CBQ* 55 (1993): 437.

15. Ronald A. Simkins, *Yahweh's Activity in History and Nature in the Book of Joel*, ANETS 10 (Lewiston: Edwin Mellen, 1991), 130. He references a similar description of a 1915 locust infestation in Jerusalem.

16. Prinsloo, *Theology*, 127.

17. Simkins, *Yahweh's Activity*, 101–20; John A. Thompson, "Joel's Locusts in the Light of Near Eastern Parallels," *JNES* 14 (1955): 54; O. R. Sellers, "Stages of Locust in Joel," *AJSL* 52 (1935–36): 81–95. Sellers suggests that each term refers to a different phase in the development of the desert locust. Thompson, however, argues that the desert locust has six stages of development instead of four. This is not an issue that should sidetrack the interpreter. In my translation, I refer to the locusts as "gnawing," "swarming," "creeping," and "stripping" mostly to emphasize different activities that locusts undertake. A precise identification of each of the locust synonyms is not necessary since their rhetorical function is to emphasize the totality of the destruction.

18. van der Merwe and Wendland, "Word Order," 117.

torical features of 1:2–4. These verses indicate that a severe crisis is at hand, which lays the foundations for the prophet's strategy to call the Judahite audience to a proper response.[19]

2. The Calls to Lament (1:5–14)

a. A Call to the Drunkards (1:5–7)

Following the announcement of the locust crisis, Joel details how the audience ought to respond through a series of four subunits that begin with imperatives (1:5–7, 8–10, 11–12, 13–14). Each of these subunits follows a similar structural pattern, building a multi-stage call to lament. Each stage consists of three elements: (1) the command to lament, (2) a vocative indicating who is to lament, and (3) the reasons for lament.[20] The first subunit is found in 1:5–7, and it initiates Joel's plan for how the Judahite audience should react to the locust invasion. The first stage of the lament in this subunit is found in 1:5, which contains three imperatives within its first four words. The prophet calls on the שִׁכּוֹרִים ("drunkards") first to הָקִיצוּ ("awake") in 1:5a and then to וּבְכוּ ("weep") in 1:5b. Joel 1:5c begins with the imperative וְהֵילִלוּ ("wail"), which is addressed to כָּל־שֹׁתֵי יָיִן ("all drinkers of wine"), paralleling the שִׁכּוֹרִים ("drunkards") in 1:5a. The sequence of imperatives suggests urgency as Joel issues short, sharp commands.

The imperatives directed at the drunkards reveal Joel's initial rhetorical strategy. First, they are the ones most affected by the lack of wine mentioned in Joel 1:5d and the destruction of the vine in 1:7a.[21] The lack of wine also makes it impossible to properly perform cultic ceremonies, which strengthens the reason to weep and wail.[22] Secondly, the imperative הָקִיצוּ ("awake") in 1:5a suggests a metaphorical understanding of drunkenness where it denotes an inability to comprehend what is happening.[23] This imperative typically refers to waking from sleep (1 Sam 26:12; 2 Kgs 4:31; Isa 29:8; Jer 31:26; Pss 3:6; 73:20), although Prov 23:35 does refer to waking from drunkenness to seek out more to drink.[24] Consequently, an address to the drunkards captures a subgroup of the community affected by the crisis and may symbolize the unresponsive posture of the audience.[25]

Using derisive terminology to address part of the audience combines the punitive and persuasive elements of prophetic speech. Jemielity comments on this rhetorical strategy, noting that "[s]atire and prophecy thus seek and despair of reform at the same time, urge change and yet expect none."[26] In essence, ridiculing drunkards requires the rest of the audience to engage with the prophetic message and assert that they do not deserve that label. Consequently, calling for drunkards and wine-drinkers to awake is appropriate to the situation. Once the prophet goads these drunkards and wine-drinkers

---

19. Chaim Perelman and L. Olbrechts-Tyteca, *The New Rhetoric: A Treatise on Argumentation* (Notre Dame: Notre Dame University Press, 1969), 21. Perelman and Olbrechts-Tyteca stress that a speaker must create a shared understanding of the situation with the audience. Joel's use of repetition 1:2–4 urges the audience to match his understanding of the magnitude of the crisis.

20. Wolff, *Joel and Amos*, 21–22.

21. Simkins, *Yahweh's Activity*, 125.

22. Kathleen S. Nash, "The Palestinian Agricultural Year and the Book of Joel" (PhD diss., Catholic University of America, 1989), 84.

23. Stuart, *Hosea—Jonah*, 242. Jemielity suggests that the text is classifying the entire audience as "drunkards," rather than referring to a specific subset. He refers to the audience of *Joel* as, "indolent, lolling drunken elders." See Thomas Jemielity, *Satire in the Hebrew Prophets* (Louisville: Westminster John Knox, 1992), 89. However, since the following imperatives refer to subsets of the Judahite community such as farmers and priests, it make sense to understand "drunkards" as a subset as well. No matter the range of the term "drunkards," its pejorative nature is a striking beginning to a prophetic call to response.

24. Dillard, "Joel," 258.

25. Assis, *Joel*, 78–79.

26. Jemielity, *Satire*, 81.

with the initial imperative, he can begin to guide them toward an appropriate response.

Joel 1:5c–d provides the reason for the prophet's calls for weeping and wailing. The drunkards must lament עַל־עָסִיס ("on account of the sweet-wine"), a potentially intoxicating drink (Isa 49:26; Song 8:2). In the current crisis, it has been נִכְרַת מִפִּיכֶם ("cut off from your mouths"). The object suffix on מִפִּיכֶם refers back to the drunkards and wine-drinkers addressed in the preceding imperatives. They experience the deleterious effects of the locust invasion quickly.

Joel 1:6–7 expands on the prophet's calls to lament by describing the damage caused by the locusts. Joel 1:6a personifies the locusts as an invading nation attacking YHWH's chosen land. The first-person suffix אַרְצִי ("my land") inserts the voice of YHWH into this discussion. This continues in 1:7a–b, which describes how the locusts devoured גַּפְנִי ("my vine") and תְאֵנָתִי ("my fig tree"). By referring to YHWH in the first person, the prophet identifies YHWH with the community that is experiencing this crisis since he too is affected by the activities of the locusts.[27] Joel thus vividly describes how the locusts have cut off the wine from its drinkers and have wrought havoc on the land that YHWH claims.

Joel 1:6 also describes the nature of the invading locusts. Their identity as a גוֹי ("nation") is deepened in 1:6b by the revelation that this nation is עָצוּם וְאֵין מִסְפָּר ("mighty and without number"). Joel 1:6c–d then reveal that not only are they an innumerable swarm, they are also built for destruction. The prophet compares their power and might to the devouring teeth and jaws of lions, emphasizing the ferocity with which locusts devour crops. These images describe the two most destructive features of locust infestations: vast numbers and voracious appetite.[28]

Joel 1:7 concludes this first lament by transitioning away from a description of the locusts to the results of their depredations.[29] The choice of vine and fig tree as the crops that the locusts destroy in 1:7a–b is significant because the abundance of these two crops symbolizes security and prosperity (1 Kgs 4:25; 2 Kgs 18:3; Isa 36:16; Mic 4:4; Zech 3:10). Consequently, the destruction of the vines and fig trees points to insecurity and poverty. Joel 1:7c stylizes the destruction through the construction חָשֹׂף חֲשָׂפָהּ ("completely stripped it bare"), which consists of an infinitive absolute followed by a suffix conjugation verb from the same root. This construction specifies the "intensity or extreme nature" of the verbal idea.[30] Here, it portrays the locusts as removing all of the protective bark from the branches, killing the plants through exposure. The scope of the devastation caused by the locusts provides ample justification for Joel's address to the drunkards and wine-drinkers.

b. A Call to Wail (1:8–10)

The next call to lament is found in 1:8–10. It begins with the imperative אֱלִי ("wail"). The addressee of this command is left unstated, but it agrees in gender with the call for the community to mourn כִּבְתוּלָה ("like young woman/virgin") who has lost her betrothed. The absence of a specific addressee occurs only in this call, although it is possible to argue that the implied addressee is Jerusalem, personified as a woman (Isa 52:1; Jer 4:14; 6:8;

---

27. Crenshaw, *Joel*, 96. It is noteworthy that the possessive suffixes identifying YHWH with the land and its people disappear as the text dives deeper into despair, only to reappear in 2:18–4:21 [3:21] when YHWH promises to bring deliverance.

28. Simkins, *Yahweh's Activity*, 129. For the non-squeamish, this video offers some perspective of the nature of a locust swarm: http://www.youtube.com/watch?v=wxHOxCmbs-8.

29. van der Merwe and Wendland, "Word Order," 118.

30. Christo H. J. van der Merwe, Jacobus A. Naudé, and Jan H. Kroeze, *A Biblical Hebrew Reference Grammar*, 2nd edition (London: Bloomsbury T & T Clark, 2017 [hereafter *BHRG*]), §20.2.2.2.

Zeph 3:14; Zech 9:13).³¹ The potential reference to Jerusalem in 1:8 may anticipate the transition to the temple as the location of mourning in the following verse. Following the imperative, Joel employs the simile of a virgin mourning the loss of her betrothed. This simile creates an image of distress as it pictures the woman garbed in sackcloth, which cruelly replaces the prospect of marriage.³² The loss of the betrothed would likely leave a woman facing a precarious future, unable to guarantee a source of social and economic stability.³³

Joel 1:9 provides the reasons behind the opening call to wail, focusing on the interruption of the cultic offering system. The totality of the devastation means that the community is unable to give its tithes to the sanctuary of YHWH. This leads to the cessation of the daily grain and drink offerings. Consequently, the temple and the priests who depend on those offerings as part of their food supply are cut off from a primary source of sustenance (cf. Lev 27:30–33; Num 18:12; Deut 14:22–29; 18:1–8; 26:1–15).³⁴ Further, the interruption of these offerings points to a breakdown in cultic communion with YHWH. Seitz captures this, stating that Joel portrays "a priesthood ready and able to exercise the vocation God has given them, who are instead in mourning because they are prevented from doing that sacred duty."³⁵ This is terrifying since it indicates that the ramifications of the locust invasion go well beyond physical deprivation.³⁶

This lament cry concludes in 1:10 with five more agricultural images that emphasize the scope of destruction wrought by the invading locusts. These images are presented succinctly since each contains only two words, beginning with a verb describing destruction or lament, followed by a subject. Only the particle כִּי between the second and third sequence interrupts this pattern. The first two images found in 1:10a–b read שֻׁדַּד שָׂדֶה אָבְלָה אֲדָמָה ("the field is destroyed, the earth mourns"). Each clause is woven together through similar words and sounds. Both words in 1:10a begin with a sibilant consonant followed by a *dalet* sound, while the two words in 1:10b are alliterative and also rhyme. The image in 1:10a is passive as the unmentioned locusts destroy the fields. The image in 1:10b is active as the earth mourns in response. Joel employs the same verb of mourning in 1:9b (אבל) to describe the response of the priests, linking human and natural realms.³⁷ This juxtaposition reinforces the idea that nothing living, whether human, animal, or agricultural, escapes the devastation of the locusts.

Joel 1:10c–e gives three reasons why the earth is mourning, following the initial כִּי. The wordplay

---

31. Dillard, "Joel," 261; Simkins, *Yahweh's Activity*, 131–35.
32. Crenshaw, *Joel*, 98.
33. On the vulnerability of widowhood see Daniel I. Block, "Marriage and Family in Ancient Israel" in *Marriage and Family in the Ancient World*, ed. Ken M. Campbell (Downers Grove, IL: IVP Academic, 2003), 71–72.
34. Sweeney, *Twelve*, 158.
35. Christopher R. Seitz, *Joel*, ITC (London: Bloomsbury, 2016), 135.
36. Prinsloo, *Theology*, 20. Prinsloo emphasizes the continuity between cultic and agricultural realms. The crops that are harvested in YHWH's land are the produce that must be offered to YHWH as part of the cultic worship experience.
37. Katherine M. Hayes, *The Earth Mourns: Prophetic Metaphor and Oral Aesthetic*, SBLAB 8 (Leiden: Brill, 2002), 192. Some suggest that there is a second root אָבַל with the meaning "to dry up" related to an Akkadian cognate *abālu* when this verb has a non-human subject. In several passages (Jer 12:4; 23:10; Joel 1:10; Amos 1:2) this root appears alongside the verb יָבֵשׁ ("to wither"). However, Clines provides examples where the non-human subject is clearly portrayed as mourning (Isa 3:26; Jer 12:10–11; Lam 1:4; 2:8). This greatly weakens the case for positing a separate root (David J. A. Clines, "Was There a '*bl* II 'be dry' in Classical Hebrew?," *VT* 42 [1992]: 1–11). Instead, the primary meaning, "to mourn," includes the sense of "drying up," when the mourner is the earth itself. See Katherine M. Hayes, "When None Repents, Earth Laments: The Chorus of Lament in Jeremiah and Joel," in *Seeking the Favor of God—Volume 1: The Origins of Penitential Prayer in Second Temple Judaism*, SBLEJL 21, ed. Mark J. Boda, Daniel K. Falk, and Rodney Werline (Atlanta: Society of Biblical Literature, 2006), 128; Assis, *Joel*, 89.

continues as 10c–d also employ a repetition of consonant sounds.³⁸ Each clause then focuses on the destruction of a particular resource. In turn, Joel addresses the loss of the דָּגָן ("grain"), תִּירוֹשׁ ("new wine"), and יִצְהָר ("oil") with three synonymous verbs. These three crops were staples of Israel's agricultural produce, and their inclusion here reflects the totality of the destruction. It also reinforces the resulting inability to properly worship YHWH since these crops were necessary parts of the sacrifices.³⁹

c. A Call to the Farmers (1:11–12)

Joel 1:11–12 consists of the third call to lament which addresses the אִכָּרִים ("farmers") and כֹּרְמִים ("vine growers") while describing the destruction of still more crops. Specifically, Joel 1:11 mentions grain and barley, along with the vines and fig trees that were mentioned in the first call to cry out in 1:7. Joel 1:12 expands on the list and adds other fruit crops including the pomegranate, date-palm, and apple trees. Nash suggests that this collection of crops may reflect a year of complete agricultural failure based on the times when the crops should have been harvested. It covers the period of winter rains to the summer harvest and culminates with the time of the celebration at Sukkoth.⁴⁰ This envisions a year of a complete breakdown of the agricultural system and threatens the community's very existence.

This subunit is also marked by lexeme repetition and an elaborate wordplay. Following the established pattern, Joel 1:11a commences with the imperative הֹבִישׁוּ ("Be ashamed"). This imperative is derived from the root בושׁ while the following clauses of this call to lament contain two uses of the verb יָבֵשׁ ("to dry up/wither") in the affix conjugation. These two verbal roots are easy to confuse in their conjugated forms since they share two consonants (*bet* and *shin*). It is likely that Joel deliberately exploits that potential in 1:12d that begins with the phrase שָׂשׂוֹן כִּי־הֹבִישׁ ("even joy is dried up"). In this instance, Joel creates a double entendre where the shame of the farmers in 1:11a results from the withering of the land and its produce.⁴¹

The joy mentioned in Joel 1:12d is related to the difficulties afflicting the cult. The cessation of these sacrifices indicates that the locusts have interrupted the relationship between the community and YHWH. Essentially, the withering of agricultural produce leads to shame because of their inability to offer the necessary sacrifices.⁴² The similarity of the two roots is another facet of how the text connects the natural and human realms since both lament what they have lost.⁴³ Consequently, 1:11–12 builds off of the preceding calls to lament and pushes another element of the audience to enter into mourning while again indicating the widespread reach of this crisis.

d. A Call to the Priests (1:13–14)

The final call to lament again shifts focus, moving from the agricultural realm to the world of cultic ritual. Joel 1:13a–e consists of five imperative clauses, three of which are followed by terms identifying the cultic leaders who are addressed by the commands.⁴⁴ Joel 1:13a–b consists of two consecutive imperatives addressed to the priests. The prophet directs them to put on mourning garb with the commands חִגְרוּ וְסִפְדוּ ("gird up and mourn"). These commands reflect the gravity of the situation since priests often were not permitted to mourn for

---

38. Assis, *Joel*, 90. There is a repetition of *daleth* sounds in 10c (דְּגָן שֻׁדַּד), and a repetition of *shin* in 10d (הוֹבִישׁ תִּירוֹשׁ).
39. Dillard, "Joel," 262.
40. Nash, "Palestinian," 68.
41. Prinsloo, *Theology*, 20.
42. Simkins, *Yahweh's Activity*, 144–45.
43. Hayes, *The Earth Mourns*, 194. See the discussion of Joel 1:8–10.
44. Assis, *Book of Joel*, 100–1.

the dead without compromising their ritual purity (Lev 10:4–7; 21:10–12).⁴⁵

Joel 1:13c advances the call for the priests to cry out with the command הֵילִילוּ ("Wail!"). Joel also directs this imperative to cultic personnel whom he identifies as the מְשָׁרְתֵי מִזְבֵּחַ ("ministers of the altar"). Variations of this phrase are found throughout Joel's calls to lament since 1:9b refers to the מְשָׁרְתֵי יהוה ("ministers of YHWH"), while 1:13e appeals to the מְשָׁרְתֵי אֱלֹהָי ("ministers of my God"). Referring to the priests with the term מְשָׁרְתֵי מִזְבֵּחַ ("ministers of the altar") draws attention to the cessation of sacrifices. These officials cannot minister at the altar if the locust invasion has destroyed the basic necessities for offering proper sacrifices.

Joel 1:13d–e completes the sequence of imperatives directed at the priests. It also moves from general commands for lament to proposing a specific course of action while maintaining the basic pattern of imperatives addressed to cultic personnel. Joel 1:13d consists simply of the imperative בֹּאוּ ("Enter"), which is followed in 1:13e with the command לִינוּ בַשַׂקִּים מְשָׁרְתֵי אֱלֹהָי ("spend the night in sackcloth, o ministers of my God"). This suggests that the situation requires an extended period of lament, marked by donning mourning garb in the presence of the sanctuary (cf. 2 Sam 12:16; 1 Kgs 21:27).⁴⁶ Further, this clause draws a parallel to 1:8 since it recalls the image of the young woman in sackcloth.

The final clause in 1:13f concludes this verse by providing the reason for the previous commands to lament. It again focuses on the lack of sacrifices, indicating that there is a cessation of the מִנְחָה וָנָסֶךְ ("grain and drink offering").⁴⁷ This phrase is found at the very end of 1:13f, well displaced from the verb נִמְנַע ("withheld") for which it is the subject.⁴⁸ Van der Merwe and Wendland suggest this separation marks these sacrifices for constituent focus, highlighting the inability of the priests to fulfill their cultic duties.⁴⁹ This builds upon the earlier command that the priests should put on sackcloth and further emphasizes the failure of proper cultic ritual. The prophet directs them to set aside their usual garments of service, which are now inappropriate given the failure of the sacrificial cycle. Instead, the priests should dress symbolically to lead the community into mourning.

Joel 1:14 moves from calling the priests to lament to issuing a plan of response. Joel commands the priests to sanctify a fast and call a sacred assembly that requires the participation of the entire community. Fasting is a standard element for both private and communal cultic expressions, thus it

---

45. Sweeney, *Twelve*, 159–60.
46. Crenshaw, *Joel*, 103; Barton, *Joel*, 55. Crenshaw and Barton disagree slightly as to the meaning of the command to spend the night at the altar. Crenshaw suggests that this command requires the priests to keep a ceaseless vigil at the temple. In contrast, Barton argues that the priests should not take off their sackcloth garments while the crisis continues. In any event, this command highlights the necessity for the priests to focus all of their energy on the unfolding crisis.
47. There is an interesting parallel to the devastation that the locusts create in an Assyrian hymn to the goddess Nanaya that is attributed to Sargon II. Notably, the hymn refers to the cessation of sacrifices on account of a locust invasion. See Victor Hurowitz, "Joel's Locust Plague in Light of Sargon II's Hymn to Nanaya," *JBL* 112 (1993): 597–603.
48. Some try to distinguish between the idea that sacrifices are "withheld" in 1:13 and the declaration that they are "cut off" in 1:9, suggesting reluctance on the part of the community to continue offering sacrifices (Simkins, *Yahweh's Activity*, 145). However, the subject of the verb "withheld" is unstated. The most likely possibility is that the subject of the verb is YHWH, which would mirror 1:9 (Barton, *Joel*, 55). The verb נִמְנַע ("withheld") is in the *niphal* stem and there are three other examples of this construction in the OT (Num 22:16; Job 38:15; Jer 3:3). Jeremiah 3:3 is especially pertinent since it refers to withholding rain as a consequence of Judah's sins. Although, no subject is identified in Jer 3:3, and context indicates that YHWH is responsible. In Joel 1:13, the context reflects the cessation of sacrifice as a result of the locusts. The "withholding" of sacrifices is a direct result of the ruined vines, trees, and fields.
49. van der Merwe and Wendland, "Word Order," 119–20.

requires other cultic terms to give it context. In this case, Joel links the call to fast with the gathering of a עֲצָרָה ("solemn assembly"), which refers generally to ritual observance.⁵⁰ Joel will offer greater specificity in the clauses that follow.

The prophet's command for the community to gather under the leadership of the priests raises the issue of his evaluation of the priests. Joel quickly connects the failure of the land's produce to the interruption of worship activities and the mourning of the priests. Some suggest that Joel is launching a subtle critique of the priestly leadership, where the call to cry out to YHWH challenges the priests' "pious self-sufficiency."⁵¹ One older commentator even detects a hint of idolatry in the priesthood which manifests further in 2:12, where YHWH implores the community שֻׁבוּ עָדַי ("return to me"), which may imply that it must first turn away from other gods.⁵²

In response to these suggestions of Joel's disapproval of the cult, it is important to consider the value that he places on cultic gathering. Joel goes to great lengths to portray the rituals of sacrifice and sacred assembly as the keys to responding to the locust invasion. He urges the audience to enter the heart of the cultic world, lamenting and fasting in the house of YHWH. In doing this, he taps into the natural response to tragedy, where the people seek solace in familiar institutions in order to gain perspective on their situation.⁵³ Joel's repeated commands for the community to go to the house of YHWH and engage in ritual lament reveal his position that the cult provides a place of reorientation.⁵⁴

Joel's insistence in grounding the community's response in a return to the temple and its rituals suggests a way of understanding this threat in the context of the relationship with YHWH. Joel's commands to seek YHWH at his house remind the Judahite audience of the central role of the temple. Not even the cessation of sacrifices can reduce the essential nature of the temple and priestly leadership. Joel's concern about the interruption of the worship rituals leads him to call the Judahite audience to redouble their commitment to maintain their relationship with YHWH. They are in desperate need of maintaining the channels of communication with their God.

Joel addresses the commands to gather to the "elders" and "all those living in the land" in 1:14c–d, using the same *merismus* found in 1:2. This returns this initial announcement of despair to its beginning. All those whom it summoned now are implored to respond as the prophet commands. Joel's call to fast is somewhat ironic since we have just seen in 1:11–12 that the lack of agricultural produce is so severe that it ends cultic offerings at the temple. The "elders" and "all those living in the land" are already engaged in involuntary fasting but the prophet attempts to sanctify the situation by using this lack as part of an appeal to YHWH.⁵⁵

Joel 1:14e spells out explicitly the purpose of this assembly in the final clause of the verse with yet another imperative clause וְזַעֲקוּ אֶל־יהוה ("then cry

---

50. Menahem Haran, *Temples and Temple-Service in Ancient Israel: An Inquiry into the Character of Cult Phenomena and the Historical Setting of the Priestly School* (Oxford: Clarendon: 1978), 296–97. Haran suggests that עֲצָרָה is a generic term indicating a gathering before YHWH. The purpose of such a gathering could range from celebratory (Amos 5:21) to supplicatory (Joel 1:14; 2:15).

51. Wolff, *Joel and Amos*, 13.

52. Gosta W. Ahlström, *Joel and the Temple Cult of Jerusalem*, VTSup XXI (Leiden: Brill, 1971), 25–26.

53. James R. Linville, "The Day of Yahweh and the Mourning of the Priests in Joel," in *The Priests in the Prophets: The Portrayal of Priests, Prophets and Other Religious Specialists in the Latter Prophets*, ed. Lester L. Grabbe and Alice Ogden Bellis, LHBOTS 408 (London: Bloomsbury, 2004), 103–6.

54. The discussion of Joel 2:12–17 will explore similar ideas.

55. Linville, "Day of Yahweh," 107.

out to YHWH"). This final imperative is "the emotive climax" and "the thematic peak" of 1:2–14.[56] The calls to fasting and sacred assembly in 1:14a–d establish the necessary conditions to cry out to YHWH since they portray the Judahite audience as desperate supplicants. Essentially, this final call to lament in 1:13–14 summarizes the preceding appeals. Joel commands the entire audience to go to the house of YHWH and submit themselves to the leadership of the priests. They are to hope that their lament elicits restoration from YHWH.

Summary

Joel 1:2–14 uses a devastating locust invasion to capture the attention of the Judahite audience. Following the superscription, 1:2–4 reveals the dramatic nature of the crisis and calls the audience to commit it to posterity. Joel first calls the entire community to hear the prophetic message. He focuses upon the devastation wrought by the locusts, emphasizing its overwhelming scope.

After announcing the crisis, 1:5–14 urgently appeals to different segments of the community to respond. He begins with the drunkards who need to understand the gravity of the situation. He then calls upon his audience to mourn with the urgency of a young woman facing the loss of her spouse. Joel then addresses the agriculturalists whose livelihoods are threatened and systematically describes the destruction of essential crops. As the devastation mounts and the entire community feels its impact, Joel then charges the priests with leading the community in lament. The priests must devote themselves to this task since the relationship between the people and their God is in jeopardy. The ruin left by the locusts threatens not only the land and its crops but the threat it poses to the sacrificial system introduces a new layer of threat. Joel 1:14 then concludes with a final imperative that encapsulates the only possible response. Under the leadership of the priests, the whole community must cry out to YHWH.

Canonical and Practical Significance

Generational Instruction

There is value in considering the call for the generational instruction expressed in 1:2–14. It is through the teaching of those who experienced great acts of God that future generations can shape their own faith and understanding. This is at the core of what it meant for Israel to be the covenant people of God who live their lives according to his instruction (Deut 6:1–3). It also stands behind the admonitions in wisdom literature to take heed of parental instruction (Prov 1:8–19). In a culture that celebrates novelty and progress, where the newest gadget is obsolete within a year, it becomes more and more important to remember the history of God's redemption of his people handed down to successive generations in Scripture. In this way, future generations may benefit from the instruction of those who experienced God in the past.

---

56. van der Merwe and Wendland, "Word Order," 120.

The Voice of Lament

The use of the imperatives in 1:2–14 connects with the broader expression of lament located throughout the canon. Joel commands weeping, wailing, mourning, and the wearing of sackcloth. All of these activities culminate in a final injunction to cry out to YHWH. Appealing to God in the midst of crisis is an important biblical theme; a theme of special importance in the psalms of lament (cf. Pss 12; 44; 58; 60; 74; 79; 80; 83; 85; 90; 94; 123; 126; 129). Brueggemann presents a four-part rubric for these psalms: (1) things are not right in this situation; (2) it is possible for the situation to change; (3) the one crying out cannot accept the situation as it stands; (4) God is obligated to change the situation.[57] The imperatives calling the audience to cry out in 1:2–14 resonate with this breakdown. Joel implores the audience to take note of the situation and how a crisis is unfolding among them, while directing them toward YHWH as the one who can enact restoration. Joel does not place an obligation upon YHWH to respond at this point,[58] but he does make it evident that only God can provide restoration.

It is worth reflecting on the necessity of appealing directly to God in the midst of crisis. While suffering and crisis may be part of God's discipline for his children (Heb 12:4–11), it is also the case that suffering arises as the result of living in a broken, sinful world. A cancer diagnosis, a tragic accident, or any number of other painful events do not have a specific inciting cause. In these situations, crying out to God for help and hope is a natural response. In doing so, we acknowledge God's sovereign power while appealing to his merciful character.[59] This permits the faith community to fully acknowledge the depths of despair. The church, as it continues to announce the kingdom of God, is not immune to the ravages of natural disasters and the despair of what seems to be the absence of divine response. Joel 1:2–14 offers one more reminder that when crisis strikes, the first response is to gather together as the community of God and to lift up voices to God, acknowledging the gravity of the situation and urgently appealing for God's presence.

---

57. Walter Brueggemann, "The Costly Loss of Lament," JSOT 36 (1986): 62.

58. But see the upcoming discussion on Joel 2:12–17.

59. The intersection of God's sovereign power and the reality of suffering and evil is the domain of theodicy. Laato and de Moor identify four fundamental premises of theodicy in the biblical world: (1) there is one God; (2) this God is the source of goodness and justice; (3) this God has authority in the world; and (4) evil and suffering exist. Biblical writers wrestle with the disjunction between the fourth premise and the first three. In some instances, it is clear that human sinfulness is the cause of suffering in a given situation. In others, the link is not so clear, and the voice of lament seeks to bridge the gap by asking the good and powerful God to respond to evil and suffering. See Antii Laato and Johannes C. de Moor, "Introduction," in *Theodicy in the World of the Bible*, ed. Antti Laato and Johannes C. de Moor (Leiden: Brill, 2003), xx.

The Role of Community

It is also important to place Joel's valuation of cultic activity into canonical context. The responses that Joel requires, most notably in 1:14, implore the whole Judahite community to come together in a sacred assembly that would require a cessation of all normal, non-cultic activity (Lev 23:36; Num 29:35; Deut 16:8; Neh 8:18).[60] The prophet thus directs the community to come to grips with the gravity of the situation and devote all their time and energy to appealing to YHWH. Interestingly, Joel's call for a sacred assembly contrasts with how other prophets use this term, especially in Amos 5:21 and Isa 1:13.[61] Those passages castigate the ritualized nature of sacred assemblies when they are not performed in the correct spirit. In contrast, Joel 1:14 requires sacred assemblies, presuming that the urgency of the situation eliminates the possibility of half-hearted observance. Ritual observance certainly has its place, but the warnings of other prophets not to let them become merely a matter of formality are also important.

This observation continues to speak to worshiping communities today. Joel's insistence in calling the people to gather in sacred community is a reminder of the value of having established worship practices that can provide comfort in times of crisis. In the midst of catastrophe or tragedy, participation in worship offers the prospect of reorientation. It provides an opportunity to see beyond the difficulties of the current situation. It also provides an occasion to respond to crisis by acknowledging the necessity for the community to assemble and "cry out to the Lord."

---

60. Sweeney, *Twelve*, 160.

61. Richard J. Coggins, *Joel and Amos*, NCBC (Sheffield: Sheffield Academic, 2000), 32–33.

Joel 1:15–20

C. Despair in the Day of YHWH—The Drought

Main Idea of the Passage

Joel reveals that the locust invasion is a harbinger of the day of YHWH. He adds further detail to the picture of devastation by invoking images of drought. Joel concludes by adding his own voice to the cry to YHWH.

Literary Context

Joel 1:15–20 builds upon the initial description of the locust invasion and the calls for response in 1:2–14. This passage provides further detail regarding the state of the land and its inhabitants before concluding with Joel's own appeal to YHWH in 1:19–20. Joel's cry provides a preliminary example of a response to his own command to call out to YHWH found in 1:14. The Judahite audience itself does not speak, but witnesses the example of Joel himself crying out in the context of the day of YHWH.[1]

Joel's introduction of the day of YHWH is critical to the progression of the prophetic discourse because it links the crisis described in 1:2–14 to this fateful day. The prophet does not explore the day of YHWH in great detail here, but this passage foreshadows its appearance in 2:1–11 and 4:1–21. Introducing the day of YHWH heightens the threat of the locust invasion and increases the urgency of the appeal to cry out to YHWH found in 1:2–14. This builds to the prophet's own cry in 1:19–20, which provides a model for the Judahite audience to follow.

Joel 1:15–20 also points forward to 2:1–11, since the prophet's cry to YHWH in 1:19–20 is unanswered within this passage. The possibility that YHWH could respond positively remains in 1:15–20, but the message of 2:1–11 diminishes those hopes by providing further visions of the day of YHWH. Joel 1:15–20 thus continues the process of describing the desperate circumstances for the Judahite audience,

---

1. Dillard, "Joel," 266.

while offering a brief glimpse of hope through its appeal to YHWH. However, this results in renewed promises of the great and dreadful day of YHWH.

> A. Superscription (1:1)
> B. Despair on Account of the Locusts (1:2–14)
> **C. Despair in the Day of YHWH—The Drought (1:15–20)**
>   **1. The Announcement of the Day of YHWH (1:15–16)**
>   **2. The Effects of the Day of YHWH (1:17–18)**
>   **3. The Appeal to YHWH (1:19–20)**
> D. Despair in the Day of YHWH—The Invasion (2:1–11)
> E. Hinge: The Call to Return to YHWH (2:12–17)
> F. Divine Deliverance from the Locusts and Drought (2:18–27)
> G. Deliverance through the Spirit of YHWH (3:1–5 [2:28–32])
> H. Deliverance through Divine Judgment on the Day of YHWH (4:1–21 [3:1–21])

Translation and Outline

(See page 66.)

Structure and Literary Form

Joel 1:15–20 describes further calamities afflicting the Judahite community. Its shift in topic and literary style demarcate it as a separate unit with images of drought and desiccation. This passage commences with the cry אֲהָהּ לַיּוֹם ("Alas for the day"), an exclamatory utterance that shifts the discourse away from the imperatives found in 1:2–14. It also raises the specter of the day of YHWH. This passage also reveals Joel's commitment to identify himself with his audience in order to shape its response. This is evident in the use of the first-person plural in 1:16, describing how food is cut off before עֵינֵינוּ ("our eyes"), and joy and gladness מִבֵּית אֱלֹהֵינוּ ("from the house of our God"). He also employs the first-person singular with the verb אֶקְרָא ("I call") in 1:19, taking on the responsibility of appealing to YHWH on behalf of his audience. These developments indicate that while 1:15–20 builds upon the calamities described in 1:2–14, it is a new literary unit.

Joel 1:15–20 consists of three short addresses (1:15–16, 17–18, 19–20). The first two are communal cries in which the prophet identifies with the audience and describes the circumstances that they face. The first address identifies the crises with the imminence of the day of YHWH. The second address explores the consequences of the day of YHWH, invoking images of famine, drought, and desiccation that

Joel 1:15–20

C. Despair in the Day of YHWH—The Drought (1:15–20)
   1. The Announcement of the Day of YHWH (1:15–16)
      a. The Day of YHWH (1:15)

      b. The Repercussions of the Day of YHWH (1:16)

   2. The Effects of the Day of YHWH (1:17–18)
      a. The Effects on Crops (1:17)

      b. The Effects on Livestock (1:18)

   3. The Appeal to YHWH (1:19–20)
      a. The Prophet's Appeal to YHWH (1:19a)
      b. The Reasons for the Appeal (1:19b–20c)

15a	אֲהָהּ לַיּוֹם	Alas for the day!
15b	כִּי קָרוֹב יוֹם יְהוָה	For near is the day of YHWH.
15c	וּכְשֹׁד מִשַּׁדַּי יָבוֹא׃	And like destruction from the Almighty it will come.
16a	הֲלוֹא נֶגֶד עֵינֵינוּ אֹכֶל נִכְרָת	Has not the food been cut off from before our eyes?
16b	מִבֵּית אֱלֹהֵינוּ שִׂמְחָה וָגִיל׃	From the house of our God, joy and mirth?
17a	עָבְשׁוּ פְרֻדוֹת תַּחַת מֶגְרְפֹתֵיהֶם	Grains of seed are withered under their furrows.
17b	נָשַׁמּוּ אֹצָרוֹת	The storehouses are desolated;
17c	נֶהֶרְסוּ מַמְּגֻרוֹת	the granaries are destroyed,
17d	כִּי הֹבִישׁ דָּגָן׃	for the corn is dried up.
18a	מַה־נֶּאֶנְחָה בְהֵמָה	How the beasts groan!
18b	נָבֹכוּ עֶדְרֵי בָקָר	Herds of cattle wander,
18c	כִּי אֵין מִרְעֶה לָהֶם	for there is no pasture for them.
18d	גַּם־עֶדְרֵי הַצֹּאן נֶאְשָׁמוּ׃	Even the flocks of sheep suffer.
19a	אֵלֶיךָ יְהוָה אֶקְרָא	To you, o YHWH, I call,
19b	כִּי אֵשׁ אָכְלָה נְאוֹת מִדְבָּר	for fire consumes the pastures of the wilderness
19c	וְלֶהָבָה לִהֲטָה כָּל־עֲצֵי הַשָּׂדֶה׃	and flame sets afire all the trees of the field.
20a	גַּם־בַּהֲמוֹת שָׂדֶה תַּעֲרוֹג אֵלֶיךָ	Even the beasts of the field are panting for you,
20b	כִּי יָבְשׁוּ אֲפִיקֵי מָיִם	for the streams of water are dried up,
20c	וְאֵשׁ אָכְלָה נְאוֹת הַמִּדְבָּר׃	and fire consumes the pastures of the wilderness.

threaten the existence of the Judahite community. The final prayer in 1:19–20 is uttered in the voice of the prophet, taking up the intercessory mantle and calling upon YHWH to respond. These cries elaborate upon the appeal to call out to YHWH in 1:14 that concluded the previous passage. Joel 1:15–20 thus provides the next step in guiding the audience in the way that it should respond to Joel's exhortations. Once Joel identifies his audience and calls them to assemble in 1:5–14, the stage is set for him to model an example of what it means to cry out to YHWH.

Structurally, 1:19–20 announces its closure by means of *epistrophe*, through the repetition of the phrase אֵשׁ אָכְלָה נְאוֹת מִדְבָּר ("fire consumes the pastures of the wilderness"), which is found in 1:19b and 1:20c. The only difference between these expressions is the presence of the definite article on הַמִּדְבָּר ("the wilderness") in 1:20c. Joel 1:19a commences with an appeal to YHWH, followed by the expression in 1:19b, which 1:20c mirrors. *Epistrophe* is a rhetorical strategy to which Joel will later return in 2:18–27.[2] Consequently, the use of repetition in 1:19–20 signals the closure of this literary unit, in which the prophet continues to discuss the difficulties that afflict the audience.

Explanation of the Text

1. The Announcement of the Day of YHWH (1:15–16)

Joel 1:15 begins with the exclamation אֲהָהּ לַיּוֹם ("Alas for the day!").[3] This interjection is appropriate given Joel's previous commands for the audience to assemble and call out to YHWH. The exhortation וְזַעֲקוּ אֶל־יהוה ("and cry out to YHWH!") in 1:14e ended this sequence of commands so Joel 1:15a now commences with an exclamation that articulates that cry.[4] This verse also ties the disaster explicitly to the day of YHWH in 1:15b.[5] As discussed in the introduction, the exact phrase יוֹם יהוה ("the day of YHWH") appears five times in *Joel* (1:15; 2:1, 11; 3:4[2:31]; 4:14[3:14]). The prophet also uses similar expressions that invoke

---

2. Wendland, *Discourse Analysis*, 50.

3. The particle אֲהָהּ is one of a set that "have the capacity to impress an emphatic flavor on the sentence." This particle typically introduces expressions of a crisis or regret. See Marco Di Giulio, "Exclamation: Biblical Hebrew," in vol. 1 of *Encyclopedia of Hebrew Language and Linguistics*, ed. Geoffrey Khan (Leiden: Brill, 2013), 875.

4. Wendland, *Discourse Analysis*, 42; van der Merwe and Wendland, "Word Order," 120.

5. There is a wealth of secondary literature for those interested in pursuing the origins and development of the day of YHWH. Essential to the origins of the day of YHWH discussion are Mowinckel and von Rad. Mowinckel connects it to a cultic enthronement festival, while von Rad proposes an original setting of holy war (Sigmund Mowinckel, *He That Cometh*, trans. G. Anderson [Oxford: Basil Blackwell, 1956], 130–45; Gerhard von Rad, "The Origin of the Concept of the Day of Yahweh," *JSS* 4 [1959] 97–108). Mowinckel's approach is no longer in favor. Instead, Stuart stresses the military nature of the day of YHWH and connects it to ancient Near Eastern traditions that describe the victory of a sovereign over an enemy in a single day (Douglas Stuart, "The Sovereign's Day of Conquest," *BASOR* 221 [1976], 159–64). Hoffman stresses that theophany is its key element (Yair Hoffman, "The Day of the Lord as a Concept and a Term in Prophetic Literature," *ZAW* 93 [1981]: 37–50). The result of these studies is that there is no established consensus concerning the origin and transmission of the idea of the day of YHWH. These studies, however, effectively convey the range of images invoked by this day. On the day of YHWH, YHWH appears, announces judgment and/or salvation, while the physical world and its habitants tremble in response.

the essence of that day (3:2[2:29]; 4:1, 18[3:1, 18]).⁶ He makes good use of the flexibility of the day of YHWH, employing it here in the discussion of calamity while later returning to it as a signal of hope. Speaking about the day of YHWH in the Book of the Twelve more broadly, Nogalski correctly notes that YHWH's intervention "does not fall neatly into a single, systematic view."⁷ The day of YHWH in prophetic literature is a time of both judgment and restoration, destruction and salvation, rooted in the expectation of YHWH's intervention into human affairs.⁸ The day of YHWH is such an overwhelming concept that the prophets who invoke it draw widely from a range of images that frequently have ominous overtones.

The range of communicative purposes of the day of YHWH is evident throughout this book. The prophet first uses it in the wake of his announcement of a locust invasion that sets off a cycle of liturgical lament, appealing for divine restitution. He later uses the day of YHWH to describe a time when Judah and Jerusalem stand aside, allowing YHWH their God to preserve their security and destroy foreign nations who threaten them.⁹ We will explore these varied uses of the day of YHWH as we encounter them.

Following the introductory exclamation, the remainder of 1:15 focuses on the imminence and divine authorization of the day of YHWH. Joel 1:15b stresses its imminence, placing the descriptor קָרוֹב ("near") after the introductory כִּי. Joel 1:15c then describes the divine sanction of the day with a simile, claiming that it comes כְּשֹׁד מִשַּׁדַּי ("like destruction from the Almighty").¹⁰ This elevates the consequences of the locust invasion and the calamities that Joel has previously described. In effect, the announcement of the imminence of the day of YHWH lends more weight to the call to cry out that concludes 1:14. Joel reveals to his audience that they are facing not only a devastating locust invasion but also the arrival of the day of YHWH.

Identifying the day of YHWH as a day of destruction also links 1:15 with 1:10, which uses the same root to describe the destruction of the fields.¹¹ The שֻׁדַּד ("destruction") that the locusts bring in 1:10c connects to the שֹׁד ("devastation") of the day of YHWH in 1:15c. This link allows Joel to invoke the presence of YHWH, not only as the one who hears the people's cries but also as the agent of the devastation. Joel does not pursue this idea any further in this passage, but the idea that the Judahite audience faces crises that are כְּשֹׁד מִשַּׁדַּי ("like destruction from the Almighty") sets an ominous tone that is picked up in 2:1–11. This brief introduction to the day of YHWH suggests that the significance of the current situation extends

---

6. See the discussion in the Introduction for the reasons to include these variations as part of the day of YHWH corpus. In the Minor Prophets specifically, this broader approach allows us to see greater unity within the collection. (Rolf Rendtorff, "How to Read the Book of the Twelve as a Theological Unity," in *Reading and Hearing the Book of the Twelve*, ed. James Nogalski and Marvin A. Sweeney, SBLSS 15 [Atlanta: Society of Biblical Literature, 2000], 75–87).

7. James Nogalski, "Recurring Themes in the Book of the Twelve: Creating Points of Contact for a Theological Reading," *Interpretation* 61 (2007): 126.

8. Usually the temporal orientation of the day of YHWH is toward the future. This is the case in *Joel*, where it is identified as קָרוֹב ("near") on the three of the five occasions in which it is used (1:15; 2:1; 4:14 [3:14]). However, other passages use the day of YHWH retrospectively to attribute significant events to YHWH's sovereignty (Lam 1:12; 2:22; Isa 22:1–14; Jer 46:2–20; Ezek 13:1–9). See A. Joseph Everson, "The Days of Yahweh," *JBL* 93 [1974] 329–37).

9. Rolf Rendtorff, "'Alas for the Day!' The 'Day of the Lord' in the Book of the Twelve," in *God in the Fray: A Tribute to Walter Brueggemann*, ed. Tod Linafelt and Timothy K. Beal (Minneapolis: Fortress, 1998), 19.

10. Joel again engages in some creative wordplay in this clause. The words "destruction" and "Almighty" both contain a *shin-daleth* consonant combination. Joel reveals that שֹׁד ("destruction") will come from שַׁדַּי ("the Almighty"), which is a memorable alliterative construction.

11. van der Merwe and Wendland, "Word Order," 120.

beyond a locust invasion and the loss of agricultural produce. It is a troubling sign of the state of YHWH's relationship with the Judahite audience.

Joel 1:16 reveals further consequences of the day of YHWH, stressing the inability of the cult to function because of the cessation of daily sacrifices. He uses two rhetorical questions to link the day of YHWH, the locust plague, and the cultic crisis.[12] The function of the rhetorical questions here is not to ask for information but rather to make a strong assertion.[13] Joel 1:16a asks הֲלוֹא נֶגֶד עֵינֵינוּ אֹכֶל נִכְרָת ("has not the food been cut off from before our eyes?"), again focusing on the destruction of agricultural produce that the community is facing. Joel 1:16b uses ellipsis to ask a parallel rhetorical question that shifts the focus from hunger to cultic practice. The two elements from 1:16a that it borrows are the interrogative particle הֲלוֹא and the verb נִכְרָת. Joel 1:16b itself then details what has been cut off. This clause begins with מִבֵּית אֱלֹהֵינוּ ("the house of our God"), the location experiencing absence. It then identifies שִׂמְחָה וָגִיל ("joy and mirth") as the elements that have been cut off. These have cultic connotations since rejoicing is the expected attitude of those bringing offerings to YHWH (cf. Deut 12:5–7). Their absence indicates a fractured relationship between YHWH and his people.

The structure of 1:16b parallels 1:13f, which gives the reasons why the priests should heed Joel's call to mourn. Joel 1:13f begins by identifying מִבֵּית אֱלֹהֵיכֶם ("from the house of your God") as the location of absence, followed by מִנְחָה וָנֶסֶךְ ("grain-offering and drink-offering"). The cessation of the מִנְחָה וָנֶסֶךְ thus parallels the loss of שִׂמְחָה וָגִיל ("joy and mirth") in 1:16b, emphasizing again that the day of YHWH has serious repercussions for worship in the community. Joel 1:16 thus reveals that in the aftermath of the day of YHWH, there will be no cultic celebrations of joy.

2. The Effects of the Day of YHWH (1:17–18)

Joel 1:17–18 follows the announcement of the day of YHWH with images of drought and desiccation. This adds detail to the rhetorical questions of 1:16, explaining why the community is struggling to find food for itself and for offering sacrifices to YHWH. The swathe of destruction left in the wake of a locust invasion may have similarities with the effects of a drought, but it is not necessary to claim that the former is the cause of the latter.[14] Rhetorically, this shift in imagery adds further weight to the crisis. The explicit announcement of the day of YHWH in 1:15 provides the foundation to expand on its effects on the entire natural realm.[15] Wave after wave of locusts have devastated the land, and now images of drought and even fire in 1:19–20 suggest even more calamitous ruin.

Joel 1:17a likely describes seeds unable to sprout in the plowed soil because of drought conditions.[16]

---

12. Simkins, *Yahweh's Activity*, 149.
13. Moshavi, "Interrogative: Biblical Hebrew," 310. Again, the principle of "reversed polarity" is at work since the implied answer to the negative question is in the affirmative. Moshavi also has an extended discussion on the function of הֲלוֹא, which introduces the rhetorical question in 1:16a. She differentiates between its use as an interrogative and as an asseverative clausal adverb. Here, the obvious nature of the answer to the question and its function of connecting the situation to the day of YHWH indicate that הֲלוֹא is introducing a rhetorical question. See Adina Moshavi, "Rhetorical Question or Assertion? The Pragmatics of הֲלוֹא in Biblical Hebrew." *JANES* 32 (2011): 91–105.

14. Simkins, *Yahweh's Activity*, 149–53.
15. Seitz, *Joel*, 144.
16. Joel 1:17a is incredibly challenging to translate since three of its four words occur only once in the OT. It reads עָבְשׁוּ פְרֻדוֹת תַּחַת מֶגְרְפֹתֵיהֶם. The basis for the translation used above is that פְרֻדוֹת has cognates in Aramaic and Syriac with words that mean "seeds." This word is derived from the Hebrew root פרד ("separate"), which in this context refers to individual kernels of grain or seed. The suggestion that מֶגְרְפֹתֵיהֶם refers to plowed earth goes back to medieval rabbinic interpretation and is followed in modern scholarship by Assis. On 1:17a as a whole, see Assis, *Book of Joel*, 112–13.

This builds upon on the description of the locusts, suggesting that any surviving plants succumb to a lack of rainfall.¹⁷ Joel 1:17b–c furthers this picture by referring to the disrepair of the storage houses for the crops, with the phrases נָשַׁמּוּ אֹצָרוֹת נֶהֶרְסוּ מַמְּגֻרוֹת ("the storehouses are desolated; the granaries are destroyed"). Both clauses contain only two words; the verb and its subject. This succinct repetition brings into focus the effects of the widespread crop failure. There is no need for storehouses and granaries when these disasters have destroyed any surplus. In 1:17d, the prophet returns to the verb יָבֵשׁ ("to wither") to describe the fate of the corn. This also recalls the wordplay on the withering of crops in 1:11–12 and further connects the locust infestation and the drought.

Joel 1:18 expands the ranks of those suffering from the drought. Not only are the storehouses in ruin while the people suffer from hunger and are unable to offer sacrifices, but the disasters also affect the animals. Joel 1:18a draws attention to their plight through the exclamation מַה־נֶּאֶנְחָה בְהֵמָה ("how the beasts groan"), which contains three rhyming words in Hebrew.¹⁸ In 1:18b–c Joel paints a picture of cattle wandering aimlessly since there is no pasture.¹⁹ The animals thus face the same threat of starvation as the people. Joel 1:18d restates the suffering of the animals with the expression גַּם־עֶדְרֵי הַצֹּאן נֶאְשָׁמוּ ("even the flocks of sheep suffer"). This clause highlights the "flocks of sheep" by placing them after the focus particle גַּם and before the verb. This stresses that even more hardy animals face serious peril.²⁰ Thus, the cry in 1:17–18 reveals that the land and its creatures face an existential threat beyond the depredations of the locusts.

3. The Appeal to YHWH (1:19–20)

This passage concludes in 1:19–20 with a direct appeal to YHWH for relief from the unrelenting series of crises. It makes use of the "I" voice, which is best equated with the voice of the prophet.²¹ It is the first of two instances where humans directly address YHWH in this book, both of which occur at climactic moments (cf. 2:17).²² Here, the tension created by the litany of disasters facing the commu-

---

17. Simkins, "God, History and the Natural World," 442.

18. Although the noun and verb in this phrase are both singular, the rest of the verse suggests that the meaning is collective, indicated by a plural object suffix on לָהֶם in 1:18c and a reference to flocks of sheep.

19. The verbal root in 1:18b is בּוּךְ, which is also used to indicate Israel's aimless wandering in Exod 14:3 and a state of general confusion in the city of Susa in Esth 4:13.

20. van der Merwe and Wendland, "Word Order," 121. Notably, Joel 2:18–27 reverses this picture when it calls upon the animals to rejoice in response to YHWH's restorative actions.

21. The equation of the "I" voice in 1:19a with the prophet is the standard position. A recent dissertation by A. Rahel Schafer proposes an alternative, arguing that this voice reflects the cries of the non-human animals introduced in 1:18. Schafer notes that the destroyed pastureland and streams in 1:19–20 are crises that first afflict non-human animals. She also suggests that the presence of singular grammatical forms in 1:18, 20 (the noun בְהֵמָה in 1:18a; and the verb תַּעֲרוֹג in 1:20a) refer to non-human animals, whereas humans are portrayed with plural nouns and pronouns throughout Joel 1. She further notes that Joel rarely explicitly introduces the implied speaker throughout the book, so the lack of identification of the non-human animals as the speaker is not a problem. Her proposal is possible but not conclusive. Alongside the singular noun referring to non-human animals in 1:18a are plural nouns and pronouns in 1:18b–d, indicating that there is no simple singular entity to equate with the "I" voice of 1:19a. Further, the voice of the prophet has already been activated in this passage through the first-person plural pronouns in 1:16. I maintain that it is at least equally plausible that Joel goes from identifying himself with the audience in 1:16 to speaking on its behalf in 1:19–20. See A. Rahel Schafer, "'You, YHWH, Save Humans and Animals': God's Response to the Vocalized Needs of Non-Human Animals as Portrayed in the Old Testament" (PhD diss., Wheaton College, 2015), 92–94.

22. Mark J. Boda, "A Deafening Call to Silence: The Rhetorical 'End' of Human Address to the Deity in the Book of the Twelve," in *The Book of the Twelve and the New Form Criticism*, ed. Mark J. Boda, Michael H. Floyd, and Colin M. Toffelmire, ANEM 10 (Atlanta: SBL Press, 2015), 188–90.

nity finds an outlet in Joel's cry to YHWH. Notably, this cry contains no specific request, suggesting that simply highlighting the terrible circumstances is sufficient.[23]

We see in Joel's address how he participates in the suffering of the audience and employs his intercessory prophetic mantle. He begins in 1:19a with the petition with אֵלֶיךָ יהוה אֶקְרָא ("to you, o YHWH, I cry"), indicating that YHWH is the only source of hope in the face of the accumulating catastrophes.[24] Adding his own voice is a natural progression from his previous appeals to different groups within the Judahite community to call upon YHWH, which concluded with the admonition וְזַעֲקוּ אֶל־יהוה ("then call out to YHWH!"). Here, he provides an example of such an appeal and awaits a response from YHWH.[25]

The specifics of the cry that Joel announces in 1:19a also contribute to the threat of the unfolding day of YHWH. In 1:19b–20c, Joel uses the image of a raging fire devouring everything in its path (cf. Amos 7:4–6), which complements the images of dried up seeds and parched grazing land from the previous verses. Such a dry and barren landscape is easily imagined as the setting for wildfires. As discussed in Structure and Literary Form, the phrase כִּי אֵשׁ אָכְלָה נְאוֹת מִדְבָּר ("fire consumes the pastures of the wilderness") is found in both 1:19b and 1:20c, signaling the closure of this passage.[26] Joel 1:19c further develops this image by envisioning flames consuming the dried-out husks of the trees in the field.

Joel heightens the power of his cry to YHWH through the example of the animals in 1:20a. The beasts of the field demonstrate their longing as they תַּעֲרוֹג ("pant") for YHWH. This expands the range of suffering animals beyond the domesticated beasts of 1:18; animals accustomed to foraging fare no better (cf. Ps 65:13; Jer 9:9; 23:10).[27] The prophet and the animals express their need for YHWH, perhaps providing an example for Joel's audience to follow. This fits with the only other occurrence of the verbal root עָרַג ("to pant"), which is in Ps 42:2 and places the panting of the deer for streams of water in parallel with the psalmist's longing for YHWH. Joel expands the range of the verb since in Ps 42 the animals pant for the liquid that sustains life, while in 1:20a the prophet grants them the human characteristic of desiring God in response to crisis.[28]

Joel 1:20b has another parallel to Ps 42:2 since both verses refer to water sources called אֲפִיקֵי מָיִם ("streams of water"). This phrase refers to seasonal water sources that draw upon the underground water table (cf. Ps 126:4).[29] If they were to dry up in a drought scenario, tremendous hardship would ensue. The deer that seeks these streams in Ps 42 is desperate to find YHWH, and when Joel reveals that the streams are already gone it points to the devastating reality of YHWH's disfavor. Joel returns to this thought in 4:18–21[3:18–21] when he declares that YHWH will cause water to flow in the streambeds of Judah. Both 1:20 and 4:18[3:18] use the same construct noun אֲפִיקֵי ("streams") to refer to water, equating the presence or absence of these waters with the state of YHWH's relationship with his people.

Summary

Joel 1:15–20 adds to the horrors of the locust plague with a warning of the coming day of YHWH

---

23. Ibid., 189.
24. van der Merwe and Wendland, "Word Order," 121.
25. Assis, *Book of Joel*, 116.
26. Wendland, *Discourse Analysis*, 50–51.
27. Crenshaw, *Joel*, 111.
28. Assis, *Book of Joel*, 117.
29. Simkins, *Yahweh's Activity*, 151–52.

as a day of destruction and devastation. This first brief mention of the day of YHWH establishes its terrifying nature to which Joel will add further detail. This passage continues to describe cultic and agricultural crises that heighten the audience's awareness of this fateful day. The withered crops, the suffering animals, and the desiccated fields that burst into flame combine with the assault of the locusts to articulate the scope of the threat posed by the day of YHWH. Consequently, Joel concludes this passage by crying out to YHWH, speaking on behalf of the human community and its suffering and groaning animals. This models the response that he desires from the listening audience. However, YHWH does not answer, leaving the situation unresolved.

Canonical and Practical Significance

The Day of YHWH Is Near

The effect of employing the day of YHWH in 1:15 fits into a pattern established in Amos 5:18, which is thought to be its earliest use. It is a day of when God's judgment can fall, even upon his own people. Amos corrects the flawed perception of his audience, who could not conceive of themselves as the intended targets for this day. The reference to the day of YHWH in 1:15 also has a close parallel in Isa 13:6. Both verses stress the nearness of the day with the clause "for the day of YHWH is near." They also describe its effects through the simile of being "like destruction from the Almighty." One important difference between Isa 13:6 and Joel 1:15 is that Isaiah targets Babylon while Joel 1:15 is directed at YHWH's people. This demonstrates the adaptability of this concept to warn of YHWH's wrath. Further, Isa 13:6 presents a picture of inescapable judgment surrounding the announcement that the day of YHWH is approaching, while the announcement in Joel 1:15 ties into later passages (specifically 2:12–17) that offer the hope of avoiding judgment.[30] Thus, while the day of YHWH resonates throughout the prophetic corpus of literature, it is necessary to understand that individual texts employ the same imagery for different purposes.

Crisis and Crying to God

Joel 1:15–20 continues to assert that the only response to the unfolding crises is to cry out to YHWH. This passage begins with the exclamatory cry אֲהָהּ ("Alas"), which occurs fifteen times throughout the OT. It evokes a sense of immediacy as the one uttering it comes to grips with an urgent crisis. On most occasions, the addressee of the cry is YHWH, with whom the speaker registers distress or pleads for help.[31] In military contexts, Joshua appeals to YHWH in the wake of the defeat at Ai (Josh 7:7), while King Joram exclaims it when faced with the potential destruction of his army

---

30. Rendtorff, "Alas for the Day," 188.
31. In 2 Kgs 6:5, 15, the cry is directed at Elisha, who is able to alleviate the crises because of his prophetic authority. In Judg 11:35 Jephthah directs it toward his daughter as the horror of his foolish vow is revealed.

on account of a lack of water (2 Kgs 3:10). Jeremiah and Ezekiel resemble Joel in their use of this cry since they express dismay concerning the fate of God's people (Jer 4:10; Ezek 9:8; 11:13). The different uses of this exclamation reveal that when the situation is bleak, the appropriate response is to turn toward YHWH since he alone is capable of rectifying it. Joel begins to do that with his own voice in 1:19–20.

Care for Creation

Joel 1:15–20 also prompts reflection on the relationship between God's activity and the natural world. The covenant curses of the OT include drought and associated agricultural disaster (Deut 28:22–24). This permits writers in the OT to link the response of the land to the state of Israel's relationship with its God. Notably, Elijah announces drought on the land in 1 Kgs 17 in response to the idolatry of Ahab, which God only alleviates after the people again swear allegiance to him after Elijah's defeat of the prophets of Baal (1 Kgs 18:39–45). Postexilic prophets also use images of drought and renewal to comment on the relationship between God and his people.[32] Haggai 1:4–11 calls on the people to reflect on their current state, typified by failing harvests, lack of rain, and an inability of the land's wealth to satisfy. The response to this situation is for the people to gather and commit to rebuilding the house of YHWH (Hag 1:12–15). Zechariah 8:9–12 calls for the workers' hands to be strong as they commit to the task. This results in fertility for the land signified by the transformation of fasts into feasts (Zech 8:19). Malachi 3:8–12 reflects similar concerns since YHWH castigates his people for not bringing to him their tithes and offerings. He even proposes that the people put him to the test by bringing him all that he is due and seeing if he will provide for their needs.[33] These passages reveal how the natural world provides a mirror for the relationship between YHWH and his people in the OT.[34]

This line of thinking must be modified since the people of God now live in every part of the world and include every ethnicity, language, and social class. A correlation of natural disasters with divine displeasure is inappropriate when God's people are not found in one particular location, and when Jesus Christ has paid the full penalty for the sin of those who turn to him in repentance.[35] Instead, when disasters strike, they remind us that despite all of our advances in knowledge, we cannot hope to control the storm and fury of the world that God has created and we have corrupted.

---

32. Nogalski, *Book of the Twelve*, 236.

33. This differs slightly from Joel 1:13 where the overwhelming number of locusts made it impossible to offer to YHWH the grain and drink offerings. Interestingly, YHWH does promise to remove אֹכֵל ("the devourer") in Mal 3:11, which is probably a reference to locusts. See Hayes, "*The Earth Mourns*," 198.

34. This issue will resurface in the discussion of Joel's call for his audience to "turn" back to YHWH in 2:12–17, even though he lists no explicit sin for which they are guilty.

35. A variety of Christian commentators continue to fall prey to this impulse, attributing disaster like Hurricane Katrina in 2005 or the earthquake in Haiti in 2010 to divine judgment for various moral failings.

However, we can mirror the response of Joel and cry out to God when grappling with the suffering created by natural disasters. The fallen nature of our world means that earthquakes, hurricanes, and even droughts and locusts will continue. It remains appropriate to appeal to God in the wake of these situations and to ask him for rescue and the strength to assist those in need.

Remembering the Creator should also push us toward a greater stewardship of the world that he has entrusted to our care. The commission to the original human pair was to exercise dominion over the created realm since they were made in the image and likeness of God (Gen 1:26–28).[36] Fulfilling this commission is part of what it means to worship the God of this creation. As ecological challenges continue to mount, it is important for believers to be deeply involved in caring for creation. This commitment gives believing communities a platform from which to demonstrate that our stewardship of creation reflects its divine source. Middleton captures the essential nature of this task, stating "[b]y our obedient exercise of power, humanity as the *imago Dei* functions like a prism, refracting the pure light of God into a rainbow of cultural activities that scintillate with the creator's glory throughout the earth."[37] The natural world is the arena in which the people of God live out their calling. Responsible, faithful stewardship of its resources is an essential part of that witness.

---

36. The Hebrew terms here are צֶלֶם ("image") and דְּמוּת ("likeness"). For an excellent study of these terms in their biblical and ancient Near Eastern contexts, see Catherine L. McDowell, *The Image of God in the Garden of Eden: The Creation of Humankind in Genesis 2:5–3:24 in Light of* mīs pî pīt pî *and* wpt-r *Rituals of Mesopotamia and Ancient Egypt* (Siphrut 15; Winona Lake, IN: Eisenbrauns, 2015), 117–37.

37. J. Richard Middleton, *A New Heaven and a New Earth: Reclaiming Biblical Eschatology* (Grand Rapids: Baker, 2014), 49.

Joel 2:1–11

D. Despair in the Day of YHWH—The Invasion

Main Idea of the Passage

Joel 2:1–11 is the nadir of the downward trajectory of the book. The previous crises culminate as Joel describes the day of YHWH as an assault on Zion by an army commanded by YHWH himself.

Literary Context

Joel 2:1–11 is the third passage that describes the desperate situation facing the Judahite community. In 1:2–14 and 1:15–20, the crises include a locust invasion and drought, which Joel uses to urge them to cry out to YHWH. He even provides a personal example of such an appeal in 1:19–20. However, YHWH does not yet respond. In 2:1–11, the ambiguity of YHWH's silence is removed in a terrifying fashion. This passage claims that the day of YHWH is near and develops it through a blend of images that combine cosmic upheaval and an invading army that targets Zion and is led by none other than YHWH.

The literary context of 2:1–11 helps to identify the invaders. Has Joel returned to the locusts of 1:2–14 or does he have another invader in view? The actions of the invader in this passage suggest a military force, leading to the argument that Joel is making a direct connection to a human invading army, typically identified as Babylon.[1] Joel uses many descriptions that seem to fit a military invasion, mentioning war horses (v. 4), chariots (v. 5a), preparations for battle (v. 5b), and details of an assault

---

1. Stuart, *Hosea—Jonah*, 233; Ogden and Deutsch, *Joel & Malachi*, 27. This view can work for different proposed dates for Joel. From a preexilic perspective, Stuart views Joel 2:1–11 as a prediction of the coming Babylonian invasion. From a postexilic perspective, Ogden suggests that Joel 2:1–11 looks back upon the Babylonian invasion and projects its memory into the present.

on a city (v. 7–9). However, these descriptions are preceded by the preposition כְּ (*kaph*), which suggests that these are similes (cf. Joel 2:2, 3, 4, 5, 7, 9).[2] If the invader is "like a mighty people arrayed for battle" (v. 5b) or "like mighty warriors" (v. 7a), it is not necessary for it to be an actual army.[3] In defense of a literal army view, some argue that Joel is using the so-called *kaph veritatis*, which would indicate that the invader is "in every respect like" the images it presents.[4] However, several of the *kaph* phrases in 2:1–11 do not fit this category, notably the description in 2:2 of the invader's arrival as "like dawn being spread upon the mountains" and the classification in 2:3 that the land is "like the garden of Eden" before the invader arrives. These are best understood as similes, which weakens the case for a literal army.

Another suggestion is that the invader described in 2:1–11 reflects a future attack from an apocalyptic army with no connection to any of the previous crises. This severs the connection to the locusts in Joel 1, suggesting that the effects that the invader has on the cosmos, such as causing the heavenly bodies to shake, is of a different order from the destruction of crops detailed in 1:2–14. Proponents of this view also stress that unlike 1:2–14, most of the verbs in 2:1–11 appear in the prefix conjugation, possibly reflecting future action.[5] The apocalyptic nature of the army may prefigure the appearance of locusts in Rev 9:2–11.[6]

This approach overemphasizes the differences between 1:2–14 and 2:1–11. The multi-generational command to commemorate this incident in 1:2–3 and the identification of the uniqueness of this moment in 2:2 adopt a similar tone. Both passages stress the unprecedented nature of the crisis, raising it above any other incidents in the past or future. Further, in Rev 9:2–11 the locusts do not behave like literal locusts since they are commanded not to devour the grass and the plants, but rather to directly afflict humans (Rev 9:3–4, 10). Meanwhile, the invading army described in 2:1–11 does mirror the behavior of locusts. The aftermath of their destruction makes it appear as though a fire has scoured the land.[7] Finally, the use of a sequence of prefix conjugation verbs in 2:1–11 suggests an ongoing threat, which does not necessitate a new peril.[8] Joel 2:1–11 portrays the advance of the invading army as a continual series of overlapping events that builds toward YHWH's terrifying arrival

---

2. For this function of כְּ, see Bruce Waltke and Michael O'Connor, *An Introduction to Biblical Hebrew Syntax* (Winona Lake, IN: Eisenbrauns, 1990 [hereafter *IBHS*]), §11.2.9; BHRG §39.10.

3. Linville, "Bugs," 290.

4. Robert B. Chisholm, *Interpreting the Minor Prophets* (Grand Rapids: Zondervan, 1990) 58. For the use of *kaph veritatis*, see *IBHS* §11.2.9b.

5. Wolff, *Joel and Amos*, 41–42. See also Crenshaw, *Joel*, 129.

6. Ibid.

7. Seitz, *Joel*, 125–26. Seitz refers to a report of a locust invasion in Egypt and Israel from 2013 to provide a sense of the devastation involved

8. Assis, *Book of Joel*, 122.

in 2:10.⁹ Consequently, it is possible for Joel to transform the locusts from 1:2–14 into harbingers of the day of YHWH, described in further detail in 2:1–11. The prevalence of imperatives and verbs belonging to the suffix conjugation in 1:2–14 contrasts with the prefix verbs of 2:1–11, but both passages likely still draw from the same image-world.

The final possibility is that Joel again refers to actual locusts in 2:1–11. The prophet may be invoking a second swarm of locusts, but this is not required.¹⁰ Joel likely uses the original locust invasion as the foundation for his exploration of what the day of YHWH entails for the Judahite audience. Joel's poetic use of activities that can be connected to locust behavior strengthens this perspective. These include their apparent discipline as they advance and the landscape that looks like it has been devasted by fire.¹¹ Consequently, the literary context suggests that 2:1–11 again refers to a locust invasion, albeit one described with "magnificent poetic hyperbole."¹²

Joel 2:1–11 clearly describes an increase in the destructive power of the locusts. They ravage the landscape (2:3), but the description of their assault on Zion adds a new and frightening element (2:7–9). Joel here engages in blending metaphors in order to heighten the sense of doom. Not only does the audience face the destruction of their crops, they also must fear for their very existence as the day of YHWH unfolds.¹³

Joel 2:10 shifts the literary context by explicitly identifying YHWH as the one who authorizes the activity of the locusts. This passage concludes with Jerusalem under assault by an attacking force, led by none other than YHWH. The overwhelming nature of the locust army's attack on Zion prepares the way for Joel to announce the day of YHWH and reveal that it does so under YHWH's authority. The day of YHWH now inspires despair as God's people come under judgment. Joel brings the audience down to its lowest point, which provides the foundation for his programmatic call for response in 2:12–17.

---

9. Interestingly, the text reverts to predominantly affix verbs in Joel 2:10–11 when describing YHWH's intervention. This may reflect what Arnold and Choi have termed the "rhetorical future" use of the tense, which "expresses a vivid future or prospective action or situation, which is not yet a reality but considered a certainty from the speaker's rhetorical point of view." Bill T. Arnold and John H. Choi, *A Guide to Biblical Hebrew Syntax*, 2nd ed (Cambridge: Cambridge University Press, 2018) §3.2.1d.

10. Simkins, *Yahweh's Activity*, 154. Simkins refers to the promise of restoration in 2:25 in which YHWH states that he will restore הַשָּׁנִים ("the years") that the locusts devoured to suggest that there were two locust attacks. However, the deleterious effects of a single locust swarm could last for longer than one year. Further, requiring that much continuity between an image and its referent is overreading the text.

11. Ibid., 165

12. Barton, *Joel*, 70.

13. Wendland, *Prophetic Rhetoric*, 22–23. Wendland meticulously details the elements of the metaphorical blend in Joel 2:1–11 and shows the synergy between the spheres of locust activity and military invasion.

> A. Superscription (1:1)
> B. Despair on Account of the Locusts (1:2–14)
> C. Despair in the Day of YHWH—The Drought (1:15–20)
> → **D. Despair in the Day of YHWH—The Invasion (2:1–11)**
>   **1. The Announcement of the Day of YHWH (2:1–2b)**
>   **2. The Advance of the Locust Army (2:2c–5c)**
>   **3. The View of the Victims (2:6)**
>   **4. The Locust Army Attacks (2:7–9)**
>   **5. The Advent of the Day of YHWH (2:10–11)**
> E. Hinge: The Call to Return to YHWH (2:12–17)
> F. Divine Deliverance from the Locusts and Drought (2:18–27)
> G. Deliverance through the Spirit of YHWH (3:1–5 [2:28–32])
> H. Deliverance through Divine Judgment on the Day of YHWH (4:1–21 [3:1–21])

Translation and Outline

Structure and Literary Form

An *inclusio* focused on the day of YHWH delimits the boundaries of 2:1–11.[14] Joel 2:1a declares that this day is near, while 2:11d–f concludes by detailing its magnitude and posing a rhetorical question about the Judahite audience's ability to survive it. Joel 2:1–11 shifts from laments and the prophet's own entreaties found in 1:15–20. It readdresses the audience through a series of imperatives that introduce the day of YHWH before it reveals what this day will entail. This passage culminates with a return to the day of YHWH, suggesting that the audience's doom is imminent. This leads into 2:12–17, which grapples with how the audience should respond.

The vision of the day of YHWH that Joel describes in 2:1–11 develops in several stages. Joel 2:1–2b introduces the *inclusio* and warns the audience that this day is coming. Joel 2:2c–5c reveals the nature of the day of YHWH by describing the advance of the invading locust army, which leaves behind a swathe of destruction before arriving at the gates of Zion. Joel 2:6 briefly shifts focus as it provides the reactions of the invader's victims. Joel 2:7–9 returns to the invading army and describes its overwhelming assault. Finally, 2:10–11 closes with the day of YHWH *inclusio*, revealing that the invasion is under the command of YHWH.

---

14. Crenshaw, *Joel*, 128. Crenshaw also focuses upon the threefold repetition פָּנָיו ("his face") in Joel 2:1–11 as an additional connecting feature (written as לְפָנָיו in 2:3, 10, and מִפָּנָיו in 2:6).

Joel 2:1–11

D. Despair in the Day of YHWH—The Invasion (2:1–11)

1. The Announcement of the Day of YHWH (2:1–2b)

   a. The Summons to Alarm (2:1a–c)

1a	תִּקְע֤וּ שׁוֹפָר֙ בְּצִיּ֔וֹן	Blow a trumpet in Zion!
1b	וְהָרִ֖יעוּ בְּהַ֣ר קָדְשִׁ֑י	Sound an alarm on my holy mountain!
1c	יִרְגְּז֕וּ כֹּ֖ל יֹשְׁבֵ֣י הָאָ֑רֶץ	Let tremble all the inhabitants of the land!

   b. The Nature of the Day of YHWH (2:1d–2b)

1d	כִּֽי־בָ֥א יוֹם־יְהוָ֖ה	For the day of YHWH is coming,
1e	כִּ֥י קָרֽוֹב׃	for it is near.
2a	י֧וֹם חֹ֣שֶׁךְ וַאֲפֵלָ֗ה	A day of darkness and gloom,
2b	י֥וֹם עָנָ֖ן וַעֲרָפֶ֑ל	a day of cloud and heavy darkness.

2. The Advance of the Locust Army (2:2c–5c)

   a. The Incomparability of the Locust Army (2:2c–e)

2c	כְּשַׁ֖חַר פָּרֻ֣שׂ עַל־הֶהָרִ֑ים עַ֚ם רַ֣ב וְעָצ֔וּם	Like dawn being spread upon the mountains, a people great and numerous.
2d	כָּמֹ֙הוּ֙ לֹ֣א נִֽהְיָ֣ה מִן־הָעוֹלָ֔ם	There has not been anything like it from before,
2e	וְאַחֲרָיו֙ לֹ֣א יוֹסֵ֔ף עַד־שְׁנֵ֖י דּ֥וֹר וָדֽוֹר׃	and after it there will not be again from generation to generation.

   b. The Locust Army's Effect on the Landscape (2:3)

3a	לְפָנָיו֙ אָ֣כְלָה אֵ֔שׁ	Before it a fire devours,
3b	וְאַחֲרָ֖יו תְּלַהֵ֣ט לֶהָבָ֑ה	after it a flame blazes.
3c	כְּגַן־עֵ֨דֶן הָאָ֜רֶץ לְפָנָ֗יו	Like the garden of Eden is the earth before it,
3d	וְאַחֲרָיו֙ מִדְבַּ֣ר שְׁמָמָ֔ה	but after it a desolate wasteland.
3e	וְגַם־פְּלֵיטָ֖ה לֹא־הָ֥יְתָה לּֽוֹ׃	There is no escape from it.

   c. The Nature of the Locust Army (2:4–5)

4a	כְּמַרְאֵ֥ה סוּסִ֖ים מַרְאֵ֑הוּ	Like the appearance of horses is their appearance,
4b	וּכְפָרָשִׁ֖ים כֵּ֥ן יְרוּצֽוּן׃	and like mighty steeds they run.
5a	כְּק֣וֹל מַרְכָּב֗וֹת עַל־רָאשֵׁ֤י הֶֽהָרִים֙ יְרַקֵּד֔וּן	Like the sound of chariots upon the tops of the mountains they leap,
5b	כְּקוֹל֙ לַ֣הַב אֵ֔שׁ אֹכְלָ֖ה קָ֑שׁ	and like the sound of a consuming fire they devour chaff,
5c	כְּעַ֣ם עָצ֔וּם עֱר֖וּךְ מִלְחָמָֽה׃	like a mighty people, being arrayed for battle.

3. The View of the Victims (2:6)

6a	מִפָּנָ֖יו יָחִ֣ילוּ עַמִּ֑ים	From before it, peoples tremble.
6b	כָּל־פָּנִ֖ים קִבְּצ֥וּ פָארֽוּר׃	All faces turn pale.

Continued on next page.

Continued from previous page.

4. The Locust Army Attacks (2:7–9)
   a. The Locust Army Assaults Zion (2:7–8)

7a	כְּגִבּוֹרִים יְרֻצוּן	Like mighty warriors they run.
7b	כְּאַנְשֵׁי מִלְחָמָה יַעֲלוּ חוֹמָה	Like men of battle they ascend the wall.
7c	וְאִישׁ בִּדְרָכָיו יֵלֵכוּן	Each goes in his own path.
7d	וְלֹא יְעַבְּטוּן אֹרְחוֹתָם׃	They do not change their way.
8a	וְאִישׁ אָחִיו לֹא יִדְחָקוּן	Each does not crowd his brother.
8b	גֶּבֶר בִּמְסִלָּתוֹ יֵלֵכוּן	Each man goes in his position.
8c	וּבְעַד הַשֶּׁלַח יִפֹּלוּ	Through the defenses they come.
8d	לֹא יִבְצָעוּ׃	They do not break ranks.

   b. The Locust Army Enters the City (2:9)

9a	בָּעִיר יָשֹׁקּוּ	In the city they rush about.
9b	בַּחוֹמָה יְרֻצוּן	Upon the walls they run.
9c	בַּבָּתִּים יַעֲלוּ	Upon the houses they climb.
9d	בְּעַד הַחַלּוֹנִים יָבֹאוּ כַּגַּנָּב	Through windows they enter like a thief.

5. The Advent of the Day of YHWH (2:10–11)
   a. The Response of the Heavenly Realm (2:10)

10a	לְפָנָיו רָגְזָה אֶרֶץ	Before them the earth trembles,
10b	רָעֲשׁוּ שָׁמָיִם	the heavens quake.
10c	שֶׁמֶשׁ וְיָרֵחַ קָדָרוּ	The sun and the moon grow dark,
10d	וְכוֹכָבִים אָסְפוּ נָגְהָם׃	and the stars gather their brightness.

   b. The Revelation of YHWH's Leadership (2:11a–c)

11a	וַיהוָה נָתַן קוֹלוֹ לִפְנֵי חֵילוֹ	Now YHWH utters his voice before his army,
11b	כִּי רַב מְאֹד מַחֲנֵהוּ	for very great is his host,
11c	כִּי עָצוּם עֹשֵׂה דְבָרוֹ	and mighty is the one who does his word.

   c. The Nature of the Day of YHWH (2:11d–f)

11d	כִּי־גָדוֹל יוֹם־יְהוָה	Indeed, great is the day of YHWH,
11e	וְנוֹרָא מְאֹד	and very terrifying.
11f	וּמִי יְכִילֶנּוּ׃	Who can withstand it?

Explanation of the Text

1. The Announcement of the Day of YHWH (2:1a–2b)

Joel 2:1a–c contains three imperatives warning of the arrival of the day of YHWH. These imperatives highlight the urgency of the situation. Joel reveals that the day of YHWH is not only evident in the ravages of locusts and drought but also threatens the very existence of Zion. The prophet places the introductory commands in the mouth of YHWH by means of the first-person pronominal suffix on the construction בְּהַר קָדְשִׁי ("on my holy mountain") in 2:1b. This is fascinating given what Joel reveals about YHWH at the end of this passage. In 2:1 the prophet has YHWH call for an alarm on his holy mountain to face an impending threat, but in 2:10–11 he indicates that YHWH leads the invasion against Zion.

The first command found in Joel 2:1a is תִּקְעוּ שׁוֹפָר בְּצִיּוֹן ("blow a trumpet in Zion"). This command serves a variety of purposes in the OT, including warning of attack (Jer 4:5; 6:1; Hos 8:1), calls to war (Judg 3:27; 6:34; 7:8; Jer 51:27), and cultic observance (Lev 25:9; Josh 6:4; Pss 47:6; 81:4; 150:3; 2 Chr 15:14).[15] In this instance, Joel's command to blow the trumpet warns of an attack since what follows is the prophet's description of an army advancing. Joel's command to blow the trumpet resonates with Jer 4:5–8 and the description of the day of YHWH in Zeph 1:14–16. Jeremiah calls for the trumpet to sound and for people to gather in Zion and other strongholds because YHWH is sending an invader from the north (Jer 4:6b).[16] These parallels suggest that Joel 2:1 echoes the statement of threat to Zion's continued security in Jer 4:6.[17] Zephaniah 1:14–16 stresses the nearness of the day of YHWH and the darkness that comes as a result. It also describes the day of YHWH in the context of an assault against fortified cities including Jerusalem, announced by a trumpet that sounds the alarm (cf. Zeph 1:16).[18] Thus, these parallels suggest that Joel's command to sound the trumpet warns of an impending attack.

The second command found in 2:1b echoes the first and directs the audience to sound the alarm, using a first-person suffix on the phrase בְּהַר קָדְשִׁי ("on my holy mountain") to establish YHWH's claim to Zion. This reflects ancient Near Eastern traditions of mountains as the dwelling place of deities. In particular, there is a helpful parallel between the Canaanite idea of Mount Zaphon and the OT understanding of Mount Zion. The deity dwells in a temple on the sacred mountain, which gives it the qualities of a fortress. The mountain may be a scene of battle, but it is impregnable since it is the home of the deity.[19] YHWH's active presence on Mount Zion is essential to its preservation in the face of invaders.[20] Psalms 2:1–12 and 48:2–7 employ this theme, picturing attackers who assault Zion, only to go down to defeat at the hands

---

15. Sweeney, *Twelve*, 162.
16. The connection of Jer 4:6 with *Joel* is strengthened when considering 2:20, which explicitly refers to the invading force of 2:1–11 as הַצְּפוֹנִי ("the northerner").
17. Strazicich, *Joel's Use of Scripture*, 115–16.
18. The passage in Zephaniah differs slightly since there is no actual command to blow a trumpet. Instead Zeph 1:16 describes the day of YHWH as a "day of the trumpet."
19. Richard J. Clifford, *The Cosmic Mountain in Canaan and the Old Testament* (Cambridge, MA: Harvard University Press, 1972) 131.
20. Ben C. Ollenburger, *Zion the City of the Great King: A Theological Symbol of the Jerusalem Cult*, JSOTSup 41 (Sheffield: JSOT Press, 1987), 66. See also how Hayes identifies links between Zion's inviolability and Israel's obedience to YHWH's commands (cf. Isa 10:5–6; 29:1–8; Jer 7:13–15; 26:4–6). John H. Hayes, "The Tradition of Zion's Inviolability," *JBL* 82 (1963): 419–26.

of YHWH.[21] Consequently, it is a shock when Joel subverts the idea of inviolability throughout the remainder of 2:1–11 by depicting an invasion that overwhelms Zion's defenses.[22] Of course, this is intricately connected to YHWH's absence from Zion and his presence with the invading force.

Joel 2:1c continues with a third command directing כֹּל יֹשְׁבֵי הָאָרֶץ ("all the inhabitants of the land") to tremble.[23] This is the same expression found in 1:2 and 14 to indicate the necessity for the entire covenant community to listen to his proclamation. By returning to this expression in Joel 2:1, the prophet again emphasizes that all should hear and respond. The specific command to tremble continues the mood established by the preceding imperatives. Blowing the trumpet and sounding the alarm create trepidation in the audience. This call to tremble sets up the prophet's description of the reasons for concern in the next three clauses.

Joel 2:1d–e follows the three commands with two clauses beginning with causal כִּי that stress the imminence of the day of YHWH. Joel 2:1d declares כִּי־בָא יוֹם־יהוה ("for the day of YHWH is coming"), and 2:1e simply states כִּי קָרוֹב ("for it is near").[24] This is identical to Joel 1:15b, stressing the proximity of the day of YHWH. Its nearness should prompt the audience to respond in a way that might mitigate its threat.[25] Consequently, Joel begins by invoking the same preliminary understanding of the day of YHWH found in the preceding passage before developing it in greater detail. The nearness of the day of YHWH is the foundation for the description of the invader that follows.

Joel 2:2a–b concludes the first subsection of this passage, using darkness imagery to describe the nature of the day of YHWH. These clauses read יוֹם חֹשֶׁךְ וַאֲפֵלָה יוֹם עָנָן וַעֲרָפֶל ("a day of darkness and gloom, a day of cloud and heavy darkness"). They are two short verbless clauses both headed by יוֹם and followed by word pairs. These clauses continue to set the tone of the day of YHWH. Their brevity is a rhetorical device stressing the imminence of the day. The word pairs חֹשֶׁךְ וַאֲפֵלָה ("darkness and gloom") and עָנָן וַעֲרָפֶל ("cloud and heavy darkness") are common images for the day of YHWH, probably building upon Amos' assertion that the day of YHWH is a day of darkness and not light (Amos 5:18–20; cf. Isa 5:30; 60:1–3; Zeph 1:15–16).[26] The prophet's emphasis on the dark nature of the day of YHWH lends credence to the calls found in Joel 2:1a–c to sound an alarm and tremble. The occurrence of these word pairs also

---

21. Clifford, *Cosmic*, 153.
22. The issue of the inviolability of Zion contributes to the discussion concerning the date of *Joel*. If *Joel* is to be dated after the Babylonian captivity, then the concept of inviolability might be shaken. However, it can be preserved by positing that YHWH commandeered the Babylonian army to punish sinful Judah (Crenshaw, *Joel*, 118). Zion's inviolability thus depends on whether or not YHWH chooses to defend it. Further, postexilic authors envision Zion as the place where YHWH dwells, even after the destruction of the temple. The return from captivity and the refoundation of the temple restores its sacred status. See Carol L. Meyers and Eric M. Meyers, "Jerusalem and Zion After the Exile: The Evidence of First Zechariah," in *"Sha'arei Talmon": Studies in the Bible, Qumran and the Ancient Near East Presented to Shemaryahu Talmon*, ed. Michael Fishbane, Emanuel Tov, and Weston W. Fields (Winona Lake: Eisenbrauns, 1992), 121.

23. The decision to translate this clause with the volitional "let tremble" has to be made from context since it is identical to the regular prefix form of the verb (יִרְגְּזוּ). The proximity of this verb to the preceding imperatives suggests that a volitional reading is likely.

24. The verb בָא in the first כִּי clause is either an affix or participial form, but the presence of a qualifying statement that stresses the imminence of the day of YHWH indicates that a participial translation ("is coming") is quite fitting.

25. On the rhetorical function of the imminence of the day of YHWH, see Robert B. Chisholm, "When Prophecy Appears to Fail, Check Your Hermeneutic" *JETS* 53 (2010): 561–78.

26. Barton, *Joel*, 72. Barton also suggests that the dark nature of the day of YHWH in Joel is suggestive of locusts covering over the landscape. This would be a sense unique to Joel since locusts are not in view in Amos, Isaiah, or Zephaniah.

prefigures the coming appearance of YHWH since the combination of horn-blasts, dark clouds, and the trembling of the people recalls other manifestations of YHWH's presence (Exod 19:16; Deut 4:11; Ps 18:10[9]; 97:2).²⁷ The descriptions of darkness also anticipate the prophet's return to the day of YHWH in Joel 2:10–11, where the heavenly bodies are darkened and the heavens and earth tremble. Consequently, Joel 2:1–2b reintroduces the day of YHWH and generates a sense of impending doom.

2. The Advance of the Locust Army (2:2c–5c)

Joel 2:2c–5 moves from announcing the nearness of the day of YHWH to describing what it entails. Joel begins with an extended description of the march of the locust army toward Zion. In accordance with the discussion found in the Literary Context, this army reflects a blend of the locusts from 1:2–14 with military images. Joel uses a number of similes to supply the locusts with new characteristics, tightening their association with an invading army. Joel 2:2c describes the arrival of the invading army with the simile כְּשַׁחַר פָּרֻשׂ עַל־הֶהָרִים ("like dawn being spread upon the mountains"). This image emphasizes the suddenness of the invader's arrival, possibly equating sunrise with an imminent disaster as the sun eliminates the places to hide from it.²⁸ This simile relating to light contrasts the four synonyms related to darkness found in the previous clause.²⁹ The rapidity of this shift from darkness to light expresses the disorienting quickness of the invader's appearance.

After this simile, 2:2d–e once again refers to the incomparability of the situation, recalling the use of rhetorical questions in 1:2. Here, Joel states that the size and power of the invader have not been seen previously and will not be seen again.³⁰ The strategy of incomparability recalls the temporal progression found in 1:2–3, where the prophet invokes both the past and future to highlight the unique nature of the current situation. There is overlap in vocabulary since both 1:3 and 2:2 refer to the progression through each דּוֹר ("generation"). In 1:2–3 the prophet asks rhetorically whether such an event had occurred in the past and then commands the audience to recount it to following generations. In 2:2d–e the prophet looks before and after the event and claims that nothing of this nature will occur in future generations.

After focusing on the incomparability of the invading horde, Joel describes its advance in detail, using "incremental repetition."³¹ He overlaps and occasionally repeats the verbs that trace the movements of the invader. The net effect is to portray a steady advance that devastates the landscape as it progresses from the mountains, down to the city, over the walls, and into the houses. The assault of the locust army is relentless and the concentration of verbs describing its movement reinforces that reality throughout 2:2c–9d.

---

27. Klein notes that עֲרָפֶל in particular points to a theophany since it occurs in a context that announces YHWH's presence. These include Exod 20:21; Deut 4:11; 2 Sam 22:10; Ps 97:2; Job 22:13. See Ralph W. Klein, "The Day of the Lord," *CTM* 39 (1968): 518.

28. Assis, *Book of Joel*, 129.

29. Some commentators read "darkness" instead of "dawn" (Wolff, *Joel and Amos*, 44; Allen, *Joel*, 68–69; Seitz, *Joel*, 152). This likely requires repointing שַׁחַר ("dawn") to read שְׁחֹר ("darkness"), which is found in Lam 4:8 This would fit better with the darkness imagery of the preceding verse, but the lack of textual support for this change argues against it. Assis also finds this revised phrase to be "awkward," and suggests that Joel may use "dawn" to indicate that disaster is about to unfold (Assis, *Book of Joel*, 129).

30. Barton, *Joel*, 72.

31. Robert Alter, *The Art of Biblical Poetry* (New York: Basic Books, 1985), 42. Alter notes how the verbs that describe the advance of the army convey a sense of growing threat. He translates the verbs in this manner: "they run, they dance, they run, they scale a wall, they go, indeed they go, they swarm, they run, they scale, they come in at the windows like thieves."

Joel focuses first on the effects of the invader upon the land that it crosses. He uses imagery suggestive of a large locust swarm on the march and the trail of destruction it leaves in its wake. Joel 2:3 consists of two pictures of the locust army, both of which employ a "before and after" strategy that describes the locusts' inexorable movement.[32] Joel 2:3a–b uses two parallel phrases to construct the "before and after" statement. The first clause is לְפָנָיו אָכְלָה אֵשׁ ("before it a fire devours"), while the second clause is וְאַחֲרָיו תְּלַהֵט לֶהָבָה ("after it a flame blazes"). The fronting of "before it" and "after it" shifts the topic from the temporal dimension of the invader to the space that it occupies, drawing focus to the ruin and destruction that it causes.[33] This description also fits into the metaphorical blend of an army and locusts since 2:2c refers to the invader as a עַם רַב וְעָצוּם ("great and mighty people"). The destruction that this עַם ("people") leaves in its wake recalls descriptions of actual locust invasions in that the aftermath of their ravaging resembles that of a wildfire.[34]

Joel 2:3c–e emphasizes the totality of devastation by means of a similar construction. The prophet uses a simile that reinforces the picture of a landscape devastated by fire. Joel declares that the land is like the garden of Eden before the arrival of the invaders and like a desert after they pass. Essentially, the invaders render fruitless what used to be fruitful. The syntax of this simile differs from the one in 2:3a–b since it is arranged as a chiasm, reading כְּגַן־עֵדֶן הָאָרֶץ לְפָנָיו וְאַחֲרָיו מִדְבַּר שְׁמָמָה. It begins with כְּגַן־עֵדֶן ("like the garden of Eden") which is paralleled at the end of the phrase with מִדְבַּר שְׁמָמָה ("a desolate wasteland"). The two prepositional phrases לְפָנָיו וְאַחֲרָיו ("before it and after it") appear in the middle of the construction. The grammatical inversion in this expression resonates with the change in the state of the land from Eden to desolate wasteland in the wake of the invader's activities.

The mention of Eden is noteworthy since such references are relatively rare in the OT.[35] Isaiah 51:3 and Ezek 36:35 use Eden similarly since they describe how YHWH will undo destruction and desolation in order to restore the land to an Edenic state.[36] Joel 2:3c–e reverses this picture since the coming of the day of YHWH, shown through the activities of the invading horde, changes the land from a paradise to a wasteland. It is also possible that the simile describing the landscape's change from a garden to a desert goes beyond describing the physical elements of destruction in the locust army's advance. Instead, the use of Eden and its "uncreation" opens up the possibility of the earth returning to a pre-creation state of chaos.[37] Further, Deut 32:10 pairs the term מִדְבַּר that Joel uses for desert with the term תֹהוּ that describes the uncreated state from which YHWH formed the earth in Gen 1:2. The ability of the invader to turn the landscape from a paradise to a scorched wilderness reflects its unmatched power, and its imminent arrival is intended to invoke fear from Joel's audience. The switch from Eden to a devastated wasteland

---

32. Ogden and Deutsch, *Joel and Malachi*, 28–29.
33. Wendland, *Prophetic Rhetoric*, 24. On fronting as a way of signaling a shift in topic, see Christo J. H. van der Merwe, "Fronting: Biblical Hebrew" in vol. 1 of *Encyclopedia of Hebrew Language and Linguistics*, ed. Geoffrey Khan (Leiden: Brill, 2013), 931–35. Van der Merwe also notes that entities that are the topic of the clause tend to be encoded pronominally, which would include the invader as the referent of the pronominal suffixes on לְפָנָיו and וְאַחֲרָיו. Christo J. H. van der Merwe, "Explaining Fronting in Biblical Hebrew," *JNSL* 25 (1999): 181–82.
34. Simkins, *Yahweh's Activity*, 150.
35. Kapelrud lists Gen 2:8, 10, 15; 3:23; 4:16; Isa 51:3; Ezek 31:9, 16, 18; 36:35 as the only other passages that employ either גַּן־עֵדֶן or עֵדֶן; Kapelrud, *Joel Studies*, 76.
36. Crenshaw, *Joel*, 120; Assis, *Book of Joel*, 130.
37. Simkins, *Yahweh's Activity*, 167. Seitz pursues this line of thought more boldly, stating "God is un-creating. Eden is replaced by wilderness/chaos." See Seitz, *Joel*, 159.

graphically expresses the totality of the destruction and may further invoke the prospect of the world returning to an unordered state.

Joel 2:3e summarizes the preceding similes. It begins with וְגַם to link this clause to the previous images of fire and desolation.[38] Joel focuses on the noun פְּלֵיטָה ("escape"), placing it before the negated verb לֹא־הָיְתָה ("there is not") and emphasizing that doom is inevitable.[39] In this verse, Joel provides a foreboding picture of a paradise turned into a desert. The invading locust horde that follows the announcement of the day of YHWH in Joel 2:1 is both incomparable and inescapable.

Joel 2:4 elaborates on the appearance of the invaders. This verse employs two similes that describe the invasion in equine terms. Joel 2:4a is verbless and twice uses the noun מַרְאֵה ("appearance"), bracketing the noun סוּסִים ("horses"). The first use of מַרְאֵה is prefixed by the preposition כְּ in order to construct the simile, and the second use appears with the third-person masculine plural suffix (מַרְאֵהוּ), in order to establish that the antecedent of this comparison is the invading force. Comparing the invasion to horses could refer to its military strength, but there are potential connections between horses and the locusts. Modern commentators draw attention to the similarities of the shapes of the heads of these creatures, while other biblical writers make use of this connection.[40] Joel 2:4b further reinforces the equine qualities of the invader through a simile that describes it in motion. The invaders are כְּפָרָשִׁים ("like steeds"), a word pair with סוּסִים ("horses") from the preceding clause. These steeds are the subject of the verb יְרוּצוּן ("they run").[41] Joel thus describes the activity of the invaders in terms suited for a cavalry charge.

Joel 2:5 continues to reveal the nature of the invading army. This verse contains three additional similes that shift from describing the appearance of the invader to the sounds that accompany its advance.[42] This allows Joel to strengthen his message by requiring the audience to engage another one of its senses. The audience now experiences the invasion with both its "mind's-eye" and its "mind's-ear." In the first simile found in 2:5a, Joel compares sound of the invaders to chariots upon the hilltops. Chariots reflect the pinnacle of military might in the ancient world, which fits what Joel seeks to

---

38. On the summarizing function of the particle גַם, see IBHS §39.3.4d.

39. van der Merwe and Wendland, "Word Order," 122. Note that Joel 3:5 [2:32] uses פְּלֵיטָה in a positive sense, promising that there is escape for those who call on the name of YHWH.

40. Crenshaw, *Joel*, 121. Crenshaw notes the German *Heupferd* and Italian *cavaletta* as modern languages that suggest an equine appearance for locusts. Revelation 9:7 portrays locusts as horses equipped for battle, while Job 39:20 reverses the comparison and pictures a horse leaping like a locust (Barton, *Joel*, 73; Assis, *Joel*, 132).

41. The verb is the first of several in 2:1–11 that uses the paragogic *nun* ending on third-person plural masculine verbs. See also יְרַקֵּדוּן in 2:5, יְרֻצוּן, יֵלֵכוּן, and יַעַבְטוּן in 2:7, יִדְחָקוּן and יֵלֵכוּן in 2:8, and יְרֻצוּן in 2:9. This ending is found roughly 300 times in the OT and it is unclear if it has a semantic purpose. Joüon suggests that it reflects a "fuller and more emphatic or expressive form" but does not explain precisely what is being emphasized or expressed. See P. Joüon, *A Grammar of Biblical Hebrew*, trans. T. Muraoka (Rome: Pontifical Biblical Institute, 1993 [hereafter Joüon]), §44.e. DeCaen and Kaufman note that it tends to appear in pausal positions and when the following word begins with *aleph* or *ayin*. See Vincent DeCaen, "Moveable *nun* and Intrusive *nun*: The Nature and Distribution of Verbal Nunation in Joel and Job," *JNSL* 29 (2003): 121–32; Stephen A. Kaufman, "Paragogic *nun* in Biblical Hebrew: Hypercorrection as a Clue to Lost Scribal Practice," in *Solving Riddles and Untying Knots: Biblical, Epigraphic, and Semitic Studies in Honor of James C. Greenfield*, ed. Ziony Zevit, Seymour Gitin, and Michael Sokoloff (Winona Lake, IN: Eisenbrauns, 1995), 95–99. Garr suggests that this ending occurs in clauses that he dubs "rhetorical satellites," which are expansions upon the backbone of the discourse. See W. Randall Garr, "The Paragogic *nun* in Rhetorical Perspective" in *Biblical Hebrew in its Northwest Semitic Setting: Typological and Historical Perspectives* (ed. Steven Ellis Fassberg and Avi Hurvitz; Winona Lake, IN: Eisenbrauns, 2006), 65–74. See also Jakob Hoftijzer, *The Function and Use of the Imperfect Forms with nun paragogicum in Classical Hebrew* (Assen: Van Gorcum, 1985).

42. Crenshaw, *Joel*, 121; Allen, *Joel*, 71.

convey about this invasion (Exod 14:6–7; Judg 4:3; 5:28; 1 Sam 13:5). Further, chariots accompany theophanies, which resonates with the forthcoming revelation of this host's divine leadership in Joel 2:11 (2 Kgs 2:11–12; 6:17; Ezek 1).[43] These chariots move frenetically, described by the verb יְרַקֵּדוּן ("leap"), which suggests that the invader is moving swiftly against Zion.

There is an unexpected twist to this use of chariot imagery. Joel describes their sound as they move about the tops of mountains, which is odd since chariots are weapons of the plains not of the hilltops. This suggests that these are no ordinary chariots and that even mountains provide no barrier to their approach. The implication is that if the attacking foe can bring chariots over the mountains, Zion's walls will not be an effective defense. Further, Joel uses the chariots to create a sense of foreboding. The audience first hears the rumble of their wheels as a harbinger of disaster, prefiguring their frightening effect when they attack.

Joel 2:5b contains another simile that compares the invaders to the sound of fire devouring stubble. This recalls Joel 2:3, which employs fire as an image for the aftermath of the passage of the locusts. This time, Joel focuses on the sound, where the blaze creates crackling hisses and pops as it devours everything in its path. The sound precedes and warns of the coming flames and their heat. In this way, Joel creates the image of an invasion that uses "scorched earth" tactics, destroying the landscape in its advance toward its final target.

Finally, Joel 2:5c uses a third simile to refer to the invading force as כְּעַם עָצוּם עֱרוּךְ מִלְחָמָה ("like mighty people, being arrayed for battle"). This simile recalls 2:2, which refers to the invader as a great and mighty people. The passive participle עֱרוּךְ follows the simile and expresses that this mighty people are prepared to attack (Gen 14:8; 1 Sam 4:2; Jer 6:23; 50:9).[44] The third simile encapsulates the threats created through the first two. The threatening sounds of the approaching chariots and crackling flames coalesce into an image of a great army ready to fight. The assault of which Joel warns in 2:1 is imminent.

3. The View of the Victims (2:6)

Joel 2:6 provides a brief pause in the description of the invaders. Joel shifts his focus to the effect that they have upon those who must endure their assault. Joel accomplishes this shift in perspective in 2:6a through a fronted modifier מִפָּנָיו ("from its face"), which precedes the verb יָחִילוּ ("writhe in anguish"), describing the response of the victims. This verb is used in contexts of childbirth and can also be a metaphor for how people respond to crisis (Isa 13:8, 21:3, 26:17; Jer 6:24, 22:23, 50:43).[45] The actions associated with the use of חיל paints a picture of an involuntary loss of control over the body's movements typically as a result of pain and fear.[46] Joel indicates that the advance of the attacking army is sufficient to inspire crippling panic. The image here is that of a city under siege, with the populace trembling behind the transient security of city walls. Interestingly, those who writhe are not

---

43. Dillard, "Joel," 275.

44. Crenshaw, *Joel*, 122. The active participle is used to describe the military capability of David's forces in 1 Chr 12:33, 35.

45. On the use of חיל in childbirth metaphors see Claudia D. Bergmann, *Childbirth as a Metaphor for Crisis: Evidence from the Ancient Near East, the Hebrew Bible, and 1 QH XI, 1–18*, BZAW 382 (Berlin: de Gruyter, 2008), 75–76. Dille also discusses this verb but would likely categorize Joel's use of it as a "dead metaphor" (Sarah J. Dille, *Mixing Metaphors: God as Mother and Father in Deutero-Isaiah*, JSOTSup 398 [London: T&T Clark, 2004], 28–29). I would argue that while Joel is not importing the full context of childbirth here, its association with a loss of bodily control resulting from pain and fear suggests that it is the foundation for Joel's description of writhing.

46. Bergmann, *Childbirth*, 76.

specifically identified as Zion-dwellers since Joel refers to them in 2:6a with the generic term עַמִּים ("peoples") and further describes them as כָּל־פָּנִים ("all faces") in 2:6b. There is some potential for confusion since Joel 2:2 and 2:5 refer to the invading locust army with the singular form עַם ("people"), but the actions of the עַמִּים ("peoples") make it clear that this is a different entity. The function of the עַמִּים is to reveal the power of the invaders by portraying the response of their intended targets. The writhing of the peoples suggests that the inhabitants of Zion should heed Joel's call to alarm.[47]

Joel 2:6b notes that as a result of the invaders' arrival, the peoples stare in anguish and have their faces transformed. This clause begins with כָּל־פָּנִים ("all faces") echoing the use of מִפָּנָיו ("from its face") in 2:6a. Joel thus engages in wordplay as the appearance of the face of the invader leads to a visible transformation of the color of the victims' faces.[48] This provides a template for the reaction of those dwelling in Zion. Joel highlights the powerlessness of the peoples in response to this army, suggesting to his audience that they should identify with the peoples and respond with similar distress. The terror-stricken response of the peoples points to the inevitability of the invader's victory and the imminent arrival of the day of YHWH.

4. The Locust Army Attacks (2:7–9)

After the brief interlude in the preceding verse, 2:7–9 shifts focus back to the invading army and its overwhelming power. In the space between 2:5 and 2:7, the invading army transitions from ravaging the landscape to launching its assault on Zion. Joel describes in detail the manner in which the army overwhelms the defenses and breaks into the city. The assault commences in 2:7a–b and employs two parallel similes that describe the invaders as being כְּגִבּוֹרִים ("like warriors") and כְּאַנְשֵׁי מִלְחָמָה ("like men of battle"), who run and climb over the city walls. Both similes appear first in their respective clauses and are followed by verbs in the prefix conjugation. This places the similes in the foreground of their clauses.[49] Joel 2:7c–d continues to recount the attack through two parallel clauses that indicate that all of the invading army's members cannot be diverted from their course.[50] Joel first states this positively by declaring that each attacker stays on its own path. He then states the same idea negatively, noting that the attackers do not swerve. This resonates with locust imagery since they move in an organized manner in both biblical (Prov 30:27) and non-biblical accounts.[51] The blend of locust and military imagery culminates here with the

---

47. Barton, *Joel*, 73.
48. The specifics of what happens to the faces here are unclear. The issue is the word פָּארוּר, which concludes 2:6b. Most commentators translate this word with "glow" or "grow pale." It is found only twice in the OT (cf. Nah 2:11). The LXX changes the image, claiming that the faces of the peoples darken like soot on a pot (Barton, *Joel*, 58). This might result from reading פָּארוּר as פָּרוּר "cooking pot" (Wolff, *Joel and Amos*, 38). It seems that both traditions are trying to express a change in facial coloration resulting from the fear created by the advancing army.
49. van der Merwe and Wendland, "Word Order," 123.
50. Joel 2:7d contains the verb וְלֹא יְעַבְּטוּן. The root עָבַט is found in the *qal* (Deut 15:6) or *hiphil* (Deut 15:6a, 8; 24:10) in a legal sense of giving or taking in pledge. Joel 2:7 is the only time that this root occurs in the *piel*, where it is usually translated with the semantic range of "swerve" or "change one's course." The LXX follows this path, using ἐκκλινῶσιν which can be translated as "to bend aside" (Assis, *Joel*, 134). This can be further supported by noting a chiastic structure in the four verbs that comprise Joel 2:7c–8b. The first and fourth verbs are both יֵלֵכוּן ("they go"), while the second and third verbs are וְלֹא יְעַבְּטוּן and לֹא יְדְחָקוּן respectively. This grammatical structure suggests that the second and third verbs are synonymous. Since לֹא יְדְחָקוּן clearly implies maintaining ranks, then it is plausible that וְלֹא יְעַבְּטוּן has a similar sense (Ahlström, *Joel*, 11–13; see also Dillard, "Joel," 275).
51. Simkins, *Yahweh's Activity*, 164–65. He notes numerous modern accounts that describe locusts appearing to move like members of a cohesive, disciplined military force. This confirms the appropriateness of the metaphorical blend of locusts and military invasion that frames 2:3–9. See Wendland, *Prophetic Rhetoric*, 25–26.

picture of a disciplined attacker able to break through defenses.

Joel 2:8 continues in this vein. The preposition כְּ disappears, indicating that Joel has moved from simile to metaphor. This may be intended to draw Joel's audience further into the scenario. The locusts are no longer "like" an army, they *are* an army that threatens the very existence of the Judahite community. Joel 2:8c develops the scene, painting a picture of this army continuing its advance while the defenders' efforts prove futile. This clause probably indicates that the weapons of the defenders are ineffectual, which is unsurprising given what has been revealed about the invading horde.[52] Joel 2:8d concludes with a clipped phrased לֹא יִבְצָעוּ ("they do not break ranks") that summarizes the preceding statements of the invaders' power and discipline. They penetrate the defenses without slowing or breaking formation, leaving them free to wreak havoc.

Joel 2:9 describes the final stages of the locust army's assault on Zion. It enters the city, runs along the top of the walls, and enters into houses.[53] Joel 2:9a–c details the invaders' actions by using a "short, staccato rhythm" in which these three clauses follow the same pattern.[54] They begin with the preposition בְּ, followed by a geographical location, and conclude with a verb of motion. The locations of the locust army's activities grow progressively more intimate. In 2:9a, the invader's assault is described as בָּעִיר יָשֹׁקּוּ ("in the city they rush about"). This is followed in 2:9b with the phrase בַּחוֹמָה יְרֻצוּן ("upon the walls they run"). Finally, in 2:9c, the invader penetrates the final sanctuary through the phrase בַּבָּתִּים יַעֲלוּ ("upon the houses they climb"). This portrayal of the locust army's final assault recalls the waves of locusts in 1:4. In both cases a threefold repetition of a grammatical pattern emphasizes the scope of the disaster.[55] Just as wave after wave of locusts devour the crops, so the attacking army systemically breaches every barrier to its advance.

Joel 2:9d adds an extra element to the previously mentioned rhythm. It reflects the most vulnerable geographical location since the invader not only climbs upon the houses but actually enters them, eliminating any illusion of sanctuary. The phrase בְּעַד הַחַלּוֹנִים יָבֹאוּ כַּגַּנָּב ("through windows they enter like a thief") uses a simile that may have a parallel in Jer 9:21, which describes death as entering through the window.[56] In both instances, the undesired intruder cannot be barred from entry.

Overall, 2:7–9 portrays the locust army as so powerful that nothing can stop its attack on Zion. Joel imagines a situation in which the invader breaches every possible refuge. The sequence resembles that of a protagonist in a horror movie trying desperately to find shelter, only for the implacable foe to discover each and every hiding place. The walls of Zion cannot hold back this invader and neither can the final refuge of houses. Joel systemically removes any hope that his audience can withstand this assault. This sets up 2:10–11,

---

52. Joel 2:8c reads וּבְעַד הַשֶּׁלַח יִפֹּלוּ. The preposition בְּעַד occurs with a verb of motion. Waltke and O'Connor suggest that in this case the preposition indicates motion away from a given object (*IBHS* §11.2.7). Therefore, the noun הַשֶּׁלַח probably refers to weapons that the defenders fire to try to stop the attack. However, the invaders are able to move through or away from them, suggesting that the defensive efforts have failed. One other possibility is that this verse uses a second meaning of הַשֶּׁלַח, which is "tunnel" or "aqueduct." In this reading, Joel provides the route through which the army attacks (Crenshaw, *Joel*, 124).

53. Locusts entering the homes resonates with the plague of locusts invading Egyptian houses in Exod 10:5–6. Joel then implies to his audience that it stands in place of Egypt as the target of God's wrath. Joel makes this point explicit in 2:10–11. See Strazicich, *Joel's Use of Scripture*, 132; Siegfried Bergler, *Joel als Schriftinterpret* (Frankfurt am Main: Peter Lang, 1988), 140.

54. Crenshaw, *Joel*, 124.

55. van der Merwe and Wendland, "Word Order," 123.

56. Barton, *Joel*, 74.

5. The Advent of the Day of YHWH (2:10–11)

Joel 2:10–11 brings this passage to a crescendo returning to the day of YHWH. The prophet casts his gaze into the heavens and elevates the blend of locust and military imagery to new heights, making the invader's assault reverberate through every corner of the cosmos.[57] Joel 2:10a begins with a fronted modifier לְפָנָיו ("before it/him"), which has an ambiguous pronominal suffix. It could refer back to the invading horde, envisioning it as a collective entity, which Joel does in 2:2 and 2:5. The suffix on מִפָּנָיו in 2:6a that refers to the locust army is also suggestive of this option. The suffix could also point forward, foreshadowing the explicit appearance of YHWH in the next verse (cf. 1:2–3, 5, 11).[58] I favor the first option since it preserves the strongest sense of surprise, delaying the revelation that YHWH leads the invading army until the following verse. However, the ambiguity may well be intentional. Assis suggests that "we can interpret the revealed meaning of this verse as relating to locusts while bearing in mind that the author also planted the possibility for a theophanic interpretation."[59] Until this point, Joel has discussed the activities of the invader in terms that suggest an unstoppable army. YHWH's prospective appearance increases the intensity of this description, with the downfall of Zion reverberating throughout the created order.[60]

Joel 2:10 draws from the realm of theophany as the trembling and darkening of heavenly bodies warn of the arrival of YHWH (cf. Ps 77:16; Isa 13:10, 13; Mic 1:4). This is fitting since YHWH does arrive in Joel 2:11, causing the natural world to convulse.[61] Joel 2:10a–b uses the verbs רָגְזָה ("it trembles") and רָעָשׁוּ ("they quake") to describe the response of the earth and the heavens. When the verb רָעַשׁ has a geographical feature like the stars or mountains as its subject it indicates that God's power causes this shaking.[62] Further, the root רָגַז ("to tremble") occurs in this passage as an imperative in 2:1, calling on the inhabitants of Zion to quiver in response to the threat. The fact that the earth itself trembles in 2:10 suggests that there is good reason to heed the earlier command. If the earth trembles at the approach of this army, then surely the audience should do likewise. These cosmic signs are harbingers of the presence of YHWH.

Joel 2:10c–d focuses upon the response of the heavenly bodies. Joel first discusses the sun and moon, using the verb קָדָרוּ ("they darken"). This verb is associated with divine judgment when its subjects are heavenly bodies.[63] Joel then uses the expression אָסְפוּ נָגְהָם ("they gather their brightness") to describe the dimming of the stars.[64] The descriptions of darkening in 2:10c–d recall the warning of the day of YHWH in 2:2, which emphasizes it

---

57. Crenshaw, *Joel*, 125–26.
58. van der Merwe and Wendland, "Word Order," 124.
59. Assis, *Book of Joel*, 135.
60. Crenshaw, *Joel*, 126.
61. Allen, *Joel*, 73. Allen notes that the standard effect of YHWH's interventions is an earthquake and other related cosmological phenomena.
62. John A. Kessler "The Shaking of the Nations: An Eschatological View." *JETS* 30 (1987): 161. For other examples see Judg 5:4; Pss 18:8; 77:18–19; Isa 13:13; Jer 10:10; Ezek 26:10.
63. The judgment can be enacted by YHWH (Ezek 32:7–8; Isa 50:3) or by a force standing in for YHWH (cf. the "foe from the north" in Jer 4:27–28).
64. Crenshaw, *Joel*, 127. Often this expression reflects the augmentation of light, but Crenshaw finds a parallel in 1 Sam 14:19 where Saul commands a priest cease his activity with a command אֱסֹף יָדֶךָ ("withdraw your hand"). See also Jer 16:5 in which YHWH removes blessing from his people through the announcement אָסַפְתִּי אֶת־שְׁלוֹמִי מֵאֵת הָעָם־הַזֶּה ("I have withdrawn my peace from this people").

as a day of darkness, gloom, and cloud. Further, the darkening of heavenly luminaries is common in announcements of the day of YHWH. They are harbingers foretelling the imminent arrival of YHWH (Amos 5:8–10; Zeph 1:15–16). Joel 2:10 thus marks the prophet's return to the themes introduced in 2:1–2. The invading locust army takes on supernatural importance as the heavenly bodies convulse and darken in response.[65]

Joel 2:11 marks the climax of this passage by explicitly stating what the previous verse foreshadows. The prophet finally reveals that YHWH is the guiding power behind the invading horde. This is evident in the third-person pronominal suffixes of 2:11a, which indicate that YHWH utters *his* voice (קוֹלוֹ) before *his* army (חֵילוֹ). This appears to give a negative answer to the appeals to YHWH found in 1:15–20.[66] It also marks a departure from 2:1 where YHWH calls for an alarm to sound on *my* holy mountain. Joel's audience can no longer trust that their God would defend them in the sanctuary secured by his presence. There is little hope of survival when God himself leads the assault.

Following the announcement that YHWH leads the invading horde, Joel 2:11b–c consists of two clauses that describe this army beginning with כִּי. These clauses operate in parallel, first describing YHWH's host as רַב מְאֹד ("very great") and declaring that the ones obeying his commands are עָצוּם ("mighty"). YHWH thus leads an army against his own people that is both numerically overwhelming and physically capable. Then, 2:11d explicitly announces the day of YHWH and declares גָדוֹל יוֹם־יהוה כִּי ("indeed, great is the day of YHWH"), before describing it as וְנוֹרָא מְאֹד ("very terrifying") in 2:11e.[67] Joel 1:15 and 2:2 both stress the imminence of the day of YHWH, but now the threat it poses here reaches new heights following Joel's images of cosmological upheaval.

YHWH's leadership of the invading army is stunning when considering the development of the relationship between YHWH and his people thus far. Joel 1:6–7 suggests that YHWH's perspective on the unfolding disasters are the same as his people through its threefold use of the first-person singular pronominal suffix (אַרְצִי ["my land"]; גַּפְנִי ["my vine"]; and וּתְאֵנָתִי ["my fig trees"]).[68] Likewise, Joel's call for response in 1:13–14 is to call the priests to lead all the people to lament in the house of "YHWH your God." Joel 1:2–14 thus stresses the reciprocal relationship between YHWH and his people. This changes dramatically in 2:11 as YHWH turns from the locust invasion to leading the invasion against Zion. YHWH's concern for the land and his people is juxtaposed with the looming threat of the day of YHWH.

The point of the revelation of YHWH's presence is to create an overwhelming sense of despair, which is captured in the final rhetorical question וּמִי יְכִילֶנּוּ ("who can withstand it?") in 2:11f.[69] If the

---

65. Locust swarms can seem to darken the sun but by including the rest of the heavenly bodies Joel is clearly giving this situation greater weight than that of locusts alone. The prophet will also return to the darkening of heavenly luminaries in Joel 4:16 [3:16], where there is no surrounding context of locusts. The darkening in 2:10 thus provides the foundation for YHWH to appear in the following verse. See Dillard, "Joel," 276; Simkins, *Yahweh's Activity*, 167.

66. Linville, "Bugs," 296.

67. The combination of the adjectives הַגָּדוֹל וְהַנּוֹרָא ("great and terrifying") has two connotations. This combination does refer to power of YHWH positively, usually calling on him to intervene in situations where a supplicant requires divine assistance (cf. Neh 1:5; 4:8; 9:32; Dan 9:4). However, these adjectives can also indicate a threat, where the audience has reason to fear YHWH. The latter connotation holds true for passages that use these adjectives to describe the day of YHWH (Joel 2:11; Mal 3:23 [4:5]).

68. Sweeney, *Twelve*, 157.

69. The verb in this final rhetorical question is in the prefix conjugation (יְכִילֶנּוּ), emphasizing the imperfective aspect of whether it is possible to withstand the day of YHWH. Leaving the verbal aspect open is appropriate since 2:12–17 addresses that question in detail.

day of YHWH involves YHWH himself leading this invading host, where can the audience turn for deliverance? Wendland rightly calls 2:11 the "emotive psychological nadir of the entire prophecy."[70]

Joel guides his audience through three passages of deepening despair, moving from the ravages of the locusts to the terrifying prospect of the day of YHWH.

Canonical and Practical Significance

Zion and the Day of YHWH

The way in which Joel links the locust invasion to the day of YHWH is at the heart of this passage. Joel 2:1–11 is replete with signs of theophany including the sound of a trumpet, darkness, fire, and the shaking of the heavens and the earth. These elements recall YHWH's first appearance to the nation of Israel at Mount Sinai where they entered into covenant relationship. The signs of the manifestation of YHWH's presence inspired such fear that the people would not approach the mountain (Exod 19:16–19).[71] Further, the response of the natural world to the appearance of YHWH is a recurring theme throughout Scripture (Job 26:10–12; Isa 13:6–13; Nah 1:4–6; Hab 3:8–15).[72] When God intervenes in the affairs of this world, the natural realm responds to his presence.

The use of the day of YHWH in this passage corresponds to its usage throughout the OT. Israel and Judah are the targets of the day of YHWH when they are disobedient (Isa 22:6–11; Jer 46:1–12; Ezek 7:1–9; 13:1–16 Amos 5:18–20; Zeph 1:7–18; 2:2–3; Mal 3:1–4), but they are the beneficiaries of his intervention when the day of YHWH is directed against hostile nations (Isa 13:6–9; 34:1–10; Ezek 30:1–4; Obad 15–17; Zech 12:1–9; 14:1–21). The possibility of YHWH acting either to protect or to judge on the day of YHWH also intersects with the portrayal of Zion, his putative abode. In a study of Zion imagery, Frederik Poulsen distinguishes between what he calls the "classical" and "dynamic" Zion motifs. The "classical" motif provides promises of deliverance for Zion when enemies attack, while the "dynamic" motif envisions a process of judgment and punishment, later leading to restoration after a period of exile.[73] Joel 2:1–11 begins with the foundation of the "classical" motif: the call for alarm on "my holy mountain." This presumes YHWH's presence to defend his people. However, by 2:11, this picture is reversed as the inhabitants of Zion face an army led by YHWH himself.[74] The inversion of what the day of YHWH means

---

70. Wendland, *Prophetic Rhetoric*, 25.
71. David W. Baker, *Joel, Obadiah, Malachi*, NIVAC (Grand Rapids: Zondervan, 2006), 76.
72. Samuel E. Loewenstamm, "The Trembling of Nature During Theophany," in *Comparative Studies in Biblical and Ancient Oriental Literature*, AOAT 24 (Neukirchen-Vluyn: Neukirchener, 1980), 173–89.
73. Frederik Poulsen, *Representing Zion: Judgement and Salvation in the Old Testament* (Abingdon: Routledge, 2015), 7.
74. Ibid., 81–82. Poulsen notes other places where YHWH wields authority over the nations and uses them to enact judgment (Ezek 23:22; 38:16; Hab 1:6; Zeph 3:8; Zech 14:2).

for Zion should prompt the audience to consider the state of its relationship with YHWH. If it hopes to experience the positive aspects of the day of YHWH, it must make sure that it is aligned with what YHWH requires.

The imagery used to describe the day of YHWH in 2:1–11 corresponds especially well with its use in Amos 5:18–20. Amos calls down woe on those who view this day positively, revealing that it is a day of doom. Amos 5:20 calls it a day characterized by חֹשֶׁךְ ("darkness") and אֲפֵל ("gloom"), which are terms used in Joel 2:2. Like Joel, Amos confounds the expectations of his audience when it comes to the day of YHWH. He takes what they appear to view as a hopeful day when God would intervene on their behalf and instead announces that God is coming in judgment rather than deliverance. Joel employs a similar strategy, beginning with a call for the trumpet to sound on God's holy mountain before stunning his audience with the revelation that God leads the attack. Joel and Amos also stress the inescapable nature of the day of YHWH. Amos compares this day to a man fleeing from a lion and a bear before succumbing to the bite of a serpent that had invaded his house. This calls to mind the final assault of the invader in 2:7–9 that penetrates city walls and homes, revealing that there is no respite from the day of YHWH. Both Joel and Amos stress to their audience that even though they claim to be the people of YHWH, they are still potential recipients of his judgment.

Joel's announcement of the day of YHWH in 2:1–11 draws from other vocabulary common to the theme.[75] This includes the declaration that the day is קָרוֹב ("near"). When other nations face the coming of the day of YHWH, its proximity conveys hope for Judah as God promises to intervene on their behalf (Isa 13:6; Obad 15). When the prophets proclaim that Judah is the target of the day of YHWH, it is a warning for the audience to avoid that fate. Zephaniah provides a useful example as the prophet twice proclaims the nearness of the day of YHWH in the first chapter (Zeph 1:7, 14). This leads to the prophet's call for response in Zeph 2:1–3, where he urges the audience to gather and seek YHWH. Joel adopts a similar strategy in 2:12–17.

Joel also shares day of YHWH vocabulary with Malachi. The adjectives גָּדוֹל ("great") and נוֹרָא ("terrible") are echoed in Mal 3:23[4:5] in the context of the promise of Elijah's return. In both cases, these adjectives describe a day targeting Judah, which the prophets use rhetorically to motivate a return to YHWH. Elijah's ministry is one of restoration and repentance as Judah awaits the looming threat of God's judgment.[76] When the prophets reveal that the day of YHWH is "great and terrible," they warn their audiences to respond appropriately to avoid it, either by obeying Elijah in Malachi or by following the program that Joel presents in 2:12–17. Adding to the urgency of response is the rhetorical question "who can endure it?" found in

---

75. See Nogalski, *Book of the Twelve*, 230.   76. Baker, *Joel*, 301.

Joel 2:11f and Mal 3:2. The implied answer to that question is "no one." The inability of the audience to endure the day of YHWH confirms God's supremacy and suggests that it must rely upon God's mercy to survive.

The ways in which the prophets employ the day of YHWH should provide a caution to those who place false confidence in their knowledge of God and his will. Joel's audience begins this passage hearing God call for the sounding of a trumpet on "my holy mountain," but then has come to grips with the stunning revelation that the God who promises security in Zion now leads an army against it. Jeremiah 7:1–11 similarly removes the audience's sense of security in Zion, declaring that God will act against it even when they proclaim that it houses the temple of YHWH. The God who shakes the heavens and the earth while dimming the heavenly bodies is not bound by our expectations and desires. He cannot be used as a tool to support personal preferences or our perspective on a pet issue. God's manifest sovereignty over all creation should inspire us to greater humility and caution in our use of his name.

Paradise Lost

Another key theme developed in this passage is the transformation from paradise to chaos. The landscape that he compared to the garden of Eden becomes a desolate wasteland on account of the invader's attack. Joel may be engaging in hyperbole, making an intertextual allusion to Eden's fertility in order to stress the effects of the invasion upon the land. His use of this image does not focus upon the element of human sinfulness but stresses the ruin of what was once a good and fruitful land.[77] This reverses the prophetic use of Eden imagery in both Isa 51:3 and Ezek 36:35. Isaiah 51:1–3 encourages those who seek YHWH to recall his faithfulness to Abraham and Sarah. God's presence among his people will manifest as he turns Zion's desolate places into Eden, leading to celebration and rejoicing. Ezekiel 36:35 proclaims that desolate land will become like the garden of Eden and ruined cities will be inhabited and protected.[78] Both Isaiah and Ezekiel turn to Edenic imagery to express hope in the aftermath of judgment. The promise of a renewed relationship with YHWH evokes the hope of a new beginning expressed with images of paradise regained. However, Joel reverses the idea of Eden and uses it to express what is lost when God moves against Zion. Whereas the promise of Eden regained represents great hope rooted in God's presence among his people, the warning of Eden lost fits the context of utter despair that this passage describes as YHWH moves against his people.[79]

---

77. The potential presence of human sinfulness will play a significant role in the discussion of 2:12–17.

78. Nogalski, *Book of the Twelve*, 232. Nogalski sees a potential direct allusion between Joel 2:3 and Ezek 36:35.

79. See Assis, *Book of Joel*, 131 who links Eden imagery and divine presence, suggesting that the loss of Eden equals the loss of divine presence. In 2:1–11 the situation is even worse than divine absence alone would suggest since it identifies YHWH as present among those who attack Zion. Fascinatingly, when Joel offers hope in 4:18–21 [3:18–21], a key sign is abundant, Edenic fertility rooted in YHWH's presence in Zion

Joel 2:12–17

E. Hinge: The Call to Return to YHWH

Main Idea of the Passage

In response to the imminent day of YHWH, Joel implores the Judahite audience to turn and cry out to God for rescue. He then supplies them with the words to address YHWH.

Literary Context

Joel 2:12–17 is the hinge that moves this prophecy from despair to deliverance. Joel 1:2–2:11 consists of three episodes of escalating crisis that begin with a locust invasion and drought, culminating with the terrifying appearance of an invading horde led by YHWH. Joel 2:12–17 builds upon earlier exhortations for the audience to assemble and cry out, notably those found in 1:5–14. While both passages summon the community to cry out to YHWH on the temple grounds, 2:12–17 reveals to the audience exactly what they ought to say to YHWH. All of the crises that Joel has described may be remedied if the audience hears and obeys the prophet's commands.

Joel's portrayal of YHWH in previous passages shapes the literary context of 2:12–17. YHWH's motivations remain opaque through 1:2–14 and 1:15–20, since Joel simply calls the audience to beseech him to intercede through their cries and fasting (1:13–14). YHWH's role in the crisis then becomes starkly clear with the revelation that YHWH thunders at the head of the invader in 2:10–11. The imminent day of YHWH appears to negate the prophet's commands for the audience to cry out. If YHWH leads the attack against Zion, what hope can there be for the audience? What is the point of crying out to YHWH if YHWH is the source of the threat? However, Joel does not counsel despair. Instead, he uses the terrifying imagery of the day of YHWH as a springboard to launch into a deeper discussion of YHWH's character in 2:12–17, where he urges the audience to appeal to YHWH one more time.

Also essential to the literary context of this passage is the fact that this is the final passage in which Joel commands his audience to act in hope of reversing the crisis.[1] Joel here offers a detailed plan of what the audience should say, rooted in his presentation of YHWH's character. Joel 1:2–2:11 makes it abundantly clear that the people cannot survive the crises of locusts, drought, and invasion through their own efforts. In 2:12–17, the prophet urges the audience to adopt the only possible response, which is to gather and cry out to YHWH. After this, 2:18–4:21[3:21] confirms Joel's judgment of YHWH's character by providing the details of YHWH's response to the appeals of the audience. The hope expressed in 2:18–4:21[3:21] indicates that the audience should follow Joel's urging in 2:12–17.

> A. Superscription (1:1)
> B. Despair on Account of the Locusts (1:2–14)
> C. Despair in the Day of YHWH—The Drought (1:15–20)
> D. Despair in the Day of YHWH—The Invasion (2:1–11)
> → **E. Hinge: The Call to Return to YHWH (2:12–17)**
>   **1. The Call to Return (2:12–14)**
>   **2. The Plan of Return (2:15–17)**
> F. Divine Deliverance from the Locusts and Drought (2:18–27)
> G. Deliverance through the Spirit of YHWH (3:1–5 [2:28–32])
> H. Deliverance through Divine Judgment on the Day of YHWH (4:1–21 [3:1–21])

Translation and Outline

(See page 96.)

Structure and Literary Form

Joel 2:12–17 consists of two interrelated appeals from the prophet to his audience.[2] The first appeal in 2:12–14 provides the general contours and rationale of Joel's proposal, while the second provides step-by-step instructions for putting it

---

[1] Joel issues a series of imperatives directed at the land, its creatures, and the people of Zion in 2:21–23 but these are commands to rejoice in response to YHWH's deliverance.

[2] Most view Joel 2:12–17 as a literary unit. See Finley, *Joel*, 51; Prinsloo, *Theology*, 49–50; Simkins, *Yahweh's Activity*, 172–74; Crenshaw, *Joel*, 132–33; Barton, *Joel*, 75–77; Allen, *Joel*, 76–77. However, there are objectors. Sweeney focuses on the imperatives in 2:15 that occur earlier in 1:14 and 2:1. He suggests that this lexical repetition is a signal to begin a new passage at Joel 2:15 (Sweeney, *Twelve*, 166–67; cf. Assis, *Joel*, 148–49). This approach minimizes the transitional nature of 2:12–14, which has already made the transition from the announcement to the day of YHWH to the prophet's proposed course of action. Dillard further notes the preponderance of cultic terminology found in both 2:12–14 and 2:15–17, suggesting there is good reason to view 2:12–17 as one literary unit. See Dillard, "Joel," 280.

Joel 2:12–17

E. Hinge: The Call to Return to YHWH (2:12–17)

1. The Call to Return

a. YHWH's Call (2:12a–13b)

12a	"Yet even now," declares YHWH,	וְגַם־עַתָּה נְאֻם־יְהוָה
12b	"Return to me with all your heart, with fasting, weeping, and mourning."	שֻׁבוּ עָדַי בְּכָל־לְבַבְכֶם וּבְצוֹם וּבִבְכִי וּבְמִסְפֵּד׃
13a	Rend your hearts and not your garments.	וְקִרְעוּ לְבַבְכֶם וְאַל־בִּגְדֵיכֶם
13b	Return to YHWH your God,	וְשׁוּבוּ אֶל־יְהוָה אֱלֹהֵיכֶם

b. YHWH's Character (2:13c–d)

13c	for gracious and compassionate is he, slow to anger and great in steadfast love,	כִּי־חַנּוּן וְרַחוּם הוּא אֶרֶךְ אַפַּיִם וְרַב־חֶסֶד
13d	and he relents from punishing."	וְנִחָם עַל־הָרָעָה׃

c. The Hope of Return (2:14)

14a	Who knows?	מִי יוֹדֵעַ
14b	He may turn	יָשׁוּב
14c	and relent.	וְנִחָם
14d	and leave after him a blessing	וְהִשְׁאִיר אַחֲרָיו בְּרָכָה
14e	a grain-offering and a drink-offering for YHWH your God.	מִנְחָה וָנֶסֶךְ לַיהוָה אֱלֹהֵיכֶם׃

2. The Plan of Return

a. The Summons to Gather (2:15–16)

15a	Blow a trumpet in Zion!	תִּקְעוּ שׁוֹפָר בְּצִיּוֹן
15b	Sanctify a fast!	קַדְּשׁוּ־צוֹם
15c	Call a sacred assembly!	קִרְאוּ עֲצָרָה׃
16a	Gather the people!	אִסְפוּ־עָם
16b	Sanctify the congregation!	קַדְּשׁוּ קָהָל
16c	Collect the elders!	קִבְצוּ זְקֵנִים
16d	Gather the children and the nursing infants!	אִסְפוּ עוֹלָלִים וְיֹנְקֵי שָׁדָיִם
16e	Let the bridegroom come out from his room,	יֵצֵא חָתָן מֵחֶדְרוֹ
16f	the bride from her chamber.	וְכַלָּה מֵחֻפָּתָהּ׃

b. The Leadership of the Priests (2:17a)

17a	Between the porch and the altar, let the priests, the ministers of YHWH, weep.	בֵּין הָאוּלָם וְלַמִּזְבֵּחַ יִבְכּוּ הַכֹּהֲנִים מְשָׁרְתֵי יְהוָה

c. The Appeal to YHWH (2:17b–f)

17b	Let them say,	וְיֹאמְרוּ
17c	"Have compassion, O YHWH, upon your people!	חוּסָה יְהוָה עַל־עַמֶּךָ
17d	Do not give your inheritance into reproach, as a byword among the nations.	וְאַל־תִּתֵּן נַחֲלָתְךָ לְחֶרְפָּה לִמְשָׁל־בָּם גּוֹיִם
17e	Why should they say among the peoples	לָמָּה יֹאמְרוּ בָעַמִּים
17f	'Where is their God?'"	אַיֵּה אֱלֹהֵיהֶם׃

into practice. Joel 2:12–14 uses three imperatives in order to urge the Judahite community to return to YHWH before the day of YHWH dawns. This appeal begins in 2:12a with a unique introductory phrase וְגַם־עַתָּה ("yet even now"), where the initial disjunctive *waw* marks a transition from the preceding passage.[3] In other words, this phrase does not reflect a logical continuation from 2:11. Instead, in this instance the use of גַם focuses attention on the temporal adverb עַתָּה, suggesting that this is a decisive moment.[4] The imminence of the day of YHWH leads to the urgency of Joel's call to respond.

A shift to divine speech, marked by the formula נְאֻם־יְהוָה ("declares YHWH") also indicates the beginning of this passage. In 2:10–11, the voice of the prophet reveals that YHWH leads the assault. Beginning in 2:12, YHWH himself speaks and offers the possibility of hope. This passage also introduces a shift in communicative strategy as the text moves away from descriptions of the invader in 2:1–11 to directives addressed to the audience. This creates a counterpoint to 2:1–11, which emphasizes YHWH's leadership of the invading army and stressed the inadequacy of any human response. Now that YHWH opens the door for the community to respond with his request for them to "return to me," Joel articulates how this return can be accomplished.

The second appeal is found in 2:15–17 and it expands upon Joel's initial call to return to YHWH in 2:12–14. Joel provides the details of exactly how the audience can turn back to YHWH, even as the threat of the day of YHWH looms. Joel grounds the audience's response in cultic practice and priestly leadership, by urging the people to gather in the temple courtyard where the priests are to lead them in crying out to YHWH, using the words that Joel provides.[5] Essentially, the prophet assumes that the audience heeded the call to return in 2:12–14. He now provides the specifics of what they should say to demonstrate their return.

Joel 2:12–17 also uses the same signal for closure as 2:1–11, ending with a poignant rhetorical question. The speech that Joel provides for his audience concludes by envisioning foreign nations looking upon the fate of YHWH's people and questioning whether YHWH is present. In this scenario, the nations derisively ask אַיֵּה אֱלֹהֵיהֶם ("where is their God?"), implying that YHWH either no longer cares for his people or is unable to rescue them. This rhetorical question creates significant tension and it sounds an ominous note for the future of God's people who are left hanging in the balance.

---

3. Prinsloo, *Theology*, 49. See the discussion in *IBHS* §39.2.3, on the function of the disjunctive *waw* when attached to a non-verbal constituent.

4. van der Merwe and Wendland, "Word Order," 126.

5. Ibid. Van der Merwe and Wendland indicate that "no less than seven imperatives are stacked in asyndetic sequence."

Explanation of the Text

As mentioned above, Joel dramatically shifts his rhetorical strategy in 2:12–17. Whereas Joel 2:1–11 focuses upon describing the imminent day of YHWH with all of its accompanying disasters, this passage moves the audience beyond despair by issuing imperatives that suggest that there is the potential for deliverance (2:12, 13, 15, 16, 17). In 2:12–13, the voices of YHWH and the prophet join together as the first command directs the audience to שֻׁבוּ עָדַי ("return to me"), before next directing them וְשׁוּבוּ אֶל־יְהוָה אֱלֹהֵיכֶם ("and return to YHWH your God"). Since the entire prophecy is defined as the "word of YHWH" in 1:1, it is not surprising that the voices of God and his chosen messenger merge throughout the text. Their shared voices are especially appropriate here since Joel is urging his audience to act to restore their relationship with YHWH.

Joel 2:12–14: A Call to Repentance?

Joel 2:12–14 begins with a general appeal to return to YHWH. It resembles the form of a prophetic call to repentance, which consists of an appeal for the audience to repent, followed by statements that should motivate repentance (cf. Isa 1:19–20; Jer 3:12–13; 4:1–2; 22:3–5; 25:5–6; Ezek 14:6–11). The prophet typically calls the people back to YHWH after they acknowledge their guilt so that they can avoid the threatened punishment.[6]

However, Joel's apparent use of this form conflicts with what the prophet has communicated to his audience in previous passages. Notably, 1:2–2:11 does not explicitly identify a particular sin from which the audience must repent. The locusts destroy the land and threaten Zion as the day of YHWH looms, but Joel has yet to charge the audience with any specific wrongdoing. This raises the question of what it means to "return to me."

Speculation regarding the nature of the audience's sin is rampant. Suggestions range from a lack of regard for the prophetic word, a critique of the Jerusalem cult, and the possibility of syncretistic or idolatrous worship.[7] Some also refer to the location of *Joel* in the Book of the Twelve to suggest that this passage is referring to repentance. Nogalski argues that its position next to Hosea means that readers should transfer the sentiments expressed in Hosea's final call to repentance into *Joel*, arguing that "Joel deliberately picks up where Hos 14:2ff leaves off."[8] Yates takes a similar approach, suggesting that there is a repeated pattern of repentance and relapse throughout the Book of the Twelve. *Joel* follows Hosea's failed calls to return to YHWH with an episode of repentance in 2:12–14, which then turns into sinful relapse in the following books (Amos, Micah, Habakkuk, Zephaniah).[9] Another suggestion is that by using the language of repentance while remaining silent on the nature of the sin, Joel makes his audience engage in self-reflection as they

---

6. Raitt further nuances this category, suggesting that the prophet's appeal for repentance may include other features such as a divine messenger formula, a vocative address and admonitions. The admonitions are essential, while the other two elements are optional. The prophet usually uses accusations of guilt as motivating features, with Joel 2:12–13 and Isa 55:6–7 being possible exceptions (Thomas Raitt, "Prophetic Summons to Repentance," *ZAW* 83 [1971]: 30–49).

7. See Wolff, *Joel and Amos*, 40–42; Paul Redditt, "The Book of Joel and Peripheral Prophecy," *CBQ* 48 (1985): 225–40; and Ahlström, *Joel*, 26. Wendland views Joel 2 as bringing judgment on "apostate Israel," without specifically defining their apostasy. Wendland, *Prophetic Rhetoric*, 23.

8. Nogalski, *Redactional*, 19.

9. Gary E. Yates, "The Problem of Repentance and Relapse as a Unifying Theme in the Book of the Twelve," *Themelios* 41 (2016): 248–62. The cycle then repeats twice more with repentance in Jonah and relapse in Nahum, followed by repentance in Haggai and Zechariah and relapse in Malachi.

consider what may be prompting this situation (cf. Lam 3:40).[10] The variety of suggestions reveals how challenging it is to identify what is meant by the call to return to YHWH.

The question of Judah's apparent sin bears further reflection since it is integral to the argument of this passage. Joel reinforces the appeal to return to YHWH by describing his gracious and compassionate character in 2:13. However, this characterization is awkward if the day of YHWH threatens a people who have not sinned. One commentator takes the lack of explicit sin at face value and declares that 2:12–14 does not give us, "sinners in the hands of an angry God; rather they are people in the hands of a megalomaniacal God."[11] This perspective disagrees with Joel's own description of YHWH's character, but the idea of judgment without explicit guilt is difficult. Given the willingness of the prophets to indict Israel and Judah for their failings, the lack of a named sin here is surprising.

In the absence of an evident sin, other proposals abound. Assis suggests that Joel has in mind a covenant renewal. In this case, "return to me" indicates a return to worshiping YHWH after the disruption caused by the Babylonian conquest. The people's sin may have led to exile, but Joel urges the people to cry out to YHWH to demonstrate that the bond between them remains unsevered.[12] In a similar vein, others view 2:12–14 through the prism of lament rather than repentance. In this case, 2:12–14 continues the string of lament cries found throughout Joel 1 (1:5, 8, 11, 13, 14, 18 and potentially 2:15–17).[13] The lament cries in Joel 1 urge the audience to cry out and the prophet's call for "fasting, weeping, and mourning" in 2:13 combine to call upon YHWH to act to restore his people from their desperate straits. The anguish of their appeal is deepened by the ambiguity of whether there is underlying sin.[14] Joel 2:12–14 lacks protestations of innocence that would strengthen this possibility (Pss 7:3–5; 59:3–4), but it does express that YHWH must act to alleviate the situation. Crenshaw notes, "[I]n times of trouble, whether deserved or undeserved, turning to YHWH was the appropriate response inasmuch as he alone could remove the adversity."[15]

Simkins goes further afield and interprets Joel 2:12–14 against the backdrop of a sociological honor/shame model. Shame arises when a particular group is unable to fulfill the expected ideals or functions of the society.[16] In essence, Simkins argues that Joel's audience experiences shame in its failures to properly fulfill its cultic duties because of the destruction wrought by the locusts. Consequently, their standing among their neighbors diminishes, which adds psychological trauma to the physical deprivation caused by the invasion of the locusts. The inability to sacrifice properly to YHWH leads to a sense of shame that requires crying out to YHWH and hoping for restoration.[17]

Interestingly, this model envisions Judah's shame in the eyes of other nations as a tool to motivate YHWH to act. This may resemble 2 Kings 18–19 when Sennacherib taunts Hezekiah, equating

---

10. Allen, *Joel*, 79.
11. H. Shapiro, "Joel," in *Congregation: Contemporary Writers Read the Jewish Bible*, ed. D. Rosenberg (San Diego: Harcourt Brace Jovanovich, 1987), 201.
12. Assis, *Joel*, 140–41.
13. Graham S. Ogden, "Joel 4 and Prophetic Responses to National Laments," *JSOT* 26 (1983): 97.
14. Ibid., 105.
15. James L. Crenshaw, "Who Knows What YHWH Will Do? The Character of God in the Book of Joel," in *Fortunate the Eyes that See: Essays in Honor of David Noel Freedman in Celebration of His Seventieth Birthday*, ed. Astrid Beck et al. (Grand Rapids: Eerdmans, 1995), 188. "
16. Lyn M. Bechtel, "The Perception of Shame within the Divine-Human Relationship in Biblical Israel," in *Uncovering Ancient Stones: Essays in Memory of H. Neil Richardson*, ed. Lewis M. Hopfe (Winona Lake, IN: Eisenbrauns, 1994), 80.
17. Simkins, "Return to Yahweh," 51–52.

YHWH with the impotent gods of other nations whom the Assyrians conquered (2 Kgs 18:35).[18] If the Judahite community falls, then YHWH is vulnerable to shame since he failed to protect what he claimed. YHWH, however, responds to this taunt by making his supremacy evident over the Assyrian king and rescuing Judah (2 Kgs 19:28). This example contains no explicit mention of Judah or Hezekiah's sin but rather focuses on YHWH's response to the arrogance and pride of the Assyrian ruler.

Further, this book does explicitly use shame language elsewhere. Joel 1:11 uses the imperative הֹבִישׁוּ ("be ashamed") to call the farmers to experience the ignominy of the agricultural failure, since this reveals YHWH's absence. This reference and the threefold occurrence of the similar root יָבֵשׁ ("to be dried up") in 1:12 links the shame of the people to the withering of joy.[19] Looking ahead to the next passage (2:18–27), 2:19 promises that YHWH will not allow his people to be an object of scorn among foreign nations. This same word occurs in 2:17 in the context of the people's plea to YHWH. Additionally, 2:26 and 27 both end with YHWH's assertion וְלֹא־יֵבֹשׁוּ עַמִּי לְעוֹלָם ("my people will not be ashamed again"). Joel 2:18–27 reveals that of the most notable results of YHWH's intervention is to remove the audience's shame, which came about as a result of the breakdown of the sacrificial system in 1:5–14. YHWH's intervention in 2:18–27 may reveal that Joel's call to "return to YHWH" is partly motivated by the opportunity to remove the audience's shame over its cultic failures.

This proposal has not received widespread support since the expected vocabulary of shame does not govern 2:12–17, although the use of חֶרְפָּה ("reproach") in v. 17 may provide some justification.[20] Further it relies upon assumptions about the nature of ancient Judahite society that may not be sustainable.[21] Studies that discuss honor and shame tend to look at relationships within a given society and do not necessarily translate into the broader context of international relations.[22] Similarly, it is unclear whether "honor" is appropriate to describe what the Judahite community experiences when it sacrifices properly and "shame" to describe sacrificial failures.[23] The cessation of sacrifice represents a grave disruption of the relationship between YHWH and his people, but it is not evident that the terminology of honor and shame accurately capture what is unfolding.

In summary, the honor/shame discussion is understandable given the lack of explicit reference to a sin that requires repentance, but it is not conclusive. A stronger case for suggesting the presence of sin may come from Joel's use of covenantal terminology in this passage. Deuteronomy 28:38–44 declares that disobedience will mean that Israel will not receive the fruit of the land, which includes destruction by locusts (cf. Deut 32:22–27). Clendenen argues that the Minor Prophets build from this covenantal foundation using a fourfold

---

18. Bechtel, "Perception of Shame," 87–89. See the discussion of YHWH's vulnerability to shame as the counterpart of the requirement to offer praise and honor to YHWH. A similar rationale is at work in Num 14:13–16 when Moses pleads with YHWH not to destroy Israel for failing to enter Canaan. He argues that the Egyptians would view it as a sign of YHWH's inability to do what he pledged.

19. See the discussion of the rhetorical strategy of Joel 1:11–12.

20. This terminology includes verbal roots such as בּוֹשׁ (to be ashamed), כָּלַם ("to be humiliated"), חָפֵר ("to be abashed"), קָלָה ("to be dishonored"), and חָרַף ("to reproach"). Lyn M. Bechtel (Huber), *The Biblical Experience of Shame/Shaming: The Social Experience of Shame/Shaming in Biblical Israel in Relation to its Use as Religious Metaphor* (PhD diss., Drew University, 1983), 53. None of these terms occur in Joel 2:12–14.

21. John K. Chance, "The Anthropology of Honour and Shame: Culture, Values and Practice," *Semeia* 68 (1996): 144. Chance questions if it is possible to apply an honor/shame model to relationships between different nations.

22. Stiebert, *Construction*, 79.

23. Ibid., 79.

scheme including: (1) indictment; (2) instruction; (3) judgment; and (4) incentive/salvation.²⁴ Joel lacks the element of indictment but contains the other three. Clendenen suggests that Joel relies upon his audience's knowledge of the covenantal cues surrounding repentance and suggests that they could be expected to infer their own guilt based on the circumstances surrounding them.²⁵

Solomon's dedicatory prayer for the temple in 1 Kgs 8:37–48 also resonates with the language found in this passage. In 1 Kgs 8:37–39, Solomon lists calamities including famine, pestilence, blight, mildew, locusts, or enemy invasions as reasons for the people of YHWH to reflect on whether or not they have sinned against YHWH.²⁶ A few verses later, 1 Kgs 8:48 uses similar language to Joel 2:12 in constructing its response, addressing YHWH and considering a scenario where Israel וְשָׁבוּ אֵלֶיךָ בְּכָל־לְבָבָם ("will return to you with all their heart") in the aftermath of their apparent sinfulness. The hope is that YHWH will remove these calamities in response to the community's repentance. Consequently, it is probable that the mere existence of the crises detailed in Joel 1:2–2:11 should prompt the audience to reflect on its behavior as it seeks to return to YHWH.

Overall, the intertextual resonances suggest that the prophet is drawing from the language of repentance even if he does not identify a specific sin. Seitz suggests that this fits the tenor of Joel 1:2–2:17 where, "it is not that sin or guilt is denied, but that the focus is elsewhere."²⁷ Instead, Joel calls his audience to respond to misfortune by crying out to YHWH with language of pain, suffering, and lamentation, while also drawing in the vocabulary of penitence and prayer in 2:12–13.²⁸ The audience must respond to the imminent day of YHWH by turning to YHWH and trusting in his character. Joel does not reveal the specifics of Judah's guilt, but the solution still lies in crying out to God, imploring him to turn from disaster to rescue in the day of YHWH.

1. The Call to Return (2:12–14)

Joel 2:12–14 seeks to persuade the audience that returning to YHWH is necessary in response to their situation. Joel 2:12a begins with the phrase וְגַם־עַתָּה ("yet even now"), which offers a reprieve from the rhetorical question וּמִי יְכִילֶנּוּ ("and who can endure it?") that summarized the effects of the day of YHWH. Joel 2:11 appears to have pronounced the final verdict, but this introductory phrase suggests that the matter is not yet concluded. The divine pronouncement formula נְאֻם־יְהוָה ("declares YHWH") follows, placing the call to return into the mouth of YHWH. This is significant since 2:11 reveals that YHWH is uttering his voice before his army, apparently sealing its fate. In this verse, the same voice that announces the imminence of the day of YHWH now reveals a means of escape: restoration "is still on divine offer."²⁹ Notably, this is one of only two occurrences of a divine speech formula in Joel (cf. 4:8[3:8]), emphasizing that the call to turn to YHWH comes from YHWH himself.³⁰

YHWH's command in 2:12b begins by calling the people to שֻׁבוּ עָדַי בְּכָל־לְבַבְכֶם ("return to me

---

24. E. Ray Clendenen, "Textlinguistics and Prophecy in the Book of the Twelve," *JETS* 46 (2003): 393–96.
25. Ibid., 395–96.
26. Strazicich, *Joel's Use of Scripture*, 156.
27. Seitz, *Joel*, 139.
28. Carol J. Dempsey, "'Turn Back, O People': Repentance in the Latter Prophets," in *Repentance in Christian Theology*, ed. Mark J. Boda and Gordon T. Smith (Collegeville, MN: Liturgical, 2006), 58–59.
29. Seitz, *Joel*, 162.
30. Crenshaw also contrasts the rarity of divine speech formulae in Joel with prophets like Haggai and Zechariah. See Crenshaw, "Who Knows," 187–88.

with all your heart"). It begins an imperative form of the root שׁוּב ("to turn/return"), which is an essential keyword for Joel's strategy in this passage.[31] This root occurs two more times in 2:12–14, first in another command for the audience to return to YHWH (2:13b), followed by a suggestion that YHWH may turn back to the audience in response (2:14b). Joel calls for a metaphorical turning, urging the Judahite audience to reorient itself by calling out to YHWH and hoping that YHWH will reciprocate. The interplay of these uses of שׁוּב offers the possibility of reversing the adversarial relationship between YHWH and his people.

Following the command to return in repentance, Joel offers a trio of activities that suggest how the people should demonstrate their sincerity. They are to return to YHWH through the actions of וּבְצוֹם וּבִבְכִי וּבְמִסְפֵּד ("with fasting, weeping, and mourning"). These words are found frequently in situations where God's people appeal to him and hope that he will reverse their circumstances.[32] In some cases, these activities are a direct response to the people's sin, whereas in others the situation is more ambiguous.[33] Interestingly, the only other occurrence of these three terms together is Esth 4:3, where the exiled Jewish community fasts, weeps, and mourns in response to Haman's plot. This parallel is intriguing since it occurs in a context of lamentation without a description of a specific prior sin, although the Judahites are in this precarious situation as a result of their previous sinfulness. In any event, the resonance of covenant language in *Joel* still suggests the presence of unspecified guilt. The essence of the command to fast, weep, and mourn is for the Judahite audience to demonstrate their dependence on YHWH and their trust in his ability to deliver, looking for hope beyond the announcement of YHWH as destroyer in Joel 2:11.

Joel's commands to the people continue in 2:13a where the prophet implores them וְקִרְעוּ לְבַבְכֶם וְאַל־בִּגְדֵיכֶם ("Rend your hearts and not your garments"). This resonates with a larger prophetic tradition that calls for genuine turning as opposed to rote genuflection to correct rituals and formulae. Amos in particular castigates the religious observances that the community does not offer in the proper spirit (Amos 4:4–5; 5:21–23; cf. Isa 58:1–12; Jer 7:1–8; Hos 6:6; Mic 6:1–8). Joel differs from these examples since his view of the priests and the norms of religious expression is much more positive. Joel is not taking aim at the religious practices of his audience since his proposed response requires the priests to lead the people in appealing to YHWH

---

31. The semantic range of the verb שׁוּב extends from simple physical turning. For a full study of its meaning, see William L. Holladay, *The Root ŠÛBH in the Old Testament* (Leiden: Brill, 1958). LeCureux identifies שׁוּב as the unifying theme of the larger Book of the Twelve, noting that it occurs eighty-nine times within this corpus. I am not persuaded that it is correct to elevate this theme above all of the richness and complexity of this corpus, but the prominence of שׁוּב throughout prophetic literature is worth noting. See Jason T. LeCureux, *The Thematic Unity of the Book of the Twelve* (Sheffield: Sheffield Phoenix, 2012), 22.

32. Wolff, *Joel and Amos*, 49.

33. A consideration of the semantic range of the three terms does not resolve the question of whether repentance is in view in Joel 2:12. The noun צוֹם ("fasting") occurs twenty-six times in the Old Testament. Certain fasts are in response to sin or guilt (2 Sam 12:16; Neh 9:1; Jer 36:6, 9; Jonah 3:5; Dan 9:3), while others reflect an appeal to YHWH for protection from enemies (2 Chr 20:3; Ezra 8:21) or as a response to mockery (Pss 35:13; 69:11; 109:24). Isaiah 58:1–12 calls for repentance to replace fasting, suggesting that the community's heart does not match its actions. Similarly בְּכִי ("weeping") is used in both contexts of repentance (Isa 22:12; Jer 3:21; Mal 2:13) and sorrow over unfortunate circumstances (Gen 45:2; Deut 34:8; 2 Sam 13:36; 2 Kgs 20:3; Ezra 3:13; Jer 31:16). Finally, מִסְפֵּד ("mourning") indicates both repentance (Isa 22:12; Jer 6:26; Zech 12:10) and lamentation in response to tragedy (Gen 50:10; Ps 30:12) or divine judgment (Ezek 27:32; Amos 5:16; Mic 1:8, 11). Consequently, the presence of these terms does not conclusively indicate whether Joel seeks to evoke repentance. We must continue to rely on cues discussed above.

(cf. 1:14; 2:15–17).[34] In this case, the command to "rend your hearts and not your garments" in 2:13a calls for the people's internal states to match the external behaviors Joel requires in 2:12b.

Joel 2:13b restates the command to return to YHWH, again using the imperative form of שׁוּב. Joel allows his own voice to govern this second command by imploring his audience to return "to YHWH your God." The people thus hear YHWH and his prophet united in urging them to turn in repentance in the hope of restoration. This second command adds greater nuance by supplying a reason for turning that is firmly rooted in the character of YHWH. Joel draws from YHWH's proclamation of his character found in Exod 34:6–7. The context is significant since these verses declare the nature of YHWH while Moses receives the second copies of the stone tablets, re-establishing God's relationship with Israel in the aftermath of the golden calf idolatry. Joel repurposes this announcement for his situation.

In Exod 34:6–7, YHWH passes before Moses and declares that he is compassionate and gracious, slow to anger, abounding in unfailing kindness, and one who both forgives iniquity and punishes the unrepentant. This summary of YHWH's character appears in several other OT passages in a variety of literary genres, suggesting that it is integral to Israel's understanding of its divine covenant partner (Num 14:18, Pss 86:15; 103:8; 145:8; Mic 7:18–19; Nah 1:3; Jonah 4:2 and Neh 9:17, 31b).[35] Boda calls it "a moment of divine self-disclosure on a level that transcends any revelation that the ancestors Abraham, Isaac, and Jacob experienced."[36] The use of Exod 34:6–7 in Joel 2:13c–d is not an exact citation since it does not include the declaration that YHWH visits punishment on successive generations. Instead, Joel inserts an additional phrase, declaring that YHWH וְנִחָם עַל־הָרָעָה ("relents from evil"). Joel probably draws this additional phrase from Exod 32:12–14 when YHWH and Moses dialogue concerning the fate of idolatrous Israel. That dialogue contains two occurrences of verbs derived from נחם ("to relent") through which Moses persuades YHWH not to destroy his people. In Exod 32:12, Moses pairs the imperative שׁוּב with the imperative וְהִנָּחֵם in order to implore YHWH to "turn" and "relent" from his anger at Israel's idolatry. Joel also combines שׁוּב and נחם, although the onus is on Israel to "turn" in hopes that YHWH may "relent." Exodus 32:14 reveals the success of Moses' entreaties, declaring through an indicative (וַיִּנָּחֶם) that YHWH has relented and will not destroy Israel.

It is likely that Joel draws together Exod 32 and 34 in order to import that narrative context into his prophecy.[37] When YHWH relents in Exod 32:14, he ceases from bringing about Israel's destruction, but the state of the covenant relationship is in question. Exodus 32:19–25 details how Moses acted first in judgment and then in intercession in order to restore their relationship with YHWH. This culminates with the giving of the second stone tablets and the pronouncement of YHWH's character in Exod 34:1–7. Throughout this narrative, YHWH's justice and mercy are in tension. YHWH remains free to

---

34. Barton, *Joel*, 80. While Joel does not attack priestly ritual, it is interesting to note that Joel's suggestion for how to return to YHWH in 2:15–17 does not invoke the sacrificial system. The internal reorientation of the community is of primary importance. See LeCureux, *Thematic Unity*, 124.

35. Crenshaw, *Joel*, 136–37. For a chart marking the variations in the reuse of Exod 34:6–7, see Gordon R. Clark, *The Word "Hesed" in the Hebrew Bible*, JSOTSup 157 (Sheffield: Sheffield Academic, 1993), 248. Joel's parallels with Jonah's use of Exod 34:6–7 will be discussed further in the "Canonical and Practical Significance" section.

36. Mark J. Boda, *The Heartbeat of Old Testament Theology: Three Creedal Expressions* (Grand Rapids: Baker, 2017), 35.

37. Thomas B. Dozeman, "Inner-Biblical Interpretation of Yahweh's Gracious and Compassionate Character," *JBL* 108 (1989): 221.

act as he deems necessary while Moses' intercession seeks to restore the human side of the equation.[38]

This context helps to shape our reading of Joel 2:12–14 in two ways. First, this parallel again strengthens the idea that Joel is calling for repentance even though he does not specifically identify the people's sin. In Exodus, Israel learns of YHWH's gracious and compassionate character in the wake of its great sin. Now Joel calls on the people to return to YHWH in the hope that YHWH will again restore rather than judge. This provides hope for a "shift in their divine covenant partner based on his gracious character."[39] Secondly, Joel strongly implies that returning to YHWH in repentance will be effective. In Exod 32:30–35, Moses interceded and preserved the community while appealing to YHWH to relent. In Joel 2:12–14 the prophet creates an opportunity for the people themselves to call out to YHWH. Focusing on YHWH's mercy and compassion advances the possibility that YHWH might act restoratively. Joel 2:15–17 depends on this prospect since the prophet offers a detailed program of exactly how the community should appeal to YHWH. YHWH may "relent" from his intention, but 2:12–14 reminds the community that they should demonstrate proper turning to YHWH, even if the text does not provide an explicit indictment.

Joel is careful not to presume too much and guarantee YHWH's response. After his citation of Exod 34:6–7, Joel puts forward a question in 2:14a that emphasizes YHWH's sovereignty. He asks מִי יוֹדֵעַ ("who knows?") what YHWH will do, which leaves open the possibility of reprieve from destruction. The implied answer to this question is negative since humanity cannot claim to know the mind of YHWH (cf. 2 Sam 12:22; Esth 4:14; Ps 90:11; Ecc 2:19; 3:21; 6:12; 8:1; Jonah 3:9).[40] Joel cannot guarantee that the above-mentioned acts of penitence will change YHWH's mind, but asking this question suggests the verdict of 2:11 is not inevitable. Fishbane states, "although YHWH 'relents' he does so for his own reasons. Thus, like oracles, the words and acts of repentance are also not magical: YHWH does not relent *because* of them."[41] This same question is found in Jon 3:9 and 2 Sam 12:22 in contexts where showing penitence before YHWH can hopefully reverse dire circumstances.[42] In these circumstances, the inability to know the mind of YHWH should result in renewed appeals to his mercy since judgment is not guaranteed.

Following this question, Joel supplies his audience with the desired outcome, using clever lexical repetition. He returns to an indicative form of the verb שׁוּב in 2:14b (יָשׁוּב), this time with YHWH as its subject. This creates a word-play in which the commands to "return" to YHWH through fasting, weeping, and mourning establish the possibility that YHWH could "return" to his people. Joel again pairs the verb יָשׁוּב with וְנִחָם in 2:14c. Reusing a form of נחם builds upon Joel's declaration of YHWH's character in 2:13c–d. Joel provides an opportunity for the God who "relents from evil" to "turn and relent" in 2:14b–c.

---

38. Clark, *The Word Hesed*, 247–52.

39. Boda, *Heartbeat*, 51.

40. James L. Crenshaw, "The Expression MÎ YÔDĒA in the Hebrew Bible," *VT* 36 (1986) 274–75. Crenshaw identifies two ways in which this question is used. The first (including Joel 2:14) suggests that the response "will change the situation for human good," while the second "seems to assume a closed door to any redeeming action." Unsurprisingly, four of the five examples that Crenshaw places in this second category come from Ecclesiastes.

41. Michael Fishbane, *Biblical Interpretation in Ancient Israel* (Oxford: Clarendon, 1989), 346–47.

42. Dillard, "Joel," 280–81. In keeping with YHWH's sovereignty, in the case of Jonah 3:9, the ones posing the question and engaging in penitence (Ninevites) did see YHWH change his mind while in 2 Sam 12:22, David's penitence failed to remove the curse on the child born from his adulterous encounter with Bathsheba.

The interplay between Joel's call for the people to "return" and the possibility that YHWH might "return" is essential. Joel creates a hypothetical situation that allows his audience to envision YHWH's "return" to them. Joel 2:14d–e envisions YHWH leaving behind a blessing, which he specifies as the מִנְחָה וָנֶסֶךְ ("grain-offering and drink-offering"). The prophet used the absence of these sacrifices in 1:9 and 13 to highlight the devastating effects of the locust invasion. Joel's suggestion that YHWH could restore them is a synecdoche standing in for a complete turning of YHWH. If the people are able to offer grain and drink offerings, then YHWH has restored the devastated land.

In summary, 2:12–14 establishes the general parameters of the response that the prophet desires from his audience. Joel implores the people to "return" to YHWH and suggests that YHWH might also "return" to them. Their return requires them to demonstrate penitential hearts through fasting, weeping, and mourning. This may result in YHWH's return to them, based on Joel's citation of YHWH's character. The God who relented from destroying his people after they worshiped the golden calf is the God who may relent from judgment even as the day of YHWH looms. Joel does not presume to guarantee YHWH's actions, but the hope that he provides should motivate his audience to "return" to YHWH their God.

2. The Plan of Return (2:15–17)

Joel 2:15–17 reveals exactly how the people are to "turn" to YHWH and how this may persuade him to "return" to them. The prophet begins by linking this call to action with earlier passages by reusing imperatives from 1:2–14 and 2:1–11. Joel 2:15a begins with the command תִּקְעוּ שׁוֹפָר בְּצִיּוֹן ("blow a trumpet in Zion"), which echoes Joel 2:1a. In this instance, Joel uses this command not to warn of an invasion but instead to summon the people. Blowing a trumpet can signal a call to cultic activity, which is what Joel desires here (Lev 25:9; 2 Sam 6:15; 1 Chr 15:28; 2 Chr 15:14; Pss 81:4; 98:6). As the day of YHWH approaches, it is necessary for people to fully commit themselves to their God. Whereas the first trumpet call announced the arrival of the terrifying day of YHWH, this second one offers the hope of surviving it.

The subsequent two imperatives in Joel 2:15b–c reinforce this cultic orientation. Joel reissues directives first found in 1:14a–b, again giving instructions to קַדְּשׁוּ־צוֹם קִרְאוּ עֲצָרָה ("sanctify a fast! Call a sacred assembly!"). The reuse of these imperatives also helps to identify their intended recipients. Joel 2:15b–c does not explicitly identify who should call the fast and gather the people, but the prophet directs these same commands in 1:14a–b to the priests. This is confirmed in 2:17 when Joel addresses the priests and directs them to lead the community in an appeal to YHWH.

The prophet's use of these imperatives has a different tone in 2:15, which can be seen by considering the proximity of the imperatives to statements concerning the grain and drink offerings in 2:14e. The reason that 1:14a–b instructs the priests to fast and call a sacred assembly is that they can no longer make the grain and drink offerings, which threatens the relationship between the people and YHWH. Here, 2:15b–c follows the possibility that YHWH may turn and bless his people, signified by restoring the grain and drink offerings. The call to fast and assemble in 1:14a–b is an attempt to avert disaster, whereas in 2:15b–c it follows a glimmer of hope.

Joel 2:16 continues to pepper the audience with imperatives. Joel issues both general and specific directives, beginning in 2:16a–b with the calls אִסְפוּ־עָם ("gather the people") and קַדְּשׁוּ קָהָל ("sanctify the congregation"). As in 1:5–14, Joel then targets various sub-groups within the congregation. He first directs the elders (2:16c) and the children (2:16d) to gather. The command to gather the young ones in 2:16d actually has two objects of the imperative verb, summoning the עוֹלְלִים וְיֹנְקֵי שָׁדָיִם ("the children and the nursing infants"). The explicit reference to nursing infants strengthens the generational *merismus* where Joel addresses the oldest and the youngest members of the congregation to indicate that everyone should assemble.[43] Joel 2:16e–f approaches the same idea from a different angle. Joel calls even those about to be married to leave their preparations and join the rest of the community in sacred assembly. The seriousness of the situation even requires the couple to depart from their private chambers.[44] This is significant since newly married couples had exemptions from elements of cultic service (Deut 20:7; 24:5). Calling the bride and bridegroom to gather thus again stresses that every member of the community is in view. This total commitment is necessary to fulfill the command to "return to me with all your heart" (2:12b).

Joel 2:17 provides the exact details of what the assembled congregation should do and say. Joel calls for the priests to lead the people in their cry to YHWH. This recalls 1:13 where he directed the priests to don sackcloth and cry out to YHWH from the temple. Joel's concern for priestly leadership reflects an attempt to preserve social cohesion even as the sacrificial system is in disarray. Returning to established rituals provides hope that the relationship between the people and YHWH can be restored.[45] The priests lead the people with the hope that YHWH will respond to their continued faithfulness and worship.

Joel 2:17a begins with very detailed directions to the priests as they lead this sacred assembly. The prophet instructs them to weep in the space בֵּין הָאוּלָם וְלַמִּזְבֵּחַ ("between the porch and the altar"). This space served as an entrance hall into the most sacred areas of the temple.[46] As such, it was a fitting location for prayer and petition.[47] Joel places this location prior to the command for the priests to weep, putting it at the foreground of its clause. He indicates that the proper response to the day of YHWH is for the people to assemble where their relationship with their God finds its fullest expression. Under the guidance of the priestly leaders, they must cry out to YHWH.

In Joel 2:17b–f, the prophet provides the exact words for the appeal to YHWH. He begins with an introductory volitional expression וְיֹאמְרוּ ("let them say") that places what follows in the mouths of the priests. Joel's proposal consists of two short petitions (2:17c–d) and a plaintive question (2:17e–f).[48] These attempt to realize the hope expressed in 2:12–14 by reflecting the community's "return" to YHWH and imploring him to "return" to them. The first petition in 2:17c beseeches YHWH חוּסָה יהוה עַל־עַמֶּךָ ("have compassion, o YHWH, upon your people!"). The second-person pronominal suffix on עַמֶּךָ ("your people") is a reminder that the people whom he has claimed are suffering (1 Sam 10:1; 1 Kgs 8:53; 2 Kgs 21:14; Isa 19:25; Micah 7:18; Pss 33:12; 68:10; 106:5). The second petition in 2:17d uses the parallel term נַחֲלָתְךָ ("your inheritance"), which is found in contexts both referring to the land and its people. This is appropriate in Joel since both a ravaged landscape and its inhabitants

---

43. Unlike Joel 1:2 and 14, the "elders" are not paired with the "inhabitants of the land," which creates a *merismus* encompassing the leaders and the rest of the people. Instead, pairing "elders" with "children" creates a generational focus. See Assis, *Book of Joel*, 150.

44. The two nouns used in 2:16e–f are חֶדֶר and חֻפָּה. Both indicate a private place where the marriage could be consummated (for חֶדֶר, see Song 1:4; Judg 15:1; 2 Sam 13:10; for חֻפָּה see Ps 19:6).

45. Linville, "The Day of Yahweh," 106.

46. Assis, *Book of Joel*, 152.

47. See Ezek 8:16–18 where priests offer idolatrous prayers in this space, leading YHWH to reject them.

48. Allen, *Joel*, 83.

require restoration from YHWH.[49] By paralleling עַמֶּךָ ("your people") and נַחֲלָתְךָ ("your inheritance"), Joel urges the people to stress the intimate relationship between YHWH, the community, and the land promised to their forefathers.

The second petition (2:17d) also moves from a positive imperative to a negated imperative that commences with the injunction וְאַל־תִּתֵּן נַחֲלָתְךָ לְחֶרְפָּה ("do not give your inheritance into reproach"). The term חֶרְפָּה ("reproach") is found in contexts of disgrace for an individual or a group. In its collective sense it often refers to the disgrace brought about by the apparent triumph of an enemy (1 Sam 11:2; Isa 54:4; Jer 23:40; Lam 3:61; Zeph 2:8).[50] In this context, no enemy has explicitly defeated God's people but the nations observing their sorry state can be seen as similar. The nations are in a position of superiority, able to look down and mock the people of YHWH. Joel now requests that YHWH act so that his people will be spared this fate.

Following the word חֶרְפָּה ("reproach"), the rest of the petition (לִמְשָׁל־בָּם גּוֹיִם) is challenging to untangle. The difficulty centers upon the infinitive construct לִמְשָׁל. It can be either a synonym for reproach or indicate dominion over another. The syntax is awkward with either reading. Those who defend the "rule over" interpretation point to the fact that מָשַׁל meaning "to rule over" can have its object introduced by the preposition בְּ.[51] This reading also has the support of ancient versions including the LXX.[52] Those who view it as a synonym for "reproach" point to the lack of nations mentioned who would rule over God's people in the aftermath of the day of YHWH and suggest that its proximity to "reproach" suggests that the synonymous reading ("byword" in my translation) is better.[53] This possibility also fits better with the rhetorical question that concludes Joel 2:17f and is the more likely option, though as Troxel suggests, the text may be intentionally playing with the ambiguity, "preserving the association of disgrace with domination."[54]

After the infinitive construct לִמְשָׁל, Joel 2:17d then reveals who would see God's people as a "reproach" if God does not intervene. The prophet first reveals that this will happen בָּם ("among them") before identifying them as גּוֹיִם ("nations"). Outside observation worsens the situation since it turns Judah into a public spectacle. By extension, this image also challenges YHWH since YHWH is the one who has brought this fate upon his people. The double reference to the reproach and shame of God's people in 2:17d places pressure on YHWH to "return" and rectify the situation. Joel carefully constructs the plea so that YHWH's character, alluded to in such glowing terms in the citation of Exod 34:6–7, is in question if he does not respond.

Similar to 2:1–11, this passage also ends with a climactic rhetorical question. Joel 2:17e–f constructs a hypothetical situation in which the surrounding nations look upon the shame of Judah and mock them and their deity. The final question is directed at YHWH, asking why these nations should be able to ask among themselves אַיֵּה אֱלֹהֵיהֶם ("where is their God?"). The implied answer to this question is that YHWH is absent or powerless.[55] This question also resonates with the Sinai tradition and Moses' pleas to preserve Israel in spite of

---

49. Assis, *Book of Joel*, 153–54.
50. Ibid., 154.
51. Garret, *Hosea, Joel*, 349.
52. The LXX reads "of being ruled over by nations" (τοῦ κατάρξαι αὐτῶν ἔθνη).
53. Barton, *Joel*, 82–83.
54. Troxel, *Joel*, 81.
55. Assis, *Book of Joel*, 154–55. Assis notes a strong parallel between Joel 2:17 and Ps 79 which is likely set against the backdrop of the Babylonian conquest of Jerusalem. In this case, YHWH's apparent absence does not lead to mockery, but rather to exile and destruction.

its apostasy (Exod 32:12; Deut 9:26–28).⁵⁶ Moses suggests that the nations will view Israel's destruction as evidence of YHWH's weakness. If YHWH's people are destroyed, then "their God" clearly is limited.

Essentially, Joel's appeal uses the unidentified nations as proxies to ask challenging questions. Those who gather in Zion do not ask whether YHWH has abandoned them, but suggest that this is the nations' perspective. This protects them from potential accusations that they lack faith. Through this rhetorical sleight-of-hand, Joel suggests that YHWH's reputation among the nations is in the balance.⁵⁷ If he restores his people, he demonstrates the truth of his gracious and compassionate character. The rest of Joel's prophecy provides the answer to this rhetorical question.

Summary

Joel 2:12–17 begins with YHWH's command to the people שֻׁבוּ עָדַי ("return to me!"). Joel guides toward this goal by calling them to assemble and cry out. He also creatively employs the verb שׁוּב to indicate that if the people demonstrate their desire to "return," the onus shifts to YHWH to "return" to his people and confirm the graciousness and compassion of his character. This passage begins to move the audience from despair to the hope of deliverance, but it hinges upon both the audience's obedience and YHWH's compassion to succeed.

Canonical and Practical Significance

The Character of God

The description of YHWH's character that the prophet cites from Exod 34:6–7 is at the heart of Joel 2:12–17. Joel's response to the imminent day of YHWH is rooted in the hope that YHWH is a God who may turn from wrath to restoration. The OT takes the Sinai revelation of YHWH's mercy and compassion and applies it to narrative, poetic, and prophetic contexts. Moses returns to it in Num 14:18 in order to plead with YHWH for forgiveness after the people refused to go to the promised land. Along with the golden calf incident, this reflects one of the most tragic moments in Israel's history where fear overrules faith and the covenant between YHWH and Israel is called into question. Only YHWH's gracious and compassionate character could repair the relationship. The penitential prayer of Neh 9 twice draws from Exod 34:6–7 (Neh 9:17, 31) as the people look back and see YHWH's forgiveness at work in their wilderness wanderings and in the events that led to the exile. Micah 7:18–20 reflects on YHWH's character to offer hope after a time of judgment and punishment, while Nah 1:2–3 looks for him to judge a wicked nation.⁵⁸ Psalmists both praise YHWH by reflecting on his character(Ps 103:8; 145:8) and implore him to intervene

---

56. Crenshaw, *Joel*, 143.
57. Barton, *Joel*, 84.
58. For a deeper discussion of these passages see Joel Barker, "From Where Does My Hope Come? Theodicy and the Character of YHWH in Allusions to Exodus 34:6–7 in the Book of the Twelve," *JETS* 61 (2018): 697–715.

in desperate circumstances (Ps 86:15). The nature of YHWH that was revealed in the aftermath of the golden calf is integral to how the OT understands its God.

The Explanation of the Text noted that Joel's citation of Exod 34:6–7 included an additional phrase וְנִחָם עַל־הָרָעָה ("he relents from punishing"), which is derived from the aftermath of the golden calf incident in Exod 32:12–14. The verb is נָחַם, and when God is its subject it deepens our understanding of his nature. It usually indicates YHWH changes his mind concerning punishment against either his people or foreign nations, although Gen 6:6 uses this verb to indicate YHWH's regret that he created humanity. This pushes back against doctrines of God's intractability, which we may be drawn to out of a concern "that God not appear weak."[59] Instead, the OT is quite comfortable attributing a dynamic nature to YHWH. In 2 Sam 24:16, YHWH relents from bringing the full weight of the announced judgment upon Israel on account of David's census, while Jer 26:13 calls for the people to obey YHWH so that he will relent and not bring disaster. Jeremiah 26:19 provides an example of YHWH relenting as he recounts Hezekiah's response to a prophecy from Micah (Mic 3:12). Amos's entreaties lead YHWH to relent from two visions of doom that he showed to the prophet (Amos 7:3, 6), though eventually further visions promise judgment (Amos 7:7–9; 8:1–3).[60] The fact that YHWH is willing to נָחַם ("relent") strengthens Joel's calls for the people to שׁוּב ("return"). The OT does not see God as static or unchanging. Instead, he is in a dynamic relationship with his covenant people, and he can freely respond when they return to him.

The closest canonical connection to Joel's use of נָחַם is found in Jonah. Jonah 4:2 also includes the phrase וְנִחָם עַל־הָרָעָה ("he relents from punishing") in its citation of Exod 34:6–7. Scholars have differing opinions on the nature of the relationship between the two texts, but it is useful to explore how both texts use this declaration of YHWH's character.[61] Joel's context more closely mirrors that found in Exodus since Joel is urging Judah to cry out to God in repentance and hope that he will rescue them. Both *Joel* and Exodus appeal to YHWH's reputation among the nations as a reason for restoration (Exod 32:12; Joel 2:17). Exodus 19:3–6 reveals that God intends for Israel to be his "kingdom of priests" and his "holy nation" whose

---

59. Nogalski, *Book of the Twelve*, 234.

60. See also Jer 20:16 and Ezek 24:14 for negated examples of נחם where YHWH claims that his punishment cannot be averted.

61. The vast majority of scholars argue for literary dependence in the use of this phrase in the books of Joel and Jonah, though it is possible that their use of this phrase comes from some common source. Numerous attempts have been made to support the priority of both Joel and Jonah. See Joseph Kelly, "Joel, Jonah, and the YHWH Creed," *JBL* 132 (2013): 810–11 for a comprehensive list. Kelly's work reveals that more scholars believe that Joel was the source for Jonah, though he argues for the opposite. For a representative selection of others who support the priority of Jonah, see Jonathan Magonet, *Form and Meaning: Studies in Literary Technique in the Book of Jonah* (Frankfurt: Peter Lang, 1976) 77–79; Thomas M. Bolin, *Freedom beyond Forgiveness: The Book of Jonah Reexamined*, JSOTSup 236 (Sheffield: Sheffield Academic, 1997) 171–72. For a selection of those who support the priority of Joel, see Allen, *Joel*, 228; Fishbane, *Biblical Interpretation*, 345–46; Nogalski, *Redactional Processes*, 273.

obedience should be an example to the nations. God declares that "the whole earth is mine" (Exod 19:5), indicating that Israel's role as the priestly kingdom is to reveal God to the nations so that they might also follow him. Israel's disobedience threatens this relationship but when God forgives his sinful people he demonstrates that he is gracious and compassionate, slow to anger and quick to forgive. This testimony to the nature of God reveals that God preserves his people, both for their own benefit and to be an example to other nations.

Jonah 4:1–4 extends the range of Exod 34:6–7. It reveals that a gentile nation also can receive YHWH's mercy, which raises a theological dilemma for Israel.[62] Jonah 4:2 turns the account of God's character into an accusation. Jonah attributes his desire to flee to Tarshish to his worry that God might dare to demonstrate his grace and mercy to Nineveh. If God is merciful toward a nation hostile to Israel, does that negate Israel's status as his kingdom of priests and holy nation? The book of Jonah does not directly answer this question but its climactic rhetorical question, "should I not pity Nineveh, that great city?" forces its audience to see that God's mercy and compassion cannot be constrained. Reading Jonah with *Joel* extends our understanding of God. The God who reveals his character in the wake of Israel's idolatry is the God to whom Joel can call his audience to return, and the God who is concerned about the fate of all nations.

Crying to God: Oracles of Woe and Doom

Joel 2:12–17 is also fascinating to consider in the broader context of oracles of woe and doom. As 2:11 ends, it appears that judgment is inevitable. The great and terrible day of YHWH looms, and the implication is that no one can endure it. Joel, however, follows with a declaration of hope if his audience will turn and repent. How is this possible? It seems that even within oracles that declare judgment there is an underlying message that turning to YHWH in repentance can avert disaster. The OT makes this case explicitly in Jeremiah's visit to a potter in Jer 18:1–10. As Jeremiah watches the potter shape and reshape the clay, he receives a divine message declaring that God relates to the nations in the same way. God reveals in Jer 18:7–10 that if he proclaims disaster for a nation and it repents, then he can relent. If, however, he proclaims peace and prosperity for a nation and it sins, then he may bring judgment. This suggests a level of interactivity to prophetic language, where a repentant response can turn aside pronouncements of imminent doom.

Terminology drawn from speech-act theory is instructive here. We can consider prophetic declarations using the categories of locution, illocution, and perlocution. Locution corresponds to the speech itself, while illocution refers to what the speech

---

62. For a discussion of the parallels between Joel and Jonah that focuses on Jonah, see Kevin J. Youngblood, *Jonah: God's Scandalous Mercy*, ZECOT 28 (Grand Rapids: Zondervan, 2013), 157–58.

is trying to accomplish, and perlocution considers its effects.[63] When speaking of oracles of doom, the illocutionary intent is to announce and activate potential judgment. This can provoke a variety of perlocutionary responses including lament and penitence from the audience of those oracles. If there is no appropriate response, then the activated judgment stands.[64] Joel 2:12–17 is the prophet's attempt to spur his audience to the proper perlocutionary response to the announcement of the day of YHWH.

Jonah again provides a strong parallel for the shift from doom to hope. In Jonah 3:4, the prophet speaks five words of prophecy to Nineveh, עוֹד אַרְבָּעִים יוֹם וְנִינְוֵה נֶהְפָּכֶת ("yet 40 days and Nineveh will be destroyed"). Jonah's prophecy leaves no room for repentance, yet Nineveh responds by fasting and crying out to God. The king of Nineveh even uses the same question, "who knows?" whether YHWH will turn and restore, also found in Joel 2:14. In response, God turns from bringing disaster, demonstrating the truth of Jer 18:7–10. A prophecy of disaster that the prophet wanted to come true was averted when its audience responded by turning to God.

In Joel 2:12–17, the capacity for repentance and return to YHWH to turn aside disaster is even stronger since the prophet openly declares that YHWH may "turn." Joel 2:12–17 provides the proper perlocutionary response to the warnings of doom. The locust plague, drought, and invasion reveal that judgment looms, but these threats are not yet fully realized. Joel urges the people to weep, fast, and mourn since judgment can still turn to restoration.

A Trustworthy God

Joel 2:12–17 masterfully combines God's mercy and compassion with his freedom to act as he sees fit. Even as the day of YHWH draws near, Joel calls Israel back to its God and offers hope rooted in the divine nature. Joel is also careful not to diminish Israel's interaction with God to the level of a mechanistic transaction. If the people fast, mourn, and weep, then "who knows" what YHWH will do? However, these actions in combination with Joel's celebration of God's attributes offer great encouragement even in the midst of crisis. The sovereign freedom of God along with faith in his character is a combination that C. S. Lewis evokes in *The Lion, the Witch, and the Wardrobe*. As the human children learn about the great lion Aslan before they struggle to break the power of the White Witch, they are told by Mr. Beaver, "'Course he isn't safe. But he's good. He's the King, I tell you."[65] Aslan cannot

---

63. See J. L. Austin, *How to Do Things with Words: 2nd Edition* (Oxford: Clarendon, 1975), 102.

64. Walter Houston, "What Did the Prophets Think They Were Doing? Speech Acts and Prophetic Discourse in the Old Testament," *Biblical Interpretation* 1 (1993): 187.

65. C. S. Lewis, *The Lion, The Witch and the Wardrobe* (Glasgow: William Collins Sons & Co, 1980), 75.

be controlled or tamed, but his character is trustworthy and true. Likewise, 2:12–17 reveals that God cannot be controlled, but he can be trusted. This trust should shape our own approaches to God in the face of trials. While there is no magic formula that will cause God to answer as we would like, there is the hope that the gracious and compassionate God will hear our prayers and respond in keeping with his character.

Joel 2:18-27

F. Divine Deliverance from the Locusts and Drought

Main Idea of the Passage

Joel 2:18–27 assumes that Israel has heeded the prophet's call from the previous passage. In response, YHWH systematically reverses the crises of locusts, agricultural disaster, and invasion presented in 1:2–2:11.

Literary Context

Joel 2:18–27 is the first of three passages that offer hope for deliverance in place of the despair found in 1:2–2:11. This passage readdresses the crises explored in previous passages and celebrates that YHWH will reverse them. Joel assumes that the people cried out to YHWH as he directs in 2:12–17, even though there is no explicit statement of obedience.[1] A similar assumption is found in the debate between Jeremiah and Hananiah in Jer 28:13–16.[2] In Jer 28:13–14, YHWH instructs Jeremiah to tell Hananiah that YHWH is placing an iron yoke on the neck of the nations, symbolizing their servitude to Babylon. In Jer 23:15–16, the prophet speaks to Hananiah but doesn't repeat YHWH's message. Instead he announces a death sentence on Hananiah for false prophecy. However, it is reasonable to assume that Jeremiah would pass on YHWH's oracle before announcing judgment. The lack of repetition of YHWH's oracle allows the text to move quickly to its outcome.[3] The apparent gap between Joel 2:17 and 2:18 is best explained in a similar fashion. Joel's omission of an explicit statement of compliance does not negate the fact that assuming such obedience makes the most sense of the text.

---

1. Assis, *Joel*, 164.
2. Ronald L. Troxel, "The Problem of Time in Joel," *JBL* 132 (2013): 83. Troxel also suggests that something similar occurs in Ezek 37:1–14, in which Ezekiel's prophecy to the whole house of Israel (v. 12–14) only makes sense if they are aware of the prophecy spoken to the dry bones (v. 1–10). Ezekiel 37:11 then directly links the dry bones and the house of Israel.
3. Strazicich, *Joel's Use of Scripture*, 163.

The link between Joel 2:18–27 and 2:12–17 means that YHWH's actions in this passage confirm the attributes of YHWH that Joel invokes in his citation of Exod 34:6–7. YHWH's grace and compassion are on display as he disperses the locust army and restores the fertility of the land. Joel's consistent warnings of the looming threat of the day of YHWH and his proposal for how to respond give him the standing to announce YHWH's renewed commitment to his people. This commitment will play out over the rest of the book as Joel makes YHWH's salvific actions his primary focus.

As discussed in the Introduction, the shift from catastrophe to renewal makes this one of the places where some divide *Joel* into two distinct halves, emanating from different situations.[4] These theories of radical discontinuity become even less likely when we closely examine the connections between 2:18–27 and preceding passages. First, 2:18–27 answers the appeal to YHWH found in 2:12–17. In 2:17 the prophet urges the people to plead with YHWH that they will not be an object of mockery or a חֶרְפָּה ("reproach") in the eyes of the nations. In 2:19, the prophet gives YHWH's answer, which promises that his people do not need to fear that fate any longer. Joel 2:17 concludes with the nations' mocking question אַיֵּה אֱלֹהֵיהֶם ("where is their God?"), which is answered in 2:27 when YHWH declares בְּקֶרֶב יִשְׂרָאֵל אָנִי ("I am in the midst of Israel"). Further, 2:12–17 considers YHWH's nature, asking מִי יוֹדֵעַ ("who knows?") whether YHWH might return and save his people. Joel 2:18–27 reveals that the answer is an emphatic "yes." This corresponds to Joel's citation of YHWH's nature from Exod 34:6–7. YHWH's mercy and compassion will lead him to save his people.

Secondly, Joel 2:18–27 has numerous lexical and thematic parallels with the crises revealed in 1:2–2:11. These include how 2:25 reuses the terms for locusts introduced in 1:4, while promising to reverse the damage they have done. Similarly, God promises a full restoration of the land and its produce that succumbed to the locusts and drought. Joel 2:23 urges the people to be glad and rejoice, using verbal forms that draw from the same roots as the "joy and gladness" (שִׂמְחָה וָגִיל) that were eliminated in 1:16. Yahweh's intervention essentially "leads to the liquidation of the lack" created by the previous crises.[5] Consequently, the literary context of Joel 2:18–27 is intertwined with Joel's previous proclamations. The locusts, the devastation of the land, and the threat of invasion provide the necessary backdrop for Joel's promises of a better future rooted in the presence of YHWH.

---

4. See the discussion in Allen, *Joel*, 39–44. Others make the primary division between Joel 1:2–2:28 and 3:1–4:21. This will be explored further in the discussion of "Literary Context" for Joel 3:1–5.

5. Deist, "Parallels and Reinterpretation," 63.

> A. Superscription (1:1)
> B. Despair on Account of the Locusts (1:2–14)
> C. Despair in the Day of YHWH—The Drought (1:15–20)
> D. Despair in the Day of YHWH—The Invasion (2:1–11)
> E. Hinge: The Call to Return to YHWH (2:12–17)
> ➡ **F. Divine Deliverance from the Locusts and Drought (2:18–27)**
>   **1. YHWH's Restoration (2:18–20)**
>   **2. Calls to Rejoice (2:21–24)**
>   **3. YHWH's Promises (2:25–27)**
> G. Deliverance through the Spirit of YHWH (3:1–5 [2:28–32])
> H. Deliverance through Divine Judgment on the Day of YHWH (4:1–21 [3:1–21])

Translation and Outline

(See pages 116–17.)

Structure and Literary Form

Joel 2:18–27 begins with an abrupt switch in topic. Joel ceases to instruct the Judahite community in how it should cry out to YHWH. Instead, he focuses on YHWH's attitude and actions, which includes the use of divine speech in the first person. Rather than urging his audience to action, Joel now addresses them as the recipients of YHWH's activity. Some older scholars attempt to include 2:18 with the prayer of 2:17 by repointing the two *waw*-consecutives + prefix conjugation verbs of 2:18 (וַיְקַנֵּא, וַיַּחְמֹל) so that they read as volitional forms ("let him be jealous, let him have compassion").[6] However, reading the verbs as they stand creates a *waw*-consecutive chain of four prefix verbs in 2:18–19. The first two reveal YHWH's state of mind concerning Israel ("YHWH was jealous," and "He had compassion") while the second two found in 2:19 introduce divine speech (וַיַּעַן יהוה וַיֹּאמֶר; "YHWH answered and he said"). Thus, following the rhetorical question that concluded 2:17, Joel 2:18 shifts the focus from urging the audience to call upon YHWH to revealing what YHWH does in response.

After walking through YHWH's promises in this passage, Joel closes this passage by means of *epistrophe*. Joel uses the phrase וְלֹא־יֵבֹשׁוּ עַמִּי לְעוֹלָם ("and my people will never again be put to shame") to conclude both 2:26 and 2:27. This reinforces YHWH's commitment to his people, indicating that he acts on their behalf. Another textual

---

6. Wolff, *Joel and Amos*, 57; Merx, *Prophetie*, 91.

Joel 2:18–27

F. Divine Deliverance from the Locusts and Drought (2:18–27)

1. YHWH's Restoration (2:18–20)
   a. YHWH's Commitment to Turn (2:18a–19b)

18a	וַיְקַנֵּא יְהוָה לְאַרְצ֑וֹ	YHWH was jealous for his land.
18b	וַיַּחְמֹ֖ל עַל־עַמּֽוֹ׃	He had compassion upon his people.
19a	וַיַּ֨עַן יְהוָ֜ה	YHWH answered
19b	וַיֹּ֣אמֶר לְעַמּ֗וֹ	and he said to his people,

   b. The Restoration of Crops (2:19c–e)

19c	הִנְנִ֣י שֹׁלֵחַ֩ לָכֶ֨ם אֶת־הַדָּגָ֤ן וְהַתִּירוֹשׁ֙ וְהַיִּצְהָ֔ר	"Look! I am sending to you the grain, the new wine and the oil,
19d	וּשְׂבַעְתֶּ֖ם אֹת֑וֹ	and you will be satisfied by them.
19e	וְלֹא־אֶתֵּ֨ן אֶתְכֶ֥ם ע֛וֹד חֶרְפָּ֖ה בַּגּוֹיִֽם׃	I will not again make you a reproach for the nations.

   c. The Destruction of the Locust Army (2:20)

20a	וְֽאֶת־הַצְּפוֹנִ֞י אַרְחִ֣יק מֵעֲלֵיכֶ֗ם	The northerner I will remove from among you.
20b	וְהִדַּחְתִּיו֙ אֶל־אֶ֣רֶץ צִיָּ֣ה וּשְׁמָמָ֔ה	I will drive it into a parched and desolate land,
20c	אֶת־פָּנָ֗יו אֶל־הַיָּם֙ הַקַּדְמֹנִ֔י	its head to the sea of the east,
20d	וְסֹפ֖וֹ אֶל־הַיָּ֣ם הָאַֽחֲר֑וֹן	its tail to the sea of the west.
20e	וְעָלָ֣ה בָאְשׁ֗וֹ	Its stench will arise,
20f	וְתַ֙עַל֙ צַחֲנָת֔וֹ	and its foul smell will go up,
20g	כִּ֥י הִגְדִּ֖יל לַעֲשֽׂוֹת׃	for it has done great things."

2. Calls to Rejoice (2:21–24)
   a. The Call to the Land (2:21)

21a	אַל־תִּֽירְאִ֖י אֲדָמָ֑ה	Do not fear, o land!
21b	גִּ֥ילִי	Shout for joy
21c	וּשְׂמָ֔חִי	and rejoice
21d	כִּֽי־הִגְדִּ֥יל יְהוָ֖ה לַעֲשֽׂוֹת׃	for YHWH has done great things!

   b. The Call to the Beasts (2:22)

22a	אַל־תִּֽירְאוּ֙ בַּהֲמ֣וֹת שָׂדַ֔י	Do not fear, o beasts of the field,
22b	כִּ֥י דָשְׁא֖וּ נְא֣וֹת מִדְבָּ֑ר	for the pastures of the wilderness have sprouted
22c	כִּי־עֵץ֙ נָשָׂ֣א פִרְי֔וֹ	for the tree has borne its fruit,
22d	תְּאֵנָ֥ה וָגֶ֖פֶן נָתְנ֥וּ חֵילָֽם׃	and the fig tree and the vine have given their wealth.

23a	בְּנֵי צִיּוֹן גִּילוּ	Children of Zion, shout!	c. The Call to the Children of Zion (2:23)
23b	וְשִׂמְחוּ בַּיהוָה אֱלֹהֵיכֶם	Rejoice in YHWH your God!	
23c	כִּי־נָתַן לָכֶם אֶת־הַמּוֹרֶה לִצְדָקָה	for he has given you the early rain for righteousness.	
23d	וַיּוֹרֶד לָכֶם גֶּשֶׁם	He has brought showers down upon you,	
23e	מוֹרֶה וּמַלְקוֹשׁ בָּרִאשׁוֹן׃	the early and later rains, as before.	
24a	וּמָלְאוּ הַגֳּרָנוֹת בָּר	The threshing floor will be full of grain.	d. A Summary of the Reasons to Rejoice (2:24)
24b	וְהֵשִׁיקוּ הַיְקָבִים תִּירוֹשׁ וְיִצְהָר׃	The wine-vats will overflow with new wine and oil.	
25a	וְשִׁלַּמְתִּי לָכֶם אֶת־הַשָּׁנִים	"I will restore to you the years	3. YHWH's Promises (2:25–27) a. The Promise of Restoration (2:25)
25b	אֲשֶׁר אָכַל הָאַרְבֶּה	which the locusts have devoured—	
25c	הַיֶּלֶק וְהֶחָסִיל וְהַגָּזָם	the creeping locusts, the stripping locust, and the gnawing locust.	
25d	חֵילִי הַגָּדוֹל	My great army	
25e	אֲשֶׁר שִׁלַּחְתִּי בָּכֶם׃	that I sent among you.	
26a	וַאֲכַלְתֶּם אָכוֹל וְשָׂבוֹעַ	You will surely eat and be satisfied.	b. The Signal of Restoration (2:26)
26b	וְהִלַּלְתֶּם אֶת־שֵׁם יְהוָה אֱלֹהֵיכֶם	Then you will praise the name of YHWH your God,	
26c	אֲשֶׁר־עָשָׂה עִמָּכֶם לְהַפְלִיא	who has done astounding things with you.	
26d	וְלֹא־יֵבֹשׁוּ עַמִּי לְעוֹלָם׃	My people will never again be put to shame.	
27a	וִידַעְתֶּם	Then you will know,	c. The Confirmation of YHWH's Presence (2:27)
27b	כִּי בְקֶרֶב יִשְׂרָאֵל אָנִי	that I am in the midst of Israel.	
27c	וַאֲנִי יְהוָה אֱלֹהֵיכֶם	I am YHWH your God,	
27d	וְאֵין עוֹד	there is no other.	
27e	וְלֹא־יֵבֹשׁוּ עַמִּי לְעוֹלָם׃	My people will never again be put to shame."	

signal that this passage concludes in 2:27 is the modified formula of divine recognition introduced by וִידַעְתֶּם ("you will know"), followed by an assurance of YHWH's presence in the midst of Israel.[7] This summarizes the intent of YHWH's actions in Joel 2:18–27. The use of this relatively well-established formula in conjunction with *epistrophe* in the final clause signals the conclusion of the passage.[8]

Joel 2:18–27 sub-divides into three separate addresses marked by the implied speaker. First, 2:18–20 reveals that YHWH is the agent of restoration. He promises to restore his people by providing them with agricultural bounty and removing the invading army from 2:1–11. Joel 2:18–20 commences with a narrative introduction that lays the foundation for divine speech (2:18–19b). YHWH then speaks in the first person and indicates what he will do on behalf of Israel (2:19c–20). Secondly, in 2:21–24 the prophet commands the Judahite audience to rejoice in response to YHWH's promises, celebrating the result of YHWH's presence among his people. Joel's commands in this section markedly contrast his previous imperatives which called for fear and lamentation. Finally, YHWH again speaks in 2:25–27, providing numerous promises of his commitment to his people. Consequently, YHWH's addresses to the Judahite community bracket Joel's commands to rejoice.

Explanation of the Text

1. YHWH's Restoration (2:18–20)

Joel begins his programmatic reversal of the previously-mentioned crises by focusing on YHWH's attitude and actions. As mentioned above, this passage assumes that the audience heeded Joel's commands to assemble and cry out. Now, Joel shifts the focus to YHWH's restoration. YHWH's activity is the subject of four successive verbs in 2:18–19b. The construction of this verbal sequence (*waw*-consecutive + prefix conjugation) is unusual since it normally refers to past action. However, the temporal orientation of this passage looks beyond the locust invasion and drought reported in 1:2–2:17 and offers YHWH's answer to these threats. The best solution is that these verses reflect a rhetorical strategy where Joel creatively projects himself into some future time where he can present what is to come as something that has already occurred.[9] Against the backdrop of the devastation portrayed in 1:2–2:17, this grammatical construction provides encouragement that YHWH will act in response to the cries of his people. This strengthens the calls for rejoicing that follow in 2:21–24.

The four *waw*-consecutive verbs found in Joel 2:18–19b begin to answer the rhetorical question "where is their God?" from Joel 2:17. They reveal that YHWH changes his attitude toward his peo-

---

7. For more on the use of the divine recognition formula, see the discussion in the Explanation of the Text section.

8. Ernst R. Wendland, "The Discourse Analysis of Hebrew Poetry: A Procedural Outline," in *Discourse Perspectives on Hebrew Poetry in the Scriptures*, ed. Ernst R. Wendland, UBS Monograph Series 7 (New York: United Bible Societies, 1994), 5.

9. On the "future" use of the *waw*-consecutive + prefix conjugation see Jan Joosten, *The Verbal System of Biblical Hebrew: A New Synthesis Elaborated on the Basis of Classical Prose*, JBS 10 (Jerusalem: Simor, 2012), 422–23. Nogalski takes a similar perspective and argues that "Joel 2:18 portrays a future reality contingent on Israel's repentance" (Nogalski, *The Book of the Twelve*, 235).

ple and promises to act on their behalf. The two verbs of Joel 2:18 describe characteristics of God. The first verb, וַיְקַנֵּא ("he was jealous"), has both negative and positive connotations. First, this verb can be used for YHWH's promises of punishment when Israel fails to worship him alone, typified in both instances of the Decalogue (Exod 20:5; Deut 5:9).[10] Secondly, YHWH's jealousy refers to his passionate commitment to Israel, asserting that no one can sever their bond (Isa 9:7; Ezek 39:25; Zech 1:14). These two senses coalesce around the covenant relationship between YHWH and Israel. YHWH is jealous when Israel turns from him, but he is also passionately committed to Israel's well-being and he intercedes when the people sincerely cry out.[11] Joel 2:18 invokes this latter sense of the verb. When Israel cries out to YHWH as Joel suggests in 2:12–17, YHWH will again "be jealous" for his people and restore their fortunes.

The second verb is וַיַּחְמֹל ("he had compassion"). This verb highlights YHWH's mercy, which is necessary in this situation given the deprivations that his people have experienced. It also indicates YHWH's renewed commitment to his people in the wake of their return to him. Negated forms of this verb occur when YHWH declares that he will no longer have compassion on his people because of their sin (cf. 2 Chron 36:17; Jer 13:14; Lam 2:2, 17, 21; Ezek 5:11; Zech 11:6).[12] Consequently, the positive use of this verb indicates that he has changed his attitude toward his people. YHWH's jealousy and compassion thus provide the foundation for the restoration celebrated in 2:18–27.

YHWH's commitment to his people is evident in the objects of the two verbs. Joel 2:18a declares that YHWH's jealousy is לְאַרְצוֹ ("for his land") while 2:18 reveals that his compassion is עַל־עַמּוֹ ("upon his people"). The combination of the land and its people is a *merismus* that indicates the totality of YHWH's commitment. It also fits with earlier warnings from 1:2–2:11 that threaten both the productivity of the land and the security of its inhabitants.

After establishing YHWH's changed attitude, Joel 2:19–20 begins to reveal the outcomes of YHWH's actions in response to the implied return of the Judahite community. Joel 2:19a–b commences with the latter two verbs of the *waw*-consecutive sequence that introduce divine speech. YHWH begins in 2:19c with a promise to restore the land and its produce. He declares הִנְנִי שֹׁלֵחַ ("Look! I am sending"), which consists of the emphatic particle with a first-person singular suffix followed by a participle. This construction is found predominantly in prophetic literature or in reports of prophetic activity in narrative. YHWH is usually the subject, and this construction introduces both promises and threats (cf. 1 Sam 25:19; 2 Sam 12:11; 1 Kgs 5:19; 11:31; Jer 1:15; 2:35; 6:21; 35:17; Ezek 4:16; 11:3; 22:19; 23:22; Hos 2:8; Amos 6:14; 7:8).[13] Joosten argues that הִנֵּה + participle refers to "processes really going on at the time of the speech," while van der Merwe, Naudé, and Kroeze note that it highlights "the immediacy of the events."[14] In Joel 2:19c that would indicate the beginning of YHWH's turn toward his people, in response to their turn to him.

Joel 2:19c also reveals what YHWH is sending. YHWH promises to restore agricultural fruitfulness specified as הַדָּגָן וְהַתִּירוֹשׁ וְהַיִּצְהָר ("the grain,

---

10. Walter Brueggemann, *Theology of the Old Testament: Testimony, Dispute, Advocacy* (Minneapolis: Fortress, 1997), 293–97.

11. Barton, *Joel*, 88.

12. Crenshaw, *Joel*, 149.

13. Paul Humbert, "La formule hebraique en hineni suivi d'un participle," *Revue des Etudes Juives* 97 (1934) 58–64. Humbert argues that 118 out of 125 examples introduce either a divine promise or threat. Jeremiah and Ezekiel both frequently employ this construction.

14. Joosten, *Verbal System*, 106; BHRG §40.22.4.1.

the new wine and oil."). These crops were both staples of the community's diet and essential to its worship offerings to YHWH. Interestingly, Nehemiah conflates these functions when he reinstitutes a temple tithe so that the Levites can eat while returning to full-time service (Neh 13:10–12).[15] Joel is also invoking both functions since 1:9–10 uses these same three crops to discuss the ravages of the locusts and the cessation of sacrifice. When YHWH returns these three crops, he reverses both the threat of starvation and the broken sacrificial system. Joel 2:19d then succinctly emphasizes the efficacy of YHWH's activity with the verb וּשְׂבַעְתֶּם ("and you will be satisfied"). YHWH's promised actions thus replace calls to fast (1:14; 2:15) with promises of feasts.

To conclude the verse, Joel 2:19e reveals a further effect of YHWH's action. In 2:17d, the prophet calls his audience to implore YHWH not to make them a חֶרְפָּה ("reproach") among the nations since this would suggest that YHWH was unable to preserve his people. In 2:19e, YHWH announces that he will not subject them to that fate, declaring וְלֹא־אֶתֵּן אֶתְכֶם עוֹד חֶרְפָּה בַּגּוֹיִם ("I will not again make you a reproach for the nations"). YHWH's gift of the grain, new wine, and fresh oil reveals his renewed commitment to preserve the standing of his people among the nations. Essentially, the return of agricultural bounty is another part of YHWH's answer to the mocking question "where is their God?" in 2:17f.[16] YHWH thus promises to alleviate both the physical and psychological distress created by the deprivation experienced in 1:2–2:17.

YHWH introduces a new element of deliverance in Joel 2:20 by eliminating the invading army that should be identified as the one that attacks Zion in 2:1–11. In an interesting twist, YHWH identifies the invader as הַצְּפוֹנִי ("the northerner"), which is a deeply symbolic expression. Some opt for a mostly literal meaning and argue that invading locusts could have arrived from the north, but that is unlikely.[17] Instead, הַצְּפוֹנִי ("the northerner") is used frequently as a metaphor to stand in for enemies of the people of YHWH. This fits with the geopolitics of the region since Mesopotamian enemies including Assyria or Babylon attacked from the north, following the sweep of the Fertile Crescent (Isa 41:25; Jer 1:13–15; 4:6; 6:22; 10:22; Ezek 26:10; 38:6, 15; Zech 2:10).[18] It is impossible to identify the intended referent in all cases, but the foe from the north implies a significant threat.[19] Joel's use of the term is ambiguous, since it could apply equally well to locusts, a foreign invader, or an apocalyptic army.[20] Further complicating the issue is that the north can reflect a dwelling for deity (Job 37:22; Ps 48:3; Isa 14:13; Ezek 1:4). Joel likely uses הַצְּפוֹנִי ("the northerner") as a motif that invokes divine judgment, in this case through the proxy of the invading horde of 2:1–11.[21] It poses a serious danger to the Judahite community that

---

15. Sweeney, *Twelve*, 169.
16. Crenshaw, *Joel*, 150.
17. For example, Allen, *Joel*, 88, argues for locusts from the north. Others, including Kapelrud note that locusts typically enter Israel from the south or east (Kapelrud, *Joel Studies*, 96–107).
18. Dillard, "Joel," 287.
19. Previous generations of scholarship sought to identify a historical antecedent for the symbolic northern enemy. Representative examples include Cazelles who suggests an invasion by Scythian raiders (Henri Cazelles, "Zephaniah, Jeremiah and the Scythians in Palestine," in *A Prophet to the Nations: Essays in Jeremiah Studies*, ed. Leo Perdue and Brian W. Kovacs [Winona Lake, IN: Eisenbrauns, 1984; repr., *RB* 74 (1967) 22–44], 129–50). Whitley looks to the battle of Carchemish as an incident that brought a Babylonian threat to the forefront (Charles Francis Whitley, "Carchemish and Jeremiah," in *A Prophet to the Nations: Essays in Jeremiah Studies*, ed. Leo. Perdue and Brian W. Kovacs [Winona Lake, IN: Eisenbrauns, 1984; repr., *ZAW* 80 (1968) 38–49], 163–73).
20. Dillard, "Joel," 286.
21. David J. Reimer, "The 'Foe' and the 'North,' in Jeremiah" *ZAW* 101 (1989): 223–32. This explains a passage like Jer 50:1–3, which speaks of the northern enemy attacking Babylon at YHWH's behest, even though Babylon itself is often associated with the northern enemy.

YHWH must eliminate as a sign of his renewed presence among his people.

Joel's use of "the northerner" motif specifically reflects the power associated with the invading army in 2:10–11. This force has YHWH thundering at its head, which means that it reflects a scenario of imminent doom as the day of YHWH is about to unfold. The heavens respond by means of the verb רָעֲשׁוּ ("shake"), which here suggests a threat to the entire created order is in peril and the possibility of a return to chaos (cf. Isa 24:18; Ezek 38:19–20).[22] Joel takes his revelation of a divinely-sanctioned locust invasion and adapts it to fit traditions of the enemy from the north in 2:18–27. The locust army is identified with "the northerner" of 2:20 since its invasion in 2:1–11 culminates in the declaration that YHWH leads the army and threatens the created order. Now, Joel's association of the invader with "the northerner" sets the stage for its destruction. After giving the invader this title, YHWH promises to destroy it. Again, Joel emphasizes YHWH's changed perspective since he promises to defeat what was portrayed as his own army in 2:10–11.

The remaining clauses in Joel 2:20 detail the particulars of YHWH's deliverance. YHWH speaks about the invader in 2:20b and utters the promise וְהִדַּחְתִּיו אֶל־אֶרֶץ צִיָּה וּשְׁמָמָה ("I will drive it in a parched and desolate land"). The verb נָדַח appears in contexts of a scattering enemy, which reverses the images of the invader as a well-disciplined military machine in 2:7–8 (cf. Jer 8:3; 24:9; Dan 9:7;

Ezek 4:13).[23] YHWH's intervention also promises poetic justice since the invader will suffer the fates of thirst and deprivation that were integral to the threats found in previous passages. Specifically, 2:3 uses the adjective שְׁמָמָה ("desolate") to describe what the invader does to a previously fertile land.[24] This same adjective recurs in 2:20b to describe YHWH's final judgment on this invader. YHWH thus promises that the invader will suffer the fate that it intended to inflict upon its victims.

Joel 2:20c–d are verbless clauses that expand upon the implications of YHWH's promise to disperse and destroy the invader. These clauses shape a geographical *merismus*, wherein YHWH's actions drive the head of the invading army אֶל־הַיָּם הַקַּדְמֹנִי ("to the sea of the east") and its tail אֶל־הַיָּם הָאַחֲרוֹן ("to the sea of the west"). These correspond to the Dead Sea and the Mediterranean respectively. With this image, Joel suggests that YHWH's intervention thus drives the invader outside of the boundaries of the land for its final destruction. Its violation of the land and its people come to an end when YHWH divides and scatters it to the winds.

Joel 2:20e–f adds to the promise of destruction by drawing on the sense of smell. These clauses both begin with *waw*-consecutive affix verbs from the root עָלָה, followed by nouns referring to the smell of the destroyed invader (בָּאְשׁוֹ ["stench"] and צַחֲנָתוֹ ["foul smell"]).[25] Both ancient and modern commentators note the putrefaction of locust bodies when the swarm dies.[26] This again contributes to the sense of total destruction accomplished by

---

22. Brevard S. Childs, "The Enemy from the North and the Chaos Tradition," *JBL* 78 (1959): 187–98. Childs suggests that this verb became associated with the "enemy from the north" tradition when this enemy took on attributes that cannot be attributed to any mere human invader.

23. Crenshaw, *Joel*, 151–52.

24. The LXX uses the verb "I will destroy" (ἀφανιῶ) to translate the adjective שְׁמָמָה found in the Masoretic tradition. The Hebrew underlying the LXX reading is probably the

first-person verb שממתי. This appears to be an attempt to construct a smoother reading by supplying a verb before the definite direct object marker.

25. The term צַחֲנָתוֹ is a *hapax legomenon*. The fact that both clauses contain the same verb and have parallel syntax provides warrant for translating it as a synonym of "stench."

26. Simkins cites Augustine who described the death of a locust swarm as toxic enough to cause plague and pestilence. Simkins, *Yahweh's Activity*, 195.

YHWH's intervention. YHWH drives the invader from the land and all that remains is the aroma of its rotting corpses.

Joel 2:20g provides the reason for YHWH's judgment. This clause reads כִּי הִגְדִּיל לַעֲשׂוֹת ("for it has done great things"). The subject of הִגְדִּיל is unexpressed, which opens up the potential for confusion since 2:21d concludes with almost exactly the same phrase. The sole difference is that 2:21d explicitly identifies YHWH as the subject. It is possible that YHWH is the subject of the clause in 2:20g and the divine name was elided during the process of transmission.[27] Another suggestion is that this verb should be changed into a first-person form (אַגְדִּיל) with YHWH as the speaker so that it refers to YHWH's actions in destroying the invader.[28]

A preferable solution is to suggest that "the northerner," which has been the focus of this entire verse is the unexpressed subject of the final clause. This does not require changing the Masoretic text, and it sets up a contrast with the "great things" that YHWH does in the following verse. The invader's "great things" suggest self-aggrandizement which merits YHWH's judgment.[29] Isaiah 10:5–19 provides a parallel in that it describes Assyria as an agent of divine judgment against whom YHWH turns when it succumbs to its own *hubris*. Psalm 35:26–27 provides further support for identifying "the northerner" as the subject of the הִגְדִּיל in 2:20g. Psalm 35:26 uses a participle from the same root (הַמַּגְדִּילִים) to refer to arrogant enemies of the psalmist. Psalm 35:27 then uses a prefix form of the root (יִגְדַּל) in a volitional sense to urge the audience to magnify YHWH for saving the psalmist. Thus, in successive verses, forms of the verb גָּדַל refer to the psalmist's enemies and then to YHWH. Joel 2:20g is the first step in the same progression. It promises that YHWH will destroy the invader because of its "great deeds," which contrast the "great deeds" of YHWH in 2:21c. The proximity of the two clauses suggests that YHWH's "great deeds" trump those of the invader.

In summary, Joel 2:18–20 reveals YHWH's turn to his people in response to Joel's call for them to return to him in 2:12–17. YHWH displays his jealousy and compassion and he begins to deliberately reverse the threats found in 1:2–2:11. His promise to send grain, new wine, and oil specifically liquidates what was lacking in 1:2–14 and 1:15–20. The promise to destroy "the northerner" reverses the threat of 2:1–11. The use of first-person speech further strengthens YHWH's commitment. YHWH no longer thunders at the head of his invading host. Instead, he promises to drive that army to its utter destruction outside of the land. These actions reverse the possibility that the nations could view his people with scorn, which answers the plea that Joel constructs for the Judahite audience in 2:17.[30]

2. Calls to Rejoice (2:21–24)

Joel 2:21 switches from first person divine speech to the voice of the prophet. Joel issues a series of imperatives that build upon YHWH's actions in 2:18–20. Now that YHWH promises to restore his people, Joel calls for celebration. Joel targets three addressees for his imperatives: the land, the beasts of the field, and the children of Zion. This progression highlights the fullness of YHWH's restorative actions. The land, the beasts, and the people have all experienced deprivation in 1:2–2:17, and now Joel urges them to celebrate. Joel's progression builds to the address to the chil-

---

27. Wolff, *Joel and Amos*, 55.
28. E. Sellin, *Das Zwölfprophetenbuch übersetzt und erklärt*, KAT 12/1 (Leipzig: A. Deichertsche, 1929), 166.
29. Prinsloo, *Theology*, 77.
30. Deist, "Parallels and Reinterpretation," 64.

dren of Zion. Even though the land and the animals cannot actually understand Joel's commands, the natural world provides a template for the expected state of YHWH's people. Consequently, Joel's audience effectively hears a three-part command to rejoice since it shares in the positive outcomes for the land and the animals.

The commands to the land, the animals, and the children of Zion follow a similar pattern, which may reflect the form of an expansion of the form of a prophetic summons to joy.[31] Each address contains one or more imperatives calling for celebration, a vocative addressee, and reasons for rejoicing introduced by כִּי.[32] Often the addressee is a personified female figure such as Daughter Zion and the reason for rejoicing is YHWH's victory over an enemy (Isa 12:6; 54:1; Zeph 3:14–15; Zech 2:14[10]; 9:9–10). Joel 2:21-24 varies slightly from this form in that it does not personify Zion itself, but it does personify the land and the beasts before addressing the children of Zion (cf. Isa 52:7–10). The land and the beasts are both addressed using feminine forms of the imperatives, which parallels addresses to Daughter Zion. Joel's reasons for rejoicing are rooted in the explicit promise of renewed fertility but this requires the removal of the locust army, which Joel describes using language reminiscent of a military victory in 2:19–20.[33] Consequently, Joel taps into the form of a prophetic summons to joy to celebrate YHWH's victory over the invader and the promise of renewed fertility.

Joel 2:21a begins this process by addressing the land with the command אַל־תִּירְאִי ("do not fear"), which opens an oracle of assurance and again reflects YHWH's favorable answer to Israel's pleas.[34] This imperative is often addressed to military leaders but it can also speak to the entire community, promising that YHWH will act as the Divine Warrior on its behalf (Isa 10:24–27; Jer 46:27–28; Zeph 3:16–18).[35] Although the immediate addressee here is the land, the progression from land, to beasts, to the children of Zion suggests that YHWH is adopting his warrior persona. The land and its inhabitants should not be afraid because YHWH will act on their behalf. Joel 2:21b-c reinforces the positive turn of events with two imperatives, addressing the land with the commands גִּילִי וּשְׂמָחִי ("shout for joy and rejoice"). These two imperatives reverse the despair of 1:16, which employed nominal forms of the same roots (שִׂמְחָה וָגִיל) to refer to the cessation of sacrifices in the temple.

Joel 2:21d provides the reason for the calls to rejoice. As mentioned above, the phrase is identical in form to 2:20f except that YHWH is now the explicit subject. Joel exhorts the land not to fear, כִּי־הִגְדִּיל יְהוָה לַעֲשׂוֹת ("for YHWH has done great things"). This sets the "great deeds" of YHWH over and above the "great deeds" of the invading locust army. This verse begins the prophet's summons to joy by calling for a celebration of YHWH's deeds, which refers to his promise of renewed grain, new wine, and oil and the destruction of the locust army in 2:19–20. YHWH's jealousy and compassion are put into action and Joel calls his audience to celebrate.

Joel 2:22 unfolds similarly. It begins with a plural

---

31. The identification of this form is attributed to Crüsemann who calls it an *Aufruf zur Freude*. See Frank Crüsemann, *Studien zur Formgeschichte von Hymnus und Danklied in Israel*, WMANT 32 (Neukirchen-Vluyn: Neukirchener Verlag, 1969), 55–65.

32. Mark J. Boda, "The Daughter's Joy," in *Daughter Zion: Her Portrait, Her Response*, SBLHB, ed. Mark J. Boda, Carol J. Dempsey, and Leanne Snow Flesher (Atlanta: SBL, 2012), 325.

33. Boda, "Daughter's," 335–37.

34. Crenshaw, *Joel*, 153.

35. Edgar Conrad, *Fear Not Warrior: A Study of the 'al tira' Pericopes in the Hebrew Scriptures*, BJS 75 (Chico: Scholars, 1985), 122–23, 168–69.

form of the command to not fear (אַל־תִּירְאוּ), followed by a vocative identification of the addressee, and concludes with reasons for assurance introduced by כִּי.[36] The plural form of the imperative is necessary since the addressees are the בַּהֲמוֹת שָׂדַי ("beasts of the field"). The beasts require this reassurance in light of their deprivation in 1:16–20 where the prophet describes their agony as their pastures and water sources dry up. Joel 2:22b–d reverses this threat by means of multiple images of renewed fertility. These assurance clauses do not explicitly attribute the restoration to YHWH, but direct mentions of his activity in 2:21, 23 suggest that he is responsible.

Joel 2:22b uses כִּי to introduce the first reason for rejoicing, which is that the pastures of the desert have sprouted. The verb דָּשְׁאוּ ("they sprouted") is found only in Gen 1:11 in YHWH's command for the earth to produce vegetation. It also recalls 2:3, which portrays the locust army as wreaking havoc upon an Edenic landscape. In employing a verb associated with the creation narrative, Joel hints at the prospect of paradise restored.[37] The subjects of the flourishing indicated by דָּשְׁאוּ are the נְאוֹת מִדְבָּר ("the pastures of the wilderness"). This reflects a complete reversal of 1:19–20 where fire had consumed these pastures. The beasts of the field need no longer fear since YHWH has transformed their scorched pastureland into fertile ground.

Joel 2:22c–d echoes and enhances the renewed fertility. Joel 2:22c again uses כִּי to reveal that trees are bearing their fruit. Joel 2:22d expands upon this phrase and specifically highlights that the תְאֵנָה וָגֶפֶן ("the fig tree and the vine") flourish. Joel uses the destruction of these same plants in 1:7 to reveal the destruction caused by the locusts. Now, the fig trees produce their fruit and the vines yield "their wealth" (חֵילָם). This is the same word that Joel uses to describe YHWH's army in 2:11, differing only in the attached suffix (חֵילוֹ). This is yet another example of how the prophet reuses vocabulary that announced threat in 1:2–2:17 to promise restoration now that YHWH acts on behalf of his people.

The summons to joy culminates in Joel 2:23, which begins with the prophet's direct address to the Judahite audience. Joel uses two parallel imperatives in 2:23a–b that echo the imperatives addressed to the land in 2:21a–b, modifying only their gender and number (גִּילוּ וְשִׂמְחוּ). These clauses employ slightly different syntax since 2:23a places the addressees, the בְּנֵי צִיּוֹן ("children of Zion"), in front of the imperative to shout for joy. Assis suggests that bringing forward the addressees more closely links their presumed response to the responses of the land and its animals. The rejoicing of the earth and its creatures provides a template that the children of Zion should follow.[38] Joel 2:23b then calls the people to rejoice בַּיהוה אֱלֹהֵיכֶם ("in YHWH your God"). The second-person suffix reinforces the tone established by the third-person suffixes in 2:18–19a that revealed YHWH's jealousy and compassion for his people. Now, Joel connects YHWH to his people by calling upon them to rejoice in "your God."

Joel 2:23c introduces the reasons for rejoicing through the particle כִּי, which mirrors the syntax of the previous two verses. Joel's first reason introduces an interpretive issue. The Masoretic text states that YHWH will give to the community הַמּוֹרֶה לִצְדָקָה, which is usually translated as "the early

---

36. The phrase בַּהֲמוֹת שָׂדַי ("beasts of the field") is actually a feminine plural construct chain so it does not agree with the gender of the imperative. This reflects the convention that the masculine plural is the base form for verbs in the second person (cf. Ruth 1:4b; Amos 4:1). See Joüon, *Grammar*, §150a.

37. This is a key theme to which Joel will return in 4:18–21 [3:18–21].

38. Assis, *Book of Joel*, 184.

rain for righteousness." The LXX instead suggests that YHWH will give "food for righteousness" (τα βρωματα εἰς δικαιοσυνην). The proposed underlying reading for this translation is either המאכל or הבריה, neither of which bear any resemblance to the Masoretic reading.[39] This suggests that the LXX is attempting to make sense of a difficult passage by offering a reading that fits with the promises made to the beasts of the field in the previous verse. This means that we must address the challenges of the Masoretic text.

The first challenge is to determine the meaning of הַמּוֹרֶה. The anarthrous form of the noun is a place name (Gen 12:6; Deut 11:30; Judg 7:1). It is also translated as "teacher" (Job 36:22; Prov 5:13; Isa 30:20), which raises intriguing possibilities when paired with the following word לִצְדָקָה. Some have made the suggestion that YHWH is promising to give the people "the teacher for righteousness," which invokes terminology from Qumran and the Dead Sea Scrolls.[40] However, this verse is not cited in extant Qumran documents and it does not fit the best possibilities for *Joel*'s date of composition.[41] Further, translating this word as "teacher" would be incredibly out of step with the surrounding context of renewed security and agricultural productivity.

The other possibility for הַמּוֹרֶה is that it means rainfall, probably the autumn rains that prepared the ground for ploughing and sowing (cf. Ps 84:7).[42] Although this meaning is rare, it best fits the context of this verse. In the very next clause, 2:23d reveals that YHWH will send rain using the common term גֶּשֶׁם (Gen 7:12; 8:2; Lev 26:4; 1 Kgs 17:7; 18:45; Isa 44:10; 55:10; Amos 4:7; Hos 6:3). Joel 2:23e expands on this term with the phrase מוֹרֶה וּמַלְקוֹשׁ בָּרִאשׁוֹן. Here the disputed term מוֹרֶה occurs in apposition with מַלְקוֹשׁ, which refers to the rains that strengthen the crops before harvest (Deut 11:14; Prov 16:15; Job 29:23; Jer 5:24; Hos 6:3; Zech 10:1). Thus Joel uses גֶּשֶׁם as a generic term for rainfall while in the next clause the phrase מוֹרֶה וּמַלְקוֹשׁ בָּרִאשׁוֹן could be understood as a *merismus*, revealing that the rainfall encompasses both expected seasons.[43] Consequently, it is likely that since מוֹרֶה refers to rains in 2:23e, it also refers to rain in 2:23c.

Identifying הַמּוֹרֶה as a synonym for rain still leaves open what is meant by attaching it to לִצְדָקָה since there is no necessary connection between rainfall and righteousness. One suggestion is that here it refers to what is right and appropriate, suggesting that God is promising the return of the rains in their allotted amounts and seasons.[44] This proposal fits with the surrounding context of renewed fertility and is possible, but those who support it fail to provide further examples of לִצְדָקָה where it has the sense of "appropriateness." A more generic proposal is that the *lamed* in לִצְדָקָה connects the

---

39. Simkins, *Yahweh's Activity*, 199; Wolff, *Joel and Amos*, 55; Dillard, "Joel," 289.

40. The Targum and Vulgate traditions follow this approach.

41. The arguments associating this verse with Qumran come mostly from older sources. Roth suggests that the Qumran community later interpreted this verse "out of its context" to appropriate the idea of a teacher of righteousness (Cecil Roth, "The Teacher of Righteousness in the Prophecy of Joel," *VT* 13 [1963]: 93–95). Sellers proposes that לִצְדָקָה was inserted by a scribe familiar with Qumran teachings on the basis of its proximity to הַמּוֹרֶה. See O. R. Sellers, "A Possible Old Testament Reference to the Teacher of Righteousness," *IEJ* 5 (1955): 93–95).

42. Allen, *Joel*, 92–93. The other noun used to describe this rain is יוֹרֶה (Deut 11:15; Jer 5:24).

43. Futato helpfully categorizes the vocabulary for rainfall. He identifies מָטָר and גֶּשֶׁם as generic terms, while מַלְקוֹשׁ and יוֹרֶה/מוֹרֶה refer to rainfall in specific seasons. Mark D. Futato, "Sense Relations in the 'Rain Domain' of the Old Testament," in *Imagery and Imagination in Biblical Literature: Essays in Honour of Aloysius Fitzgerald, F. S. C.*, ed. Lawrence Boadt and Mark S. Smith (Washington: Catholic Biblical Association of America, 2001), 82–94.

44. Coggins, *Joel*, 48; Sweeney, *Twelve*, 172.

two words by suggesting YHWH will send rain in accordance with his own righteousness.[45] Rainfall reflects YHWH's righteousness as part of his answer to how Israel turned to him in 2:12–17. This suggestion resonates with passages where the gift of rain represents covenant blessing (Lev 26:3–4; Deut 11:13–15), while the lack of rainfall represents covenant sanction (Lev 26:18–20; Deut 28:23–24; 1 Kgs 8:35–36).[46] According to this reading, YHWH's gift of rain is part of the zeal and compassion that he promises to show beginning in 2:18.

This discussion provides the framework for Joel's rhetorical strategy in this verse. Joel 2:23 offers more images of the complete restoration through these images of rainfall, building on renewed fertility of the fields that causes the animals to rejoice. This reverses Joel's earlier descriptions of the complete breakdown of the natural order as locusts and droughts ravage the land. Specifically, 1:15–20 suggested a drought severe enough for wildfires to destroy the pastureland. In response, 2:23 refers to abundant rains, guaranteeing a return to prosperity. The total desolation brought on by the crises of 1:2–2:17 give way to a celebration of restoration in 2:18–27.

Joel's call for the children of Zion to rejoice concludes in 2:24 with even more images of prosperity. The prophet returns to vocabulary found in 2:19 by discussing grain, new wine, and oil. There is some minor variation as 2:19 and 24 use different words for grain (הַדָּגָן in 2:19, and בָּר in 2:24) but use the same terms for new wine (תִּירוֹשׁ) and oil (יִצְהָר). It is likely that בָּר refers to grain that has undergone the winnowing process (Gen 41:35, 49; Amos 8:5, 6).[47] The variation in terms for grain fits with the mention of places of manufacture in this verse. Joel 2:24a reveals that הַגֳּרָנוֹת ("the threshing floor") will be full of this grain, while 2:24b declares that הַגֳּרָנוֹת ("the wine-vats") will overflow with new wine and oil. The verbs associated with the threshing floor and the wine-vats stress the abundance of YHWH's provision. The first is מָלֵא, which is a common verb referring to filling. The second is שׁוּק, which occurs only three times and refers to being filled to overflowing (Joel 4:13[3:13]; Ps 65:10).[48] Essentially, this is the logical consequence of the renewed rains promised in the previous verse. Rainfall leads to a richly overflowing harvest that the Judahite audience can process into edible grain and wine.

In summary, 2:21–24 reveals YHWH's zeal and compassion for his people. It calls the Judahite community to rejoice and celebrate since YHWH promises to act powerfully on its behalf. The return to prosperity reverses announcements of deprivation from the first half of the book. In 1:10, sacrifices to YHWH cease because of the lack of grain, new wine, and oil, while in 1:17 the empty storehouses bear witness to their absence.[49] Now, in 2:21–24 YHWH provides these staples in abundance. In response, Joel calls for full-throated celebration, first from the land, then from the beasts, culminating with the children of Zion. The commands to the land and the beasts provide proof of YHWH's zeal and compassion, which YHWH's people ought to echo as they revel in these signs of YHWH's renewed favor.

3. YHWH's Promises (2:25–27)

Joel 2:25 returns to first-person divine speech. In 2:25a–b YHWH promises to make restitution

---

45. Kapelrud, *Joel Studies*, 116. Kapelrud notes that "this solution, besides being the easiest, is also probably correct."
46. Dillard, "Joel," 289.
47. Oded Borowski, *Agriculture in Iron Age Israel* (Winona Lake, IN: Eisenbrauns, 1987), 65–69.
48. Crenshaw, *Joel*, 156–57.
49. Assis, *Book of Joel*, 190–91.

for the destruction caused by the locusts. The verb וְשִׁלַּמְתִּי ("I will restore") in 2:25a indicates that YHWH is returning matters to their proper arrangement (Exod 21:34, 36–37; 22:1–5, 12–13). The object of YHWH's restoration is אֶת־הַשָּׁנִים ("the years") that the locusts devoured.[50] This may reflect a disruption of the agricultural cycle in which the locusts devour all of the crops and affect the planting and harvesting of the following season.[51] YHWH now reveals that his restoration is intentionally calibrated to reverse the devastation described in earlier passages.

Joel 2:25c–e further discusses the identity of the locusts and interacts with Joel's previous discussions. Joel 2:25c is a verbless clause, consisting only of three synonyms for locust הַיֶּלֶק וְהֶחָסִיל וְהַגָּזָם). These expand on yet another word for locust (הָאַרְבֶּה) that was the subject of the verb אָכַל ("devour") in the relative clause of 2:25b. These are the same words for locust that Joel used in 1:4 to describe the assault of wave after wave of locusts. Joel 1:4 and 2:25 list the locust synonyms in different orders, which further indicates that Joel is not referring to the life-cycle of the locusts. Instead, his purpose in reusing this vocabulary is to stress the completeness of YHWH's reversal. The locusts attack in four waves in 1:4 and in 2:25 YHWH promises restitution for each one.

Joel 2:25d–e further specifies the locusts as חֵילִי הַגָּדוֹל אֲשֶׁר שִׁלַּחְתִּי בָּכֶם ("my great army that I sent among you"). The same word חַיִל was used in 2:11, in the context of YHWH uttering his voice before his army. By reusing it here, YHWH confirms his leadership of the locusts and their portrayal as an invading army.[52] Joel 2:25e closes by mirroring 2:25a, which began with YHWH's promise וְשִׁלַּמְתִּי לָכֶם ("I will restore to you"). YHWH's actions reverse the effects of the army that שִׁלַּחְתִּי בָּכֶם ("I sent among you"). Essentially, YHWH's promised actions match his past deeds now that he promises to bring deliverance rather than punishment.[53]

Joel 2:26 details the consequences of YHWH's promise to restore what the locusts devoured. Joel 2:26a announces that the Judahite community will find satiation as a result of YHWH's provision. This clause consists of a *waw*-consecutive + affix conjugation verb (וַאֲכַלְתֶּם) followed by two infinitive absolutes (אָכוֹל וְשָׂבוֹעַ). The first infinitive absolute comes from the same root as the initial conjugated verb, creating a paranomastic construction that emphasizes that YHWH's people will eat abundantly. The use of two infinitive absolutes suggests simultaneous action, in this case indicating that Israel will experience satiation immediately upon eating what YHWH has provided.[54] The use of the verb אָכַל ("to eat") is noteworthy since this verb is found four times in Joel 1:4 to describe the destruction that the locusts caused. Joel begins his prophecy by talking about what the locusts ate, which threatens the ability of the people to feed themselves. He now presents YHWH's promise that the people will eat plentifully.

Joel 2:26b–c provides the appropriate response to YHWH's promise of provision. First, 2:26b

---

50. Nash, "Palestinian," 126. Nash suggests that it should instead be read as "double" (שְׁנַיִם), indicating that the restitution will double the deprivations. This is unlikely since this word is anarthrous on the occasions when it refers to a double amount (Exod 22:3, 6, 8; Deut 21:17; 2 Kgs 2:9). The word that more commonly means "double" is מִשְׁנֶה.

51. Dillard, "Joel," 292. See also Simkins, *Yahweh's Activity*, 193. Simkins argues that Joel's use of "years" implies that 1:2–14 and 2:1–11 refer to two different waves of locusts. I think this assumes too specific of a connection between the imagery of the text and its historical circumstances. It is more likely that Joel is creating a metaphorical blend between the locusts in 1:2–14 and the invading host in 2:1–11.

52. This verse also links the locusts in 1:2–14 with the invader in 2:1–11 by equating the synonyms for locusts with "my great army."

53. Crenshaw, *Joel*, 158.

54. Joüon §123m.

declares וְהִלַּלְתֶּם אֶת־שֵׁם יהוה אֱלֹהֵיכֶם ("you will praise the name of YHWH your God"). Again, Joel attaches the second-person plural pronominal suffix to the mention of God (אֱלֹהֵיכֶם), reinforcing the restored relationship between the community and its God. YHWH's promises of food reveal the continuing bond between him and his people. Joel 2:26c is a relative clause that stresses the magnificence of YHWH's restorative actions through a *lamed* + infinitive construct (לְהַפְלִיא). This verb is often used in contexts describing YHWH's wondrous deeds, and it could even be an epithet celebrating his essence (cf. Judg 13:19).[55] Joel 2:26 thus makes the transition from promises of satiation to the response of praise that YHWH's actions should evoke.[56]

Joel 2:27 provides the capstone of YHWH's promises of restoration. Joel 2:27a–d celebrates YHWH's presence among his people, his claim to be their God, and his incomparability.[57] Joel 2:27a–b promises YHWH's presence in the midst of Israel, which 2:27c–d follows with the pronouncement וַאֲנִי יהוה אֱלֹהֵיכֶם וְאֵין עוֹד ("I am YHWH your God, there is no other").[58] These clauses reflect a modified version of the "divine recognition formula," found frequently in Ezekiel and Zechariah (cf. Exod 6:7; 10:2; 16:12; Ezek 6:7, 13–14; 7:4; 11:10, 15:7; 16:22; 29:6, 9, 16; Zech 2:9; 4:9; 6:15). The essence of this formula is the declaration "you will know that I am YHWH," which frequently follows a description of what YHWH has done on behalf of his people.[59] In the case of Joel, this formula indicates that YHWH will fulfill the promises made in this passage. Essentially, the people experience YHWH's presence through the renewed fertility of the land as famine turns into feasting. This provides an opportunity for tactile learning in which Israel can literally "taste and see" that YHWH is present.

Joel modifies the formula by inserting the claim that YHWH is in the midst of his people (2:27b) prior to the declaration that he is the God (2:27c). This again suggests an intentional inversion of crises from 1:2–2:17. Joel 1:15–20 concludes with an unanswered cry, suggesting that YHWH is not among his people, while 2:1–11 goes further and reveals that YHWH leads an invader against Zion. The modified divine recognition formula thus emphasizes that now YHWH is among them, working to deliver them from despair.

After the declaration of YHWH's presence, 2:27c–d continues with the divine recognition formula as YHWH stakes his claim to his people and stresses his incomparability. Joel places extra emphasis on revealing that YHWH is the speaker by repeating the first-person pronoun אֲנִי. This pronoun concludes 2:27b, operating as the subject of the phrase בְּקֶרֶב יִשְׂרָאֵל ("in the midst of Israel"). It is then the first word of 2:27c, introducing YHWH's declaration of his status as אֱלֹהֵיכֶם ("your God"). The short phrase וְאֵין עוֹד ("there is no other") in 2:27d then emphasizes YHWH's unique status. Again, YHWH links himself to his people as his presence in their midst reinforces his commitment.

Joel 2:27e concludes with a phrase summarizing the results of YHWH's renewed presence. YHWH promises וְלֹא־יֵבֹשׁוּ עַמִּי לְעוֹלָם ("and my people will never again be put to shame"). This same phrase is also found in 2:26d. While some suggest dittography, it is more plausible that this is deliberate

---

55. Crenshaw, *Joel*, 159.
56. Joel 2:26 ends with a final summation indicating that YHWH's people will not be put to shame. I will discuss it in greater detail below since it is repeated at the end of Joel 2:27.
57. Ogden and Deutsch, *Joel & Malachi*, 26.
58. Assuming a postexilic date for this book, Israel here is a generic reference to the people of YHWH whom I have referred to as the Judahite community throughout this commentary.
59. Prinsloo, *Theology*, 74–75; Dillard, "Joel," 292.

repetition, celebrating YHWH's promises.⁶⁰ It also calls to mind the conclusion of 1:15–20, where 1:19 and 20 both concluded with identical phrases. In both cases, these phrases are set at the end of their respective passages and encapsulate the content.⁶¹ YHWH's claim that the Judahite community is עַמִּי ("my people") is significant. It contrasts with the use of the first-person singular suffix in 2:25, where YHWH referred to the locusts as חֵילִי ("my army"). YHWH's orientation toward the Judahite community has changed and they are now "my people," who are called to worship "YHWH your God."

This final repeated summary statement in 2:26 and 2:27 also answers the challenges raised in 2:12–17. Joel has urged the people to plead with YHWH so that they will not become a reproach among the nations. While Joel does not provide evidence that the people obeyed his commands, he envisions a scenario in which YHWH responds to their cries. Joel assures his audience that YHWH will not let them be put to shame, which provides confidence that he is acting on their behalf. This statement provides the desired answer to the rhetorical question "where is their God?" in 2:17. Joel 2:18–27 declares and describes YHWH's zeal and compassion, culminating with the assurance that YHWH is present in their midst, which guarantees that they will no longer be ashamed. One commentator eloquently states, "what was a mere hope in the previous pericope is now realized, the 'perhaps' of 2:14 has been fulfilled; the prayer has been heard."⁶² This renewed commitment between YHWH and his people is worthy of celebration.

Canonical and Practical Significance

The Fertility of the Land

Joel 2:18–27 returns us to the broader motif of the land mirroring the relationship between YHWH and Israel. When YHWH was silent or promising judgment in 1:2–2:17, locusts, fires, and an invading army turned the land into a desolate wasteland. Now, YHWH's renewed commitment to his people results in the land bearing abundant fruit. These images are rooted in the covenant blessings and curses. Obedience is linked to fertility, prosperity, and victory, while disobedience leads to opposite outcomes. The same considerations that shape our reading of 1:15–20 are germane to 2:18–27 since the return of rainfall is necessary for the covenant blessings to come to fruition (Lev 26:4; Deut 28:12). Meanwhile, the absence of rain reflects YHWH's displeasure with his people (Lev 26:18–20; Deut 28:23–24).

Deuteronomy 11:13–15 bears close resemblance to the use of the rainfall motif in *Joel*. It promises that if Israel obeys YHWH's commands to love and serve him wholeheartedly, YHWH will respond by providing rain in the appropriate seasons. Deuteronomy 11:14 uses יוֹרֶה וּמַלְקוֹשׁ to refer to the early and latter rains, which

---

60. Wolff, *Joel and Amos*, 56. Wolff claims the phrase originally was found only in Joel 2:27. Barton remains on the fence, suggesting that it could be dittography, but it produces a rhetorically pleasing effect (Barton, *Joel*, 90).

61. Thompson, "Use of Repetition," 107. See also Wendland, *Discourse Analysis*, 50.

62. Prinsloo, *Theology*, 76.

parallels the terminology in *Joel*. The result of this rainfall is that Israel will be able to gather in its grain, new wine, and oil, which are the products that YHWH promises to restore in 2:18–27. Further, Deut 11:15 reveals that the restoration of these products will permit Israel to eat and be satisfied, using the same verbs found in YHWH's promise in Joel 2:26. Joel's promises of YHWH's provision thus resonate with covenantal language of blessing and cursing.[63] This suggests that turning to YHWH as Joel commands in 2:12–17 provides the opportunity for YHWH to reciprocate and demonstrate his turn to his people through signs of divine blessing.

Deuteronomy 8:10–14 takes a different tack and warns of potential dangers living in the midst of bounty. After discussing YHWH's provision in leading Israel into a fertile land, Deut 8:10 informs the people וְאָכַלְתָּ וְשָׂבָעְתָּ ("you will eat and be satisfied"), using the same verbs found in Joel 2:26. Deuteronomy 8:11–14 goes on, however, to warn against complacency, where Israel forgets the supplier of these riches.[64] In the wake of calamity, the hope of renewed fertility is inextricably linked to the work of YHWH. This passage shows the danger of taking for granted YHWH's gift of the good land. The promise of satiation is desperately needed in the context of *Joel*, and the prophet goes to great lengths to emphasize that YHWH has made it possible.

The presence of agricultural produce or its lack is a common theme in prophetic literature.[65] Hosea 2 personifies the land of Israel as YHWH's wife and uses this combination of images to show both blessing and curse. In Hos 2:10–11[2:8–9], Israel does not recognize that its grain, new wine, and oil come from YHWH, which results in YHWH removing them. Later, Hos 2:23–25[2:21–23] looks toward a future in which YHWH draws Israel back to himself, which will yield renewed agricultural prosperity. In a series of escalating curses, Amos 4:6–11 invokes images of hunger, withheld rain, and destroyed crops in an attempt to cause Israel to recognize its sins. The lack of rain means that Israel would not be satisfied (Amos 4:8), which is the opposite of what Joel promises. As the situation worsens, YHWH repeatedly laments "you have not returned to me" (Amos 4:6, 8, 9, 10, 11), which means that the curses must continue. In contrast, Joel 2:18–27 reflects a scenario in which Israel does "return to YHWH" in response to the prophet's pleading in 2:12–17. Amos thus provides a warning of what happens when Israel fails to heed a call to repentance. Images of agricultural productivity and fertility give way to increasing devastation.[66]

Joel 2:18–27 thus taps into some of the richest images of the covenant relationship between YHWH and his people. YHWH promises to Israel through Abraham land,

---

63. Allen, *Joel*, 92–93.
64. Assis, *Book of Joel*, 195.
65. Nogalski, *Book of the Twelve*, 236.
66. It is fascinating to note that when Amos finally turns to hope, he casts it in terms of renewed fertility. Amos 9:13–15 gives images of such overwhelming abundance that the people cannot even harvest all of it. The impetus for Amos' restoration is slightly different in that it is set after a time of punishment, when YHWH chooses to restore Israel, using the synecdoche of the house of David. The people may not have explicitly returned to YHWH, but eventually he promises to restore them.

relationship, and descendants. As YHWH interacts with Abraham's descendants, he uses the state of the land as a barometer of the relationship. Joel 2:18–27 gives the hopeful side of the equation as the people's return to YHWH prompts YHWH's return, which is celebrated in the calls to celebrate as the land pours forth its bounty.

In their biblical theology of creation care, Douglas and Jonathan Moo use YHWH's zeal in Joel 2:18 in response to the people's return in 2:12–13 to ask "what might such repentance, cries for God's mercy, and a return to justice and righteousness mean in our day for ourselves, our societies and the earth itself?"[67] As mentioned in the Canonical and Practical Significance of 1:15–20, believers who are found all over the globe cannot draw a simple link between the state of their own land and God's pleasure or displeasure. However, the church can model careful stewardship of the resources that God has granted and call on surrounding societies and countries to do the same. This is in keeping with the creational mandate given to humanity and could provide a way to speak prophetically to the ecological challenges that the world faces.

The Presence of YHWH

Joel 2:27 uses a well-known divine recognition formula, promising that Israel will know that YHWH is its God. This knowledge comes in the wake of YHWH's actions on behalf of his people. Joel modifies the formula slightly by inserting the expression "I am in the midst of Israel." This expansion is a form of reassurance that is necessary after YHWH's evident absence in the first half of the book. YHWH's leadership of an invading army starkly contrasts the assurance found in passages including hymns of Zion in Pss 46 and 48 that promise that YHWH dwells in his temple. Assis sets Joel's promise of YHWH's presence against passages that presume it.[68] Micah 3:11 recounts the moral failures of Israel's leaders while they blithely ask, "Is not YHWH in our midst?" Jeremiah similarly challenges the confidence of the people in YHWH's presence when they oppress the widow, the orphan, and the foreigner (Jer 7:4–8).

The assumptions of YHWH's presence are shattered in the wake of the trauma of exile. The most poignant image is that of the departure of YHWH's glory from Zion in Ezek 10:18–19. If YHWH's glory can depart, then the growing number of crises in Joel 1:2–2:17, YHWH's silence and ultimately the question "where is their God?" (Joel 2:17), take on increasing urgency. Is YHWH absent? Will catastrophe overtake his people? Will the mockery of the nations be proved true? In response, YHWH provides fantastic promises of his presence. The restoration of the land and the destruction of the invader permit Israel to know once again that YHWH dwells among them.

---

67. Douglas J. Moo and Jonathan A. Moo, *Creation Care: A Biblical Theology of the Natural World* (Grand Rapids: Zondervan, 2018), 111.

68. Assis, *Book of Joel*, 191–92.

Joel 2:27 also declares that the audience will know that "I am YHWH your God, there is no other." The Judahite community acquires this knowledge in the context of God's actions on their behalf. In Exod 6:7, YHWH reveals to Moses that the people will know that he is their God when he delivers them from Egypt's yoke (cf. Exod 29:46; Deut 5:6). Isaiah 45 stresses YHWH's unique standing as he asserts his claim over the entire created order. This chapter reveals that Cyrus is only a tool of YHWH and promises release for his people. Punctuating YHWH's claims of authority is the repeated statement "I am YHWH" (Isa 45:5, 6, 14, 18, 21, 22). Ezekiel looks to a time when Israel will know that YHWH is their God when he brings them back out of captivity and into their own land (Ezek 28:26; 39:28–29).[69] Zechariah looks ahead to YHWH's salvation of Judah on account of his compassion (Zech 10:6). This confirms that YHWH is their God and that he has not rejected them. When YHWH acts on behalf of his people it confirms the reality of the covenant and allows Israel to know again the nature of its God.

The Judahite community's knowledge that YHWH is its God entails certain obligations. Declaring that he is its God and that he brooks no rivals stresses the exclusive nature of the relationship. Both iterations of the Decalogue begin with YHWH's declaration that he is its God who brought them out of slavery (Exod 20:2; Deut 5:6). Consequently, the Judahite community is to have no other gods before him and must not bow down to any images because YHWH is a jealous God (Exod 20:3–5, Deut 5:7–9). This linkage between YHWH's claim to be its God and its reciprocal commitment to him continues throughout the Pentateuch. "I am YHWH your God" also occurs multiple times throughout Leviticus, including seven occurrences in Lev 19 alone (Lev 19:3, 4, 10, 25, 21, 34, 36). As YHWH teaches his people how to be holy, he continually reminds his people that he is their God. The assurances of YHWH's presence ultimately require his people to respond in covenantal obedience.

YHWH's Zeal and Compassion

Ultimately, the meaning of this passage takes its cue from the initial two verbs in 2:18 that confirm YHWH's zeal and compassion for his people. The outpouring of YHWH's power and the affirmation of his presence are rooted in these aspects of the divine character. In the wake of Joel's call to cry out to YHWH in 2:12–17, this passage calls us once again to trust in the commitment of God to his people. Joel establishes God alone as the source of deliverance, reversing crises that God's people could not address in their own strength.[70] Joel makes God the active agent of this entire passage, while he calls the people of YHWH simply to rejoice and celebrate as they see the power of God at work. Paul later calls the church to have similar confi-

---

69. See Wolff, *Joel and Amos*, 65.   70. Baker, *Joel*, 111.

dence that nothing can possibly separate God from his people (Rom 8:38–39). This is always a welcome reassurance for the people of God. Even when crises arise, Joel's announcement of God's zeal and compassion rings true. Trusting in the zealous and compassionate God also calls God's people to rely on his strength. In a society that worships at the altar of self-help and self-reliance, acknowledging God's authority is a necessary gesture of humility. The God who sees the desperate plight of Israel in Joel remains the same God who promises a passionate commitment to his people.

CHAPTER 7

Joel 3:1–5[2:28–32]

G. Deliverance through the Spirit of YHWH

Main Idea of the Passage

Joel 3:1–5[2:28–32] promises spiritual renewal through an outpouring of YHWH's spirit that matches the physical restoration described in the previous passage. This renewal continues to build hope that the people will find deliverance rather than destruction during the day of YHWH.

Literary Context

Along with 2:18–27, this passage is the other place where Joel appears to make a dramatic break with preceding material. Joel 3:1–5[2:28–32] moves away from the concerns surrounding the locust invasion, the devastation of the land and their remedy. Instead this passage promises an outpouring of YHWH's spirit and hope for rescue on the day of YHWH. However, 3:1–5[2:28–32] also displays significant continuity with earlier passages by redressing the fractured relationship between YHWH and his people. The broken sacrificial system in 1:9, 13, YHWH's silence in the wake of the prophet's cries in 1:19–20, and his leadership of the assault on Zion in 2:10–11 all indicate a severed connection. Now, as YHWH pours out his spirit in abundance, Joel celebrates the restoration of this relationship.

Joel 3:1–5[2:28–32] is also a necessary counterpart to 2:18–27. While the latter focuses on a restoration of material prosperity, the former emphasizes a renewal of the spiritual connection between YHWH and his people. This juxtaposition provides a fuller picture of the turn that YHWH has taken toward the Judahite community (cf. 2:12–14).[1] Joel 2:26–27 argues that YHWH's provision is a sign of his presence,

---

1. Moore connects the combination of material and spiritual restoration here to other texts that note a relationship between the activity of God's spirit and creation/recreation (Gen 1:2; Pss 33:5; 104:30; Isa 32:15). From this list, Isa 32:15 resonates most closely with Joel 2:18–27 and 3:1–5 [2:28–32] since the larger oracle of Isa 32:9–20 moves from judgment conveyed through images of material destruction to restoration by God's spirit that is accompanied by renewed material prosperity. See Erika

which is reinforced by the promised outpouring of the divine spirit in 3:1–2[2:28–29]. Not only will YHWH satisfy the need for sustenance and security, he will provide continued intermediation through the presence of his spirit. The renewed connection between YHWH and his people culminates with yet another mention of the day of YHWH in 3:4[2:31], which explicitly provides hope that Judah will be spared its devastation.

> A. Superscription (1:1)
> B. Despair on Account of the Locusts (1:2–14)
> C. Despair in the Day of YHWH—The Drought (1:15–20)
> D. Despair in the Day of YHWH—The Invasion (2:1–11)
> E. Hinge: The Call to Return to YHWH (2:12–17)
> F. Divine Deliverance from the Locusts and Drought (2:18–27)
> **G. Deliverance through the Spirit of YHWH (3:1–5 [2:28–32])**
>   **1. YHWH's Gift of the Spirit (3:1–2 [2:28–29])**
>   **2. The Signs of the Day of YHWH (3:3–4 [2:30–31])**
>   **3. Security in Zion (3:5 [2:32])**
> H. Deliverance through Divine Judgment on the Day of YHWH (4:1–21 [3:1–21])

Translation and Outline

(See pages 136.)

Structure and Literary Form

Joel 3:1–5[2:28–32] begins with the phrase וְהָיָה אַחֲרֵי־כֵן ("and it will happen after this"). This is the only occurrence of this particular construction in the OT. There is some debate concerning the relationship between 3:1–5[2:28–32] and 2:18–27 created by this unique expression.[2] Some focus on the logical connection between material and spiritual restoration, suggesting that the events in these passages unfold simultaneously.[3] The outpouring of the divine spirit in 3:1–5[2:28–32] thus directly and immediately complements the material blessings and renewed relationship with

---

Moore, "Joel's Promise of the Spirit," in *Presence, Power, and Promise: The Role of the Spirit of God in the Old Testament*, ed. David G. Firth and Paul D. Wegner (Downers Grove, IL: IVP Academic; 2011), 250.

2. On the semantic function of phrases beginning with וְהָיָה, see *BHRG* §40.24.

3. Willem A. VanGemeren, "The Spirit of Restoration," *WTJ* 50 (1988): 84–87. He looks at Isa 1:26 and comments on the promised restoration of judges and counselors that will be followed "after this" (אַחֲרֵי־כֵן), by a declaration of the people's righteousness. He suggests that the logical connection between the people's behavior and the restoration of their leaders is more important than the temporal sequence of these events.

Joel 3:1–5[2:28–32]

G. Deliverance Through the Spirit of YHWH (3:1–5[2:28–32])

1. YHWH's Gift of the Spirit (3:1–2)
   a. The Introductory Formula (3:1a)
   b. The Outpouring of YHWH's Spirit (3:1b–2b)

1a	וְהָיָה אַחֲרֵי־כֵן	It will happen after this:
1b	אֶשְׁפּוֹךְ אֶת־רוּחִי עַל־כָּל־בָּשָׂר	"I will pour out my spirit upon all flesh,
1c	וְנִבְּאוּ בְּנֵיכֶם וּבְנוֹתֵיכֶם	and your sons and your daughters will prophesy.
1d	זִקְנֵיכֶם חֲלֹמוֹת יַחֲלֹמוּן	Your elders will dream dreams,
1e	בַּחוּרֵיכֶם חֶזְיֹנוֹת יִרְאוּ׃	your young men will see visions.
2a	וְגַם עַל־הָעֲבָדִים וְעַל־הַשְּׁפָחוֹת בַּיָּמִים הָהֵמָּה	Even upon male and female servants in those days,
2b	אֶשְׁפּוֹךְ אֶת־רוּחִי׃	I will pour out my spirit.

2. The Signs of the Day of YHWH (3:3–4)

3a	וְנָתַתִּי מוֹפְתִים בַּשָּׁמַיִם וּבָאָרֶץ	I will give signs in the heavens and the earth—
3b	דָּם וָאֵשׁ וְתִימֲרוֹת עָשָׁן׃	blood, fire, and pillars of smoke.
4a	הַשֶּׁמֶשׁ יֵהָפֵךְ לְחֹשֶׁךְ	The sun will be turned to darkness
4b	וְהַיָּרֵחַ לְדָם	and the moon to blood,
4c	לִפְנֵי בּוֹא יוֹם יְהוָה הַגָּדוֹל וְהַנּוֹרָא׃	before the coming of the great and terrible day of YHWH."

3. Security in Zion (3:5)

5a	וְהָיָה	And it will happen,
5b	כֹּל אֲשֶׁר־יִקְרָא בְּשֵׁם יְהוָה יִמָּלֵט	[that] all who call upon the name of YHWH will escape.
5c	כִּי בְּהַר־צִיּוֹן וּבִירוּשָׁלַ͏ִם תִּהְיֶה פְלֵיטָה	For upon Mount Zion and in Jerusalem there will be an escaped group,
5d	כַּאֲשֶׁר אָמַר יְהוָה	just as YHWH said,
5e	וּבַשְּׂרִידִים	including the survivors,
5f	אֲשֶׁר יְהוָה קֹרֵא׃	whom YHWH is calling.

YHWH in 2:18–27. However, this introductory phrase likely functions as a sequential indicator, which would suggest that the events mentioned in 3:1–5[2:28–32] follow the restoration of 2:18–27.[4] The gift of material restoration is then the first stage, which YHWH then supplements with the outpouring of his spirit. Other occurrences of אַחֲרֵי־כֵן ("after this") signify temporal sequence (Gen 41:31; 1 Sam 24:9[8]; 2 Sam 2:1; 2 Chr 20:35; Jer 16:16; 34:11).[5] A similar introduction is found in Isa 2:2 (cf. Mic 4:1) that reads וְהָיָה בְּאַחֲרִית הַיָּמִים ("It will be after the days), which commentators typically take to indicate temporal progression as Isaiah looks to the future to envision a time of idyllic peace.[6] This expression, like the one in Joel 3:1[2:28], is introduced by וְהָיָה and contains a form of אַחֲרֵי. It suggests that the phrase in Joel 3:1[2:28] also indicates temporal progression.[7]

Ultimately, it is unnecessary to maintain a hard and fast distinction between the logical and sequential approaches. Instead, the outpouring of the spirit and the heavenly shaking that occurs in 3:1–5[2:28–32] are "subsequent to, as well as consequent upon, the foregoing blessings."[8] YHWH's guarantee of material restoration in 2:18–27 thus lays the foundation for spiritual renewal. Given the crises faced by the Judahite community, it is impossible to imagine one form of restoration without the other.

Following the introductory phrase, Joel 3:1–5[2:28–32] consists of three interrelated sub-units. An *inclusio*, employing YHWH's promise to pour out his spirit, is the defining feature of 3:1–2[2:28–29]. YHWH continues to speak in 3:3–4[2:30–31] and introduces upheaval in the cosmos that announces the day of YHWH. Joel 3:5[2:32] concludes this chapter by shifting the point of view and speaking about YHWH in the third person. It focuses on the hope of survival on the day of YHWH for those who call upon his name. Troxel notes that this verse summarizes the statements of 3:1–4 (2:28–31): the outpouring of the prophetic spirit (3:1–2[2:28–29]) leads the people to interpret the cosmological signs as evidence of the day of YHWH (3:3–4[2:30–31]), which should prompt them to call on the name of YHWH (3:5[2:32]).[9] The summarizing function of 3:5[2:32] signals the end of this passage. This is helpful since there is no obvious discourse marker of closure. The presence of another obvious introductory phrase in 4:1[3:1] and the abrupt shift in topic in that verse also indicates that this passage concludes in 3:5[2:32].

---

4. See for example Wolff, *Joel and Amos*, 58–59; Ahlström, *Joel*, 133; Finley, *Joel*, 77; Allen, *Joel*, 97–98.

5. VanGemeren, "Spirit," 84; Dillard, "Joel," 294.

6. See Joseph Blenkinsopp, *Isaiah 1–39*, AB 19 (New York: Doubleday, 2000), 190; Walter Brueggemann, *Isaiah 1–39*, Westminster Bible Companion (Louisville: Westminster John Knox, 1998), 23–34.

7. In the history of reception, Dillard notes that temporal succession is assumed when Acts 2:17 alludes to Joel 3:1–5 [2:28–32] since it introduces the prophecy with ἐν ταῖς ἐσχάταις ἡμέραις ("in the last days") rather than the LXX's more generic ἔσται μετὰ ταῦτα ("it will be after this"). See Dillard, "Joel," 294.

8. Simon J. De Vries, *From Old Revelation to New: A Tradition-History and Redaction-Critical Study of Temporal Transitions in Prophetic Prediction* (Grand Rapids: Eerdmans, 1995), 87.

9. Troxel, *Joel*, 74.

Explanation of the Text

1. YHWH's Gift of the Spirit (3:1–2[2:28–29])

Joel 3:1–2[2:28–29] focuses upon YHWH's promise to pour out his spirit, building upon the assurances of material prosperity and the removal of shame found in 2:18–27. The presence of YHWH's spirit means that the nations cannot look upon them with scorn as 2:17 warned. YHWH declares his intentions twice through the verb אֶשְׁפּוֹךְ ("I will pour out") in 3:1b and 2b[2:28b and 29b]. This creates an *inclusio* and re-emphasizes YHWH's agency in responding to his people.[10] The use of first-person verbs in 2:18–27 stresses YHWH's commitment to restoring their material situation, which is matched here by YHWH's initiative in rebuilding the spiritual connection with his people.

Within the *inclusio* framework, 3:1–2[2:28–29] discusses the impact of the outpouring of YHWH's spirit. The focus is on the magnitude of the outpouring, which is revealed when YHWH lists different types of spirit-filled responses. There are three different types of intermediation described in 3:1c–e[2:28c–e], as Joel uses three different verbs to describe what the recipients of YHWH's spirit will do: וְנִבְּאוּ ("will prophesy"), חֲלֹמוֹת יַחֲלֹמוּן ("will dream dreams"), and חֶזְיֹנוֹת יִרְאוּ ("will see visions"). The celebration of dreams and visions is consistent with other passages that portray these modes of intermediation positively (cf. Gen 28:12–17; 37:5–11; 40:8–23; 41:14–27; 1 Sam 28:6; Hos 12:11; Amos 7:1–8).[11] The promise of multiple modes of intermediation in Joel 3:1 stresses the magnitude of the gift of YHWH's spirit.

The other key element to YHWH's promise of his spirit is the range of people upon whom it falls. Joel 3:1b[2:28b] states that YHWH will pour out his spirit upon כָּל־בָּשָׂר ("all flesh"). This terms usually refers to all people without ethnic or geographical restrictions (Deut 5:26; Job 12:10; Isa 49:26; 66:16), or to all living beings (Gen 6:12, 13; 7:21; Num 18:15). Consequently, the magnitude of this outpouring of YHWH's spirit appears to know no human or geographical limitations. However, most argue that כָּל־בָּשָׂר here only refers to an outpouring of YHWH's spirit among the Judahite audience.[12] This argument depends upon the surrounding context of 3:1–5[2:28–32] since there are few occasions where the intended referents of this phrase are restricted (cf. Jer 12:12).[13] Support for this approach comes from Joel's use of second-person pronominal suffixes in 3:1c–e[2:28c–e]. YHWH declares that the outpouring of his spirit will cause בְּנֵיכֶם וּבְנוֹתֵיכֶם ("your sons and your daughters") to prophesy, while זִקְנֵיכֶם ("your elders") and בַּחוּרֵיכֶם ("your young men") will dream and see visions. The implied antecedent of the second-person

---

10. Thompson, "Use of Repetition," 103; David Marcus, "Nonrecurring Doublets in the Book of Joel," *CBQ* 56 (1994): 61.

11. The Old Testament does portray dreams and divination as invalid modes of intermediation (cf. Jer 23:25–26; 27:9; 29:8; Zech 10:2). However, the negative judgment is not on the mode itself. It is a result of a false claim to be an intermediary or from an attempt to manipulate the spiritual realm. First Samuel 28 offers a useful test case. Saul's fear of the Philistines leads him to inquire of YHWH who does not answer "by dreams or Urim or prophets" (1 Sam 28:6). YHWH's silence leads Saul to attempt to illegitimately acquire knowledge from the spiritual realm by consulting a medium (1 Sam 28:8–10). YHWH can employ a number of valid modes of intermediation, but the attempt to force communication from a silent YHWH is worthy of condemnation.

12. Examples include Assis, *Book of Joel*, 202–4; Dillard, "Joel," 295; Crenshaw, *Joel*, 165; Allen, *Joel*, 98; Wolff, *Joel and Amos*, 67.

13. Strazicich, *Joel's Use of Scripture*, 209. Jeremiah 12:12 occurs in the context of YHWH pronouncing judgment against Judah. In this instance, כָּל־בָּשָׂר likely refers to the totality of the devastation that YHWH will bring against it.

pronominal suffixes is the Judahite community, the people who receive this prophecy.

Other support for limiting the scope of YHWH's spirit to Judah is found in Ezek 39:29, where YHWH promises to שָׁפַכְתִּי ("pour out") his spirit upon the house of Israel when they return from exile, using the same verb found in Joel 3:1–2[2:28–29] (cf. Isa 32:15; 44:1–5; Zech 12:10).[14] Block argues that in Ezek 39:29 "[T]he poured-out Spirit represents Yahweh's mark of ownership," which guarantees the continuation of his covenant relationship with his people.[15] The covenantal association of this expression in Ezekiel thus supports limiting its scope in Joel 3:1–2[2:28–29] to a Judahite audience. Joel's use of כָּל־בָּשָׂר as opposed to a term like "house of Israel" may suggest that all members of community can receive the spirit, including those servants who may not be ethnically Judahite.[16] When announcing deliverance from the day of YHWH, Joel 3:5[2:32] differentiates between those who call on the name of YHWH and those who do not, which suggests that not everyone receives YHWH's spirit. Consequently, if כָּל־בָּשָׂר is universalized in Joel 3:1[2:28], then it would be out of step with the division between those who call on the name of YHWH and those who do not in 3:5[2:32].

Within these ethnic boundaries, Joel's focus is on the tremendous scope of the outpouring of YHWH's spirit. Joel 3:1c–e[2:28c–e] emphasizes its comprehensiveness through two occurrences of *merismus*. The first indicates YHWH's gift of the spirit is for both men and women since it comes upon both the sons and daughters of the Judahite community. The second is generational, promising that both the elders and the young men of the community will manifest the presence of YHWH's spirit.[17] Joel 3:2a extends the outpouring of YHWH's spirit even further by claiming that it affects even those of low social standing since it will come עַל־הָעֲבָדִים וְעַל־הַשְּׁפָחוֹת ("upon male and female servants"). This encompasses the entire social order, while again emphasizing access for both genders since servants are included as "marginal members," in the kinship structure that makes them part of the community of YHWH-worshipers (Deut 5:12–15; 16:11, 14).[18] Interestingly, there is no second-person pronominal suffix on the reference to the servants, which probably indicates that non-Judahite servants can also receive YHWH's spirit.[19] Ultimately, the purpose of 3:1–2[2:28–29] is to establish the contours of "all flesh". Joel mentions all of these sub-groups in order to indicate that everyone within the Judahite community has access to the outpouring of YHWH's spirit.

2. The Signs of the Day of YHWH (3:3–4[2:30–31])

Joel 3:3–4[2:30–31] ties YHWH's gift of the spirit to warning signs of cosmic upheaval that again announce the day of YHWH. The verb וְנָתַתִּי ("I will give") indicates that YHWH continues to

---

14. Assis pursues the connection even farther and sees in Joel a restatement of the Ezek 37 prophecy to the dry bones. Joel uses the phrase כָּל־בָּשָׂר ("all flesh") to match the בָּשָׂר ("flesh") that clothes the Judahite community in Ezek 37:6 when Ezekiel's prophecy reanimates them. See Assis, *Book of Joel*, 203.

15. Daniel I. Block, *The Book of Ezekiel: Chapters 25–48*, NICOT (Grand Rapids: Eerdmans, 1998), 488.

16. Strazicich, *Joel's Use of Scripture*, 210.

17. Prinsloo, *Theology*, 81. This echoes the *merismus* used to urge the whole community, from elders to children, to cry to YHWH in Joel 2:16. Joel 3:2 [2:29] uses a different term for youths (בַּחוּרֵיכֶם), but its function is to complement the use of elders (cf. Deut 32:25; Ps 148:12).

18. For the sociology of the family unit, see Shunya Bendor, *The Social Structure of Ancient Israel: The Institution of the Family (beit 'ab) From the Settlement to the End of the Monarchy*, JBS 7 (Jerusalem: Simor, 1996) 230–32. On the protection that these marginal members were to receive within the family unit, see Block, "Marriage and Family," 58–60.

19. Strazicich, *Joel's Use of Scripture*, 211–12.

speak.[20] YHWH now promises מוֹפְתִים ("signs") in the heavens and the earth that announce the imminent day of YHWH, which he then identifies as blood, fire, and columns of cloud. The keyword מוֹפְתִים resonates with the Exodus plagues (cf. Exod 7:14–24; 10:21–29), since around half of its occurrences are found in those narratives or in later reflection upon them.[21] However, the promised outpouring of the spirit mitigates their terrifying nature for the Judahite community. Strazicich captures the effect of the Exodus allusions, stating "the resignification of Yahweh's great power, exerted for purpose of freeing the Israelites from the power of the Egyptians, is now recontextualized into Yahweh freeing the Judeans from foreign powers."[22]

Joel 3:4a–b[2:31a–b] then directs these signs toward the coming of the day of YHWH by creatively re-interpreting its announcement in 2:10–11. Both 2:10 and 3:4a–b[2:31a–b] announce that the heavenly bodies will grow dark in anticipation of the day of YHWH. Joel emphasizes the parallel between 2:11 and 3:4c[2:31c], in both cases referring to the day of YHWH as הַגָּדוֹל וְהַנּוֹרָא ("great and terrible"). This shared description takes on a radically different connotation in 3:4[2:31] since it follows the promise of YHWH's spirit rather than an announcement of YHWH leading an assault against Zion. Joel returns to the day of YHWH, reusing language that reminds his audience that YHWH can shake the cosmos, but provides a context where it offers hope rather than despair. The outpouring of YHWH's spirit transforms the meaning of the day of YHWH, even though its signs remain the same. This transition provides the foundation for the promise of rescue found in Joel 3:5[2:32].

3. Security in Zion (3:5[2:32])

Joel 3:5[2:32] builds upon the portents of the day of YHWH and further emphasizes the shift in context from 2:10–11. Joel 2:11 concluded with the despairing rhetorical question "who can endure it?" In response, 3:5[2:32] provides hope for escape. In this verse, the prophet summarizes YHWH's declarations. Joel 3:5a[2:32a] marks the shift through the introductory phrase וְהָיָה כֹּל אֲשֶׁר־יִקְרָא ("and it will be that all who call"). This phrase is a discourse marker that concludes literary units by means of the arrangement "wĕhāyâ + Noun Phrase + yiqtol." There are thirty-five uses of this construction in the OT, thirty of which are found at the end of a speech unit and introduce consequences or logical inferences from the preceding speech.[23] This demonstrates the coherence of Joel 3:1–5[2:28–32], and it suggests that the purpose of Joel 3:5 is for the prophet to work out the implications of YHWH's speech in Joel 3:1–4[2:28–31].

The first implication that Joel reveals is that all who call upon the name of YHWH will escape the terrifying cosmological phenomena that signal the day of YHWH. Similar to 3:1[2:28], the interpretation of "all" in 3:5b[2:32b] requires discussion. Since the reference to "all flesh" in 3:1[2:28] probably has ethno-religious restrictions, it is reasonable to suppose the same limitations apply here. Further, the concept of "calling on the name of YHWH" denotes worship, restricting the likely

---

20. YHWH remains the speaker through Joel 3:4, even though it refers to the "day of YHWH" in the third person. It is a fixed, technical expression that does not need to be modified (cf. Ezek 13:5; 30:3; Mal 3:23).

21. Bergler directly connects the reference to מוֹפְתִים with the Exodus plagues, noting the plague of blood and the plague of darkness that Joel 3:3 activates (Bergler, *Joel als Schriftinterpret*, 268–73). Also see S. Wagner, "מוֹפֵת," *TDOT* 8:174–81. Wagner notes that nineteen of the thirty-six uses of this word are connected to the Exodus and the plagues.

22. Strazicich, *Joel's Use of Scripture*, 213.

23. Ronald L. Troxel, "Confirming Coherence in Joel 3 with Cognitive Grammar," *ZAW* 125 (2013): 579.

audience to the Judahite community (cf. Gen 12:8; 13:4; 21:33; 26:25; Exod 33:19; 34:5; 1 Kgs 18:24; Isa 12:4; Zeph 3:9; Zech 13:9). Within this range, some have argued that those who call on the name of YHWH represent a subset of the Judahite community.[24] However, after an extensive look at the semantic range of כֹּל, Troxel convincingly suggests that its use in 3:5[2:32] is intended to cover the same group as the כָּל־בָּשָׂר in 3:1[2:28].[25] He finds further support for this in Joel's summons in 1:5–14 and 2:16, which use the subsets of the audience as building blocks to address the entire community. Consequently, Joel has the full Judahite community in mind as recipients of this offer of deliverance from the terrifying signs of the day of YHWH.

Joel 3:5c[2:28c] highlights the Judah-centric emphasis of this passage by identifying the place of refuge as Mount Zion or Jerusalem. There are parallels between Joel's reference to sanctuary in Zion and Obad 17 (cf. Isa 4:2).[26] The first clause of Obad 17 declares that "on Mount Zion there will be an escaped group." The only difference between the occurrences of this phrase in the two books is that Obadiah omits Jerusalem as a phrase in parallel with Mount Zion. The day of YHWH informs both passages, with Obadiah explicitly casting judgment on a foreign nation (Edom) in Obad 18, while Joel 3:5c[2:32c] focuses on the existence of a group who can escape the day of YHWH. The association with Obad 17 and its judgment of Edom prefigures the judgment of the nations that occurs in Joel 4:1–20[3:1–20]. In 3:5[2:32], the day of YHWH rescues those who call on the name of YHWH while preparing the ground for the explicit judgment of foreign nations in the next chapter.

Joel 3:5c[2:32c] also returns to an expected use of the Zion tradition. Joel uses Zion here to indicate security and stability while the heavenly portents announce the day of YHWH.[27] Zion is the only location that provides refuge from the cosmos-rending power of the day of YHWH. Again, this reflects a significant contrast from the portrayal of the day of YHWH in 2:1–11. In that passage, YHWH leads the invading army against Zion, easily breaching its defenses and announcing destruction. In this passage Zion/Jerusalem is now an inviolable fortress into which YHWH is calling people to gather to escape the day of YHWH. Poulsen connects this picture of security to the trajectory from despair to deliverance throughout Joel. He suggests that the people can be secure "in their future salvation on Mount Zion and in Jerusalem. In other words, the preceding repentance, acknowledgment and outpouring of the spirit determine the salvation on Zion."[28]

This verse also links to the use of the day of YHWH in 2:1–11 through the reference to a פְּלֵיטָה ("escaped group"), which again refers to those who call on the name of YHWH. Joel 2:3 refers to the inability to escape the invading locust army whereas

---

24. Jorg Jeremias, "'Denn auf dem Berg Zion und in Jerusalem wird Rettung sein' (Joel 3:5): Zur Heilserwartung des Joelbuches," in *Zion-Ort der Begegnung: Festschrift für Laurentius Klein zur Vollendung des 65 Lebensjahres*, ed. F. Hahn et al. (Bodenheim: Hanstein, 1993), 41. See also Ahlström and Plöger who argue that "calling on the name of YHWH" implies that some may not do it correctly (Ahlström, *Joel*, 54–55; Otto Plöger, *Theocracy and Eschatology*, trans. S. Rudman [Richmond: John Knox, 1968], 125). Redditt suggests that the democratization of YHWH's spirit in this section reflects the book's growing disillusionment with priestly leadership (Redditt, "Book of Joel," 240–41). These suggestions depend on a different view of the literary unity of the book. They are also highly speculative since Joel's concern throughout the prophecy has been to unify the audience and have it respond together (Joel 1:5–14; 2:15–17).

25. Troxel, *Joel*, 75–81.

26. Sweeney, *Twelve*, 175; Crenshaw, *Joel*, 169. Some suggest that Joel uses a specific quotation formula following the reference to the escaped group. This group escapes כַּאֲשֶׁר אָמַר יְהוָה ("as YHWH has said"). This likely cites Obad 17 (Strazicich, *Joel's Use of Scripture*, 218–19; Wolff, *Joel and Amos*, 68).

27. Prinsloo, *Theology*, 87.

28. Poulsen, *Representing Zion*, 106.

in this case YHWH himself declares that some will survive. There is a hopeful progression here since the portrayal of the day of YHWH in 2:1–11 permits no escape whereas in 3:5d[2:28d], YHWH announces that there will be those who endure.

Joel strengthens the hope of deliverance in 3:5e-f[2:28e-f] with a reference to this group as שְׂרִידִים ("survivors") whom YHWH will call.[29] This word is found in parallel with the noun פְּלֵיטָה ("escaped group") on several occasions in the OT. Often, they are found in a negated form, emphasizing a total defeat (Josh 8:22; Jer 42:17; 44:14). The presence of survivors and an escaped group is significant in how Joel conceives of the day of YHWH. While this day continues to shake the heavens and the earth, 3:1–5[2:28–32] moves from the hopelessness of 2:1–11 to offer the possibility of survival to those who respond by crying out to YHWH. Joel thus "provides reassurance ... that salvation awaits those in Jerusalem, as the Lord has promised."[30] Although Joel does not give his audience any direct commands, the implicit suggestion is that they should call upon the name of YHWH in order to take advantage of this hope.

Summary

Joel 3:1–5[2:28–32] is the second unit in the trajectory toward hope that follows after the hinge of 2:12–17. This passage works in concert with 2:18–27, providing spiritual blessing through the outpouring of YHWH's spirit that matches the return to material prosperity. Joel 3:1–5[2:28–32] also continues to answer the mocking question "where is their God?" that concludes 2:17. Joel declares that YHWH is among his people, empowering them through his spirit. Further, 3:1–5[2:28–32] advances the portrayal of the day of YHWH. It shifts the primary target of the wrath from YHWH's own people to those who refuse to call upon his name. Consequently, Joel now indicates that those who do call upon the name of YHWH receive the promise of sanctuary during the day of YHWH, even as YHWH's power shakes the foundations of the cosmos.

Canonical and Practical Significance

The Promise of the Spirit

The promised outpouring of YHWH's spirit in this passage echoes other biblical literature in which this metaphor for the gift of YHWH's spirit is a sign of divine favor.[31] Isaiah 32:15–20 brings together the different arenas of restoration mentioned

---

29. In the Greek tradition, those who escape the destruction of the day of YHWH are called εὐαγγελιζόμενοι ("the ones receiving good news"). The underlying Hebrew would be ומבשרים. This is probably an erroneous reading, as the Aquila and Theodotion recensions read καὶ ἐν τοῖς καταλελειμμένοις, a participial form of the verb καταλειπω whose semantic range covers the idea "survivors" (cf. Gen 7:23; Num 21:35; Deut 2:34; Josh 23:4); Prinsloo, *Theology*, 81. Crenshaw observes that Peter's citation of this passage in Acts 2 does not use εὐαγγελιζόμενοι even though that would be an excellent fit with his proclamation of the good news of the resurrection (Crenshaw, *Joel*, 172).

30. Troxel, *Joel*, 98.

31. Another way to consider the gift of YHWH's spirit is to contrast this passage with those that discuss the absence of YHWH's presence. For example, 1 Sam 3:1 follows the announcement from an unnamed "man of God" that Eli's house will face judgment (1 Sam 2:27–36). This lays the groundwork for YHWH's silence, which elevates the status of Samuel when YHWH chooses to speak directly to him. One of the punishments for Israel's disobedience that Amos articulates is a famine of hearing the word of YHWH (Amos 8:11–12; cf. Jer 18:18; Ezek 7:26; Mic 3:6–7), which reflects a cessation of prophetic activity.

in Joel 2:18–27 and 3:1–5[2:28–32] as the outpouring of YHWH's spirit leads to fertility in the desert and the promise of YHWH's justice and righteousness. Similarly, Isa 44:1–5 links the outpouring of YHWH's spirit to a divine outpouring of water upon the arid landscape, which symbolizes a restored covenant between YHWH and his people. This is evident in the confident claim ליהוה אָנִי ("I belong to YHWH") in Isa 44:5.[32] Most notably, Ezekiel's use of the expression "pour out my spirit" was mentioned above in terms of limiting the recipients of YHWH's spirit to the Judahite community (Ezek 39:28–29). Ezekiel 39:28–29 and Joel 3:1–2[2:28–29] are also connected on a deeper thematic level since they both promise hope to follow disaster, rooted in the renewed presence of YHWH. Ezekiel 39 includes the revelation that YHWH hid his face on account of Judah's sins (Ezek 29:23–24), which brought them into disgrace (Ezek 39:26).[33] By pouring out his spirit, YHWH now "seals them as his covenant people," which guarantees his presence among them.[34] The trajectory from divine absence and shame to presence and restoration follows the pattern used by Joel. The question of YHWH's presence that Joel calls the people to ask in 2:17 is answered positively here as YHWH provides an endowment of his spirit, affirming their covenant relationship.

The outpouring of YHWH's spirit also resonates with Moses's desire to share the burden of leadership that prompts YHWH to provide the spirit to seventy elders in Num 11:10–30.[35] These elders gather around the tent of meeting and demonstrate that they have received the spirit through prophetic activity (Num 11:25). The connection between Num 11 and Joel 3:1–15[2:28–32] grows as the narrative discusses the case of the elders Eldad and Medad who prophesy away from the tent of meeting. Joshua perceives a threat to Moses's position on account of this apparently unauthorized manifestation of YHWH's spirit, but Moses responds by declaring his desire that all Israel would prophesy and receive the gift of YHWH's spirit (Num 11:29). Joel 3:1–5[2:28–32] offers a scenario in which Moses's wish could come to fruition. As part of the response to the threats faced in the first half of the book, Joel 3:1–5[2:28–32] reflects upon a key narrative from its past and builds upon Moses's desire for a universal manifestation of YHWH's spirit. This promise of YHWH's presence marks the transition of the day of YHWH from a day of destruction to a day of deliverance.

The discussion of the gift of the spirit then moves into the NT through its use in the opening stage of Peter's Pentecost sermon of Acts 2:14–21. This is a pivotal

---

32. Daniel I. Block, "The View from the Top: The Holy Spirit in the Prophets," in *Presence, Power, and Promise: The Role of the Spirit of God in the Old Testament*, ed. David G. Firth and Paul D. Wegner (Downers Grove, IL: IVP Academic; 2011), 202–3.

33. Strazicich, *Joel's Use of Scripture*, 208.

34. Block, "View," 205.

35. Dillard, "Joel," 294. Dillard notes a number of parallels between the two passages, including the fact that they share the same means of revelation and that the gift of the spirit is meant to be widely spread.

moment in the launch of the church since the gift of the Holy Spirit follows Christ's ascension and provides the apostles with the authority they require to fulfill the mandate that he gave them (Acts 1:8). After receiving this gift and facing both incredulity and mockery from the crowd in Jerusalem, Peter appeals to Joel 3:1–5[2:28–32] to explain what is unfolding. Through an explicit citation, Peter connects the gift of the Holy Spirit and the apostles' ability to communicate with the crowd in their own languages to the fulfillment of the hope of the widespread manifestation of the spirit found in Joel 3:1–5[2:28–32]. While signs like the darkening of the heavenly bodies are absent from the Pentecost event, the visible manifestation of God's spirit in the speech of the apostles provides confirmation for Peter's use of this citation.[36]

As the church expands throughout Acts, it is marked by further outpourings of the Holy Spirit. The gift of the Spirit marks each time the gospel advances and incorporates new groups into the covenant community. This includes the Samaritans (Acts 8:14–17), gentile proselytes such as Cornelius and his household (Acts 10:44–48), and even believers in Ephesus, many of whom would have no previous spiritual or ethnic connection of Jerusalem (Acts 19:6).[37] This sequence reveals that while the outpouring of the Holy Spirit that preceded that sermon appears to have taken place among the apostles and their Jewish audience (cf. Acts 2:5–21), it is not long afterwards that there is an unequivocal gifting of the Spirit to gentiles (cf. Acts 10:44–48), which stresses the universal promise of God's spirit. Consequently, all of the people who join God's new community receive the capacity to minister through the Spirit and carry the obligation to proclaim the good news of Jesus's resurrection.[38] This continues throughout the narrative of Acts and into the history of the church. Essentially, the fulfillment of Joel 3:1–5[2:28–32] happens in "slow motion," with the gift of the Holy Spirit being poured out upon each new believer, while the final manifestation of the apocalyptic signs awaits its ultimate fulfillment.[39]

Overall, the promise of the outpouring of YHWH's spirit in Joel 3:1–5[2:28–32] fits into a narrative of God's commitment to his people that can be traced throughout the canon. Block captures this connection, noting simply "[W]hen the divine *rûaḥ* (Spirit) acts, God acts."[40] The burden that Moses carried in leading the people through their grumbling and complaints caused YHWH to give an endowment of his spirit to elders in the community. This prompts Moses's fervent wish that this gift

---

36. Daniel J. Treier, "The Fulfillment of Joel 2:28–32: A Multiple-Lens Approach," *JETS* 40 (1997): 20–21. Trier has an informative discussion concerning how the eschatological signs found in Joel 3:1–5 fit into the context of Acts 2, suggesting that the best approach is to view them as an "advance typology," announcing the coming of the *eschaton* that has been inaugurated in anticipation of Christ's return.

37. Ibid." 23–24. See also Block, "View," 206.

38. Dillard, "Joel," 295. Dillard phrases it well, noting that "rich and poor, young and old, male and female; the privilege of proclaiming God's truth to a waiting world is not the province of the special office alone."

39. Robert B. Chisholm, *Handbook of the Prophets* (Grand Rapids: Baker, 2009), 374.

40. Block, "View," 207.

could be given to the entire nation. Later, in response to the cosmos-rending power of the day of YHWH, Joel prophesies that YHWH will pour out his spirit on the entire community in order to secure his covenant relationship with them. Peter's sermon in Acts then expresses that the outpouring of YHWH's spirit finds its manifestation in the Pentecost event. The spirit-fueled launch of the church is an indicator that YHWH is acting to secure for himself a new covenant community.

Joel 4:1–21[3:1–21]

H. Deliverance through Divine Judgment on the Day of YHWH

Main Idea of the Passage

Joel 4:1–21[3:1–21] provides further hope that YHWH will rescue his people by addressing external threats. This complements the promises of material and spiritual restoration found in 2:18–27 and 3:1–5[2:28–32]. This chapter gives the final answer to the question "where is their God?" asked by the nations in 2:17.

Literary Context

Joel 4:1–21[3:1–21] concludes the prophecy by further developing the hopeful trajectory begun in 2:18 with YHWH's promises of renewed material (2:18–27) and spiritual blessing (3:1–5[2:28–32]). The hopeful mood continues in 4:1[3:1] when YHWH makes the promise אָשׁוּב אֶת־שְׁבוּת ("I will restore the fortunes") of Judah and Jerusalem by addressing the threat posed by outside nations. This opens up a new line of thought since previously the focus of this book had been on renewing the relationship between YHWH and the Judahite community. Joel 1:2–3:5[2:32] mentions the nations only in passing and only in generic terms (Joel 2:6; 2:17). In contrast, Joel 4:1–21[3:1–21] refers to the nations as a collective and indicates that specific nations will face YHWH's judgment (Tyre, Sidon, Philistia, Egypt, and Edom). Even though these nations are not central to the text thus far, they serve an important purpose in its final act. Now that the internal relationship between YHWH and his people is on a hopeful footing, Joel addresses external challenges as a logical extension of YHWH's promises of restoration.

The means by which this new context is addressed involves expanding the audience. YHWH discusses the fate of the nations throughout this chapter, even addressing them directly through second-person verb forms in 4:4–8[3:4–8] and 4:9–11[3:9–11]. While there is no evidence that these foreign nations ever heard the oracles spoken against them, YHWH's announcements of judgment provide further promises of hope to the Judahite community.[1] This is made evident in 4:17[3:17] where Joel summarizes YHWH's actions against the nations as proof for the Judahite community to know that "YHWH your God" is acting on their behalf. Consequently, this section of the book addresses two audiences simultaneously.[2] The Judahite community witnesses the prophetic address to the nations, and it learns that YHWH's announcements of judgment are signs of hope.

Another element of the literary context of this passage is the reoccurrence of the day of YHWH in 4:14[3:14]. The language and imagery surrounding the day of YHWH is similar to the descriptions of it in 1:2–2:17, but its consequences are quite different. Joel 4:14[3:14] is the third occasion on which the day of YHWH is described as קָרוֹב ("near"). However, while Joel uses its nearness in 1:15 and 2:1 to prompt the Judahite audience to cry out to YHWH in hopes of alleviating catastrophe, in 4:14[3:14] the threat posed by the imminence of the day targets those hostile to YHWH and his people. The nearness of the day of YHWH now prompts thanksgiving rather than fear. Joel 4:15–16[3:15–16] also appropriates the imagery of the day of YHWH found in 2:10–11. In both passages, the celestial luminaries darken while the heavens and the earth shake. The order of events is reversed since in 4:15–16[3:15–16] the darkening of the luminaries precedes the trembling of the heavens and the earth. This coincides with the reversal of the context since Joel 2:10–11 reveals YHWH as the leader of the army assaulting Zion, while 4:15–16[3:15–16] promises YHWH's presence in Zion, which makes it a stronghold in which the Judahite community finds refuge. The literary context of Joel 4:1–21[3:1–21] thus interacts closely with earlier announcements of the day of YHWH, sharing vocabulary and imagery while reversing its significance.

---

1. Paul R. Raabe, "Why Prophetic Oracles Against the Nations?" in *Fortunate the Eyes that See: Essays in Honour of David Noel Freedman in Celebration of His Seventieth Birthday*, ed. Astrid B. Beck et al. (Grand Rapids: Eerdmans, 1995), 252. Raabe offers useful insight on the purpose of prophetic oracles against foreign nations, even suggesting the possibility that some oracles may have gone out into the wider world. He also highlights the injunction "so that they will know that I am YHWH" that concludes oracles against the nations in Ezekiel to suggest that part of the function of these oracles is to reveal YHWH to the nations. See Paul R. Raabe, "Transforming the International *Status Quo*: Ezekiel's Oracles Against the Nations," in *Transforming Vision: Transformations of Text, Tradition, and Theology in Ezekiel*, ed. William A. Tooman and Michael A. Lyons (Eugene: Pickwick, 2010), 187–207.

2. Block uses the term "hypothetical addressee" to refer to the foreign nation and "real addressee" to refer to the Judahite audience that hears the prophet's denunciations. See Block, *Obadiah*, 30.

- A. Superscription (1:1)
- B. Despair on Account of the Locusts (1:2–14)
- C. Despair in the Day of YHWH—The Drought (1:15–20)
- D. Despair in the Day of YHWH—The Invasion (2:1–11)
- E. Hinge: The Call to Return to YHWH (2:12–17)
- F. Divine Deliverance from the Locusts and Drought (2:18–27)
- G. Deliverance through the Spirit of YHWH (3:1–5 [2:28–32])
- **H. Deliverance through Divine Judgment on the Day of YHWH (4:1–21 [3:1–21])**
  - **1. The Introduction of YHWH's Judgment on the Nations (4:1–3 [3:1–3])**
  - **2. YHWH's Judgment on Tyre, Sidon, and Philistia (4:4–8 [3:4–8])**
  - **3. YHWH's Judgment on the Nations (4:9–17 [3:9–17])**
  - **4. YHWH's Restoration of Judah and Jerusalem (4:18–21 [3:18–21])**

Translation and Outline

(See pages 149–51.)

Structure and Literary Form

The structure and literary form of Joel 4:1–21[3:1–21] is shaped by references to the nations, both as a general entity and as specific people-groups. This passage can be dived into four subunits (4:1–3[3:1–3]; 4:4–8[3:4–8]; 4:9–17[3:9–17], and 4:18–21[3:18–21]), each of which bring a slightly different focus to the interplay between YHWH, Judah, and the nations. The first subunit is 4:1–3[3:1–3], which promises that YHWH will summon the nations to face divine judgment. It also provides the foundation for considering 4:1–21[3:1–21] as a single passage since the following three subunits develop themes that it introduces.[3] Joel 4:4–8[3:4–8] provides YHWH's response to Judah's enslavement described in 4:3[3:3], while 4:9–17[3:9–17] elaborates on YHWH's commitment in 4:2[3:2] to judge the nations in the Valley of Jehoshaphat. Finally, 4:18–21[3:18–21] employs vivid imagery to reveal what it would mean for YHWH to "restore the fortunes of Judah and Jerusalem" (4:1[3:1]).

The second subunit is 4:4–8[3:4–8], which adopts a confrontational tone, with YHWH speaking directly to specific nations who enslaved his people in 4:3[3:3]. YHWH promises that Tyre, Sidon, and Philistia will face judgment for their mistreatment of Judah and Jerusalem. Some consider these verses to be a later redactional

---

3. I am following Nogalski's division of Joel 4, though I do not subscribe to his theory that these reflect different "source blocks." See James Nogalski, "Where *Are* the Prophets in the Book of the Twelve?" in *The Book of the Twelve and the New Form Criticism*, ed. Mark J. Boda, Michael H. Floyd, and Colin M. Toffelmire, ANEM 10 (Atlanta: SBL Press, 2015), 175–76.

Joel 4:1–21[3:1–21]

H. Deliverance through Divine Judgment on the Day of YHWH (4:1–21[3:1–21])

1. The Introduction of YHWH's Judgment on the Nations (4:1–3)
   a. The Introductory Formula (4:1a)
   b. The Declaration of Intent (4:1b)
   c. YHWH's Place of Judgment (4:2a–b)
   d. The Reasons of Judgment (4:2c–3d)

1a	כִּי הִנֵּה בַּיָּמִים הָהֵמָּה וּבָעֵת הַהִיא	"For behold, in those days and at that time
1b	אֲשֶׁר אָשִׁיב אֶת־שְׁבוּת יְהוּדָה וִירוּשָׁלָ͏ִם:	when I restore the fortunes of Judah and Jerusalem,
2a	וְקִבַּצְתִּי אֶת־כָּל־הַגּוֹיִם	I will gather all nations
2b	וְהוֹרַדְתִּים אֶל־עֵמֶק יְהוֹשָׁפָט	and I will bring them to the valley of Jehoshaphat.
2c	וְנִשְׁפַּטְתִּי עִמָּם שָׁם עַל־עַמִּי וְנַחֲלָתִי יִשְׂרָאֵל	I will judge them there on behalf of my people and my inheritance, Israel,
2d	אֲשֶׁר פִּזְּרוּ בַגּוֹיִם	whom they scattered among the nations.
2e	וְאֶת־אַרְצִי חִלֵּקוּ:	My land, they divided.
3a	וְאֶל־עַמִּי יַדּוּ גוֹרָל	For my people, they cast lots.
3b	וַיִּתְּנוּ הַיֶּלֶד בַּזּוֹנָה	They exchanged the young men for prostitutes.
3c	וְהַיַּלְדָּה מָכְרוּ בַיַּיִן	The young women they sold for wine,
3d	וַיִּשְׁתּוּ:	and they drank it."

2. YHWH's Judgment on Tyre, Sidon, and Philistia (4:4–8)
   a. The Nations' Challenge (4:4)

4a	וְגַם מָה־אַתֶּם לִי צֹר וְצִידוֹן וְכֹל גְּלִילוֹת פְּלָשֶׁת	"Now, what are you to me, Tyre, Sidon, and all the regions of Philistia?
4b	הַגְּמוּל אַתֶּם מְשַׁלְּמִים עָלָי	Are you seeking a recompense against me?
4c	וְאִם־גֹּמְלִים אַתֶּם עָלַי	If you are paying me back,
4d	קַל מְהֵרָה אָשִׁיב גְּמֻלְכֶם בְּרֹאשְׁכֶם:	swiftly and speedily I will return your recompense upon your head.

   b. The Nations' Crimes (4:5–6)

5a	אֲשֶׁר־כַּסְפִּי וּזְהָבִי לְקַחְתֶּם	For my silver and my gold you have taken,
5b	וּמַחֲמַדַּי הַטֹּבִים הֲבֵאתֶם לְהֵיכְלֵיכֶם:	my good precious items you have brought into your temples.
6a	וּבְנֵי יְהוּדָה וּבְנֵי יְרוּשָׁלַ͏ִם מְכַרְתֶּם לִבְנֵי הַיְּוָנִים	The children of Judah and Jerusalem you sold to the children of Javan,
6b	לְמַעַן הַרְחִיקָם מֵעַל גְּבוּלָם:	in order to send them away from their borders.

   c. YHWH's Retributive Justice (4:7–8)

7a	הִנְנִי מְעִירָם מִן־הַמָּקוֹם אֲשֶׁר־מְכַרְתֶּם אֹתָם שָׁמָּה	Look, I am rousing them from the place where you sold them
7b	וַהֲשִׁבֹתִי גְמֻלְכֶם בְּרֹאשְׁכֶם:	I will return your recompense upon your head.
8a	וּמָכַרְתִּי אֶת־בְּנֵיכֶם וְאֶת־בְּנוֹתֵיכֶם בְּיַד בְּנֵי יְהוּדָה	I will sell your sons and daughters into the hands of the children of Judah,
8b	וּמְכָרוּם לִשְׁבָאיִם אֶל־גּוֹי רָחוֹק	and they will sell them to the Sabeans, to a nation far off."
8c	כִּי יְהוָה דִּבֵּר:	YHWH has spoken.

Continued on next page.

Continued from previous page.

			3. YHWH's Judgment on the Nations (4:9–17)
			a. The Summons to Battle (4:9a–11c)
9a	קִרְאוּ־זֹאת בַּגּוֹיִם	Proclaim this among the nations!	
9b	קַדְּשׁוּ מִלְחָמָה	Sanctify a battle!	
9c	הָעִירוּ הַגִּבּוֹרִים	Rouse the warriors!	
9d	יִגְּשׁוּ	Let draw near	
9e	יַעֲלוּ כֹּל אַנְשֵׁי הַמִּלְחָמָה׃	and go up all the men of battle!	
10a	כֹּתּוּ אִתֵּיכֶם לַחֲרָבוֹת	Beat your plowshares into swords,	
10b	וּמַזְמְרֹתֵיכֶם לִרְמָחִים	and your pruning hooks into spears!	
10c	הַחַלָּשׁ יֹאמַר	Let the weak say	
10d	גִּבּוֹר אָנִי׃	"I am a mighty man."	
11a	עוּשׁוּ	Hasten	
11b	וָבֹאוּ כָל־הַגּוֹיִם מִסָּבִיב	and come, all nations from all around!	
11c	וְנִקְבָּצוּ	Gather yourself there.	
11d	שָׁמָּה הַנְחַת יְהוָה גִּבּוֹרֶיךָ׃	Bring down your warriors, O YHWH!	b. The Appeal to YHWH (4:11d)
12a	יֵעוֹרוּ	"[Let them] be roused!	c. The Pronouncement of Judgment (4:12)
12b	וְיַעֲלוּ הַגּוֹיִם אֶל־עֵמֶק יְהוֹשָׁפָט	Let the nations ascend to the valley of Jehoshaphat,	
12c	כִּי שָׁם אֵשֵׁב לִשְׁפֹּט אֶת־כָּל־הַגּוֹיִם מִסָּבִיב׃	for there I will sit to judge all the nations from all around."	
13a	שִׁלְחוּ מַגָּל	Send in the sickle,	d. The Images of Judgment (4:13)
13b	כִּי בָשַׁל קָצִיר	for the harvest is ripe.	
13c	בֹּאוּ	Come,	
13d	רְדוּ	tread	
13e	כִּי־מָלְאָה גַּת	for the winepress is full.	
13f	הֵשִׁיקוּ הַיְקָבִים	The wine-vats overflow,	
13g	כִּי רַבָּה רָעָתָם׃	for great is their wickedness.	
14a	הֲמוֹנִים הֲמוֹנִים בְּעֵמֶק הֶחָרוּץ	Multitudes, multitudes in the Valley of Decision,	e. Judgment Through the Day of YHWH (4:14–15)
14b	כִּי קָרוֹב יוֹם יְהוָה בְּעֵמֶק הֶחָרוּץ׃	for the day of YHWH is near in the Valley of Decision.	
15a	שֶׁמֶשׁ וְיָרֵחַ קָדָרוּ	The sun and moon darken,	
15b	וְכוֹכָבִים אָסְפוּ נָגְהָם׃	the stars gather in their light.	

16a		YHWH roars from Zion	f. YHWH's Presence in Zion (4:16–17)
16b		and from Jerusalem he utters his voice.	
16c		The heavens and the earth quake.	
16d		But YHWH is a shelter for his people,	
16e		a refuge for the children of Israel.	
17a		You will know	
17b		that I am YHWH your God,	
17c		dwelling in Zion, my holy mountain.	
17d		Jerusalem will be holy,	
17e		strangers will no longer pass through her.	
18a		It will be on that day,	4. YHWH's Restoration of Judah and Jerusalem (4:18–21)
			a. The Introductory Formula (4:18a)
18b		the mountains will drip sweet wine.	b. Images of Edenic Restoration (4:18b–f)
18c		The hills will flow with milk.	
18d		All the streams of Judah will flow with water.	
18e		And a stream will flow from the house of YHWH,	
18f		which will water the wadi of Shittim.	
19a		Egypt will become a desolation.	c. The Desolation of Egypt and Edom (4:19)
19b		Edom will become a desert of desolation,	
19c		because of the violence against the children of Judah	
19d		whose innocent blood they poured out upon their land.	
20a		But Judah will be inhabited forever,	d. Security for YHWH's People (4:20a–21a)
20b		and Jerusalem from generation to generation.	
21a		I will avenge their blood [that] I have not avenged.	
21b		YHWH dwells in Zion!	e. The Declaration of Divine Presence (4:21b)

insertion on the basis of vocabulary and literary style.[4] Wolff stresses the way in which YHWH refers to the Judahite audience. YHWH speaks in the first person in 4:1–3[3:1–3], referring to עַמִּי ("my people") and נַחֲלָתִי ("my inheritance"), while calling them the בְּנֵי יְהוּדָה ("children of Judah") and the בְּנֵי יְרוּשָׁלָם ("children of Jerusalem") in 4:4–8[3:4–8]. However, both sections also make frequent use of terms describing economic transactions, notably slave-trading, which suggests continuity.[5] The question of style is similarly fraught. Those who argue that Joel 4:4–8[3:4–8] is an insertion argue that these verses are more prose-like than the rest of the chapter.[6] This is difficult to sustain in a section composed entirely of divine address, especially when YHWH's speech has numerous examples of parallelism describing both the crimes of the nations (v. 5, 6) and YHWH's response (v. 7, 8).

Joel 4:9–17[3:9–17] comprises the third subunit and it widens the scope of the text by addressing the nations as a collective entity and summons them to be judged in the Valley of Jehoshaphat. The literary style changes since the text directs imperatives at these nations, summoning to assemble for a fruitless challenge to YHWH's authority. Finally, 4:18–21[3:18–21] looks beyond the climactic confrontation of YHWH and the nations and reveals what it would mean for YHWH to restore the fortunes of his people. It combines promises of paradisiacal blessing for Judah and Jerusalem with proclamations of doom for Egypt and Edom, which mirrors the transition from general to specific found in 4:1–3[3:1–3] and 4:4–8[3:4–8]. Joel 4:18–21 further coheres around imagery of flowing liquids including wine, water, and milk, which provides a sharp contrast to the images of desiccation found in 1:2–20.[7]

Explanation of the Text

1. The Introduction of YHWH's Judgment on the Nations (4:1–3)

These few verses provide a short summary of the hope found in the whole of Joel 4[3] by announcing both the restoration of the Judahite community and the judgment that the nations will face. The introductory phrase בַּיָּמִים הָהֵמָּה וּבָעֵת הַהִיא ("in those days and at that time") points the audience toward YHWH's yet to be realized acts of salvation (cf. Jer 33:15; 50:4, 20). This phrase serves the same rhetorical function to the declaration וְהָיָה אַחֲרֵי־כֵן ("it will be after this") in 3:1[2:28] by pointing to an unspecified but guaranteed time when YHWH will dramatically intervene.

After the introductory formula, YHWH speaks in 4:1b[3:1b], declaring אָשׁוּב אֶת־שְׁבוּת ("I will restore the fortunes") of Judah and Jerusalem. This phrase is found twenty-seven times in the OT in literary contexts where YHWH turns from judgment

---

4. See Wolff, *Joel and Amos*, 74–78.
5. For example, see the use of מָכַר ("to sell") in Joel 4:3, 6, 8; and שׁוּב ("to return") in Joel 4:1, 4, 7. Colin Toffelmire, *A Discourse and Register Analysis of the Prophetic Book of Joel*, SSN 66 (Leiden: Brill, 2016), 76–77.
6. Barton, *Joel and Obadiah*, 100.
7. Wendland, *Discourse Analysis*, 301.

to restoration (e.g. Jer 30:3, 18; 31:23; 32:44; 33:7, 11).[8] Joel 4:2-3[3:2-3] then describes the manner and the rationale for YHWH's actions. YHWH begins in 4:2a-b[3:2a-b] by gathering all of the nations and drawing them together to the Valley of Jehoshaphat. No specific nations are identified here, suggesting that YHWH is sovereign over all of them. YHWH's interaction with the nations creates a play on words since both the place and the activity are derived from the verb שָׁפַט ("to judge"). The עֵמֶק יְהוֹשָׁפָט ("Valley of Jehoshaphat") becomes the place where YHWH asserts in 4:2c that וְנִשְׁפַּטְתִּי ("I will judge") the nations for what they have done.

The location of the Valley of Jehoshaphat remains unclear and it is more fruitful to focus on the purpose of the name rather than its potential geographical referents.[9] YHWH's judgments are often set in valleys, presumably since they provide the necessary space for the nations to assemble and hear the verdict YHWH brings from on high (Isa 22:1-5; Ezek 38-39; Zech 14). These valleys are not easily mapped since Isa 22:1 refers to a גֵּיא חִזָּיוֹן ("valley of vision") while Zech 14:4 gives the image of a new valley being created from the splitting of the Mount of Olives as YHWH goes forth to battle the nations. Ezekiel 38-39 is connected lexically to Joel 4:2[3:2] since the judgment on Gog in the Valley of Hamon-Gog is based off YHWH's declaration of intention וְנִשְׁפַּטְתִּי ("I will judge") in Ezek 38:22. Further, the description of Gog's destruction contains images of blood and fire that evoke the results of the day of YHWH described throughout Joel.[10] Placing YHWH's judgment in the unspecified Valley of Jehoshaphat thus follows prophetic tradition in subordinating the geography of the places of judgment to their symbolic significance.

This symbolism is heightened when reflecting on the parallels between judgment in a valley and the day of YHWH. All four of the texts (Isa 22:1-5; Ezek 38-39; Joel 4:1-21[3:1-21]; Zech 14) refer to the day of YHWH, even if the non-Joel texts do not have the exact phrase יהוה יום.[11] The connection in Joel is through the Valley of Jehoshaphat in 4:1[3:1]. It is placed in parallel to the Valley of Decision in 4:12[3:12], which is the setting for the day of YHWH in 4:14[3:14]. In all four of these cases the targets of the day of YHWH are foreign nations. Consequently, announcing that YHWH will judge in the Valley of Jehoshaphat anticipates the day of YHWH and further establishes that YHWH's own people are no longer the targets of his wrath.

Joel 4:2c-3d[3:2c-3d] moves from the announcement of judgment to a discussion of the crimes of the nations. Joel stresses YHWH's identification with the Judahite community through first-person suffixes, as YHWH redresses the wrongs done to עַמִּי וְנַחֲלָתִי ("my people and my inheritance") and אַרְצִי ("my land").[12] These suffixes

---

8. The origins of the phrase are disputed. Scholars trace the etymology of the noun שְׁבוּת to both the roots שׁוב ("to return") and שָׁבָה ("to take captive"). If the latter suggestion is correct, it might provide further evidence to date Joel in the postexilic period but this is not assured. Given the thrust of Joel 2:18-4:21 [3:21], it is possible to see a broader restoration in view here, rather than focusing it simply on a return from exile. See Simkins, *Yahweh's Activity*, 225.

9. The most common suggestions for the location of this valley are the Valley of Berekah where King Jehoshaphat defeated a Transjordanian coalition in 2 Chron 20:20-26 or the Kidron Valley, which is a prominent geographical feature in the vicinity of Jerusalem. Dillard, "Joel," 301.

10. Strazicich, *Joel's Use of Scripture*, 226.

11. Isaiah 22:5 refers to a "day of panic, confusion and subjugation for YHWH God of Hosts," while Ezek 39:11 looks to the destruction of God, "on that day" and Zech 14:1 speaks of a "day coming to YHWH."

12. Ogden and Deutsch, *Joel & Malachi*, 41. Ogden comments on the use of "my inheritance," noting that lament psalms call upon YHWH to remember "your inheritance," in their urgency for him to rescue his people (Pss 28:9; 74:2; 79:1). Thus, YHWH's use of "my inheritance" here reflects a success appeal on the part of the community.

reflect the state of YHWH's relationship with the Judahite community. In 2:17, Joel urges the people to cry out to YHWH and implore him to intervene on behalf of עַמֶּךָ ("your people") and נַחֲלָתְךָ ("your inheritance"). This was an aspiration of the part of the community since at that stage the relationship between YHWH and this people was in jeopardy. YHWH's use of "my people and my inheritance" in 4:2c[3:2c] indicates that relationship has been restored, which is central to the renewal of hope for the Judahite community.

The actual list of crimes covers 4:2d–3d[3:2d–3d]. YHWH is going to judge the nations for scattering his people, seizing their land, and engaging in the slave trade. The third charge is the most prominent since the text describes it in three different ways in 4:3a–d. First, the nations cast lots for YHWH's people, using a verb (יַדּוּ) that occurs only on two other occasions in the OT (Obad 11; Nah 3:10).[13] The contexts of Obad 11 and Nah 3:10 also evoke the enslavement of captives after the fall of a fortress. Obadiah 11 references the actions of Edom in the wake of the fall of Jerusalem, while Nah 3:10 reflects on the Assyrian conquest of Thebes. Joel further heightens the offense of the nations with two images of them using Judahite children as a means of barter, whereby the captors exchange the boys for the services of prostitutes and the girls for wine.[14]

In summary, 4:1–3[3:1–3] provides a thematic introduction for the rest of the chapter. It interacts with previous passages by revealing that YHWH is actively laying claim to his people, but it focuses on the crimes of the foreign nations. It is interesting to note that Joel specifically identifies the crimes of the nations in light of the ambiguity surrounding the guilt of the Judahite community in 1:2–2:17. Judah's potential guilt remains undefined and the threatened judgment is averted when YHWH chooses to show compassion on his people. On the other hand, YHWH charges the nations with specific crimes for which he will unleash deserved judgment.

2. YHWH's Judgment on Tyre, Sidon, and Philistia (4:4–8)

The next subsection singles out specific nations for divine judgment, targeting Tyre, Sidon, and Philistia. Joel 4:4a[3:4a] begins with the focus particle גַּם, which here marks the connection between YHWH's generic intentions and their specific application in these verses.[15] YHWH indicts these nations with the crimes listed in 4:1–3[3:1–3], invoking images of them carrying off treasures and people. YHWH then declares that he will fully redress the crimes committed against his people. This fulfills one of the functions of prophetic oracles against foreign nations since it provides hope for the Judahite audience as they see their God promising to judge their persecutors.[16] The interplay of audiences is significant for the rhetorical strategy of these verses since although YHWH directly addresses Tyre, Sidon, and Philistia, the actual in-

---

13. Crenshaw, *Joel*, 176. Amos also employs the theme of casting lots in his condemnation of the rich exploiting the poor (Amos 2:6).

14. Dillard, "Joel," 301. The preposition in בַּזּוֹנָה is probably a *bet* of price (cf. Ps 44:13; Amos 2:6). This differs from the LXX reading which takes the preposition as indicating that the boys were forced into prostitution. Reading it as a *bet* of price better parallels in the next phrase in which girls are sold in order to purchase wine.

15. Christo H. J. van der Merwe, "Another Look at the Biblical Hebrew Focus Particle גַּם," *JSS* 54 (2009): 320–21. Van der Merwe classifies this as a relatively rare use of גַּם where it functions as a macro-syntactical connective, governing more than one sentence. See also BHRG §40.20. The connection between Joel 4:1–3 [3:1–3] and 4:4–8 [3:4–8] is evident since YHWH judges Tyre, Sidon, and Philistia for the crimes introduced in 4:1–3, but YHWH's switch to direct address in 4:4–8 [3:4–8] provides sufficient distinction between these subunits.

16. Raabe, "Why Prophetic Oracles?" 249.

tended audience is the Judahite community. They hear YHWH's specific proclamations of judgment as promises that he will restore their fortunes as he promised in 4:1–3[3:1–3].

The rationale for targeting these nations in particular is difficult to determine since in comparison with Assyria or Babylon, the threat posed by these nations seems minor. However, the themes of captivity and the slave trade provide a link. In the preexilic period, Amos 1:6–10 condemns Philistia and Phoenicia for selling Israelites into slavery. In Ezek 25:15–17, the prophet condemns Philistia for taking vengeance against Judah in the context of the destruction of Jerusalem. Further, both Philistia and Phoenicia sit on trade routes that extend to the northwestern (Greece) and southeastern (Sabea) extremities mentioned in 4:4–8[3:4–8].[17] Consequently, in view of the crimes of the nations that are YHWH's focus in 4:1–3[3:1–3], the nations mentioned in 4:4–8[3:4–8] deserve to face YHWH's judgment.

After the introductory וְגַם, YHWH directs two rhetorical questions to Tyre, Sidon, and Philistia in Joel 4:4a–b[3:4a–b].[18] The first question is general and asks simply מָה־אַתֶּם לִי ("what are you to me")? The second question provides further specificity as YHWH asks הַגְּמוּל אַתֶּם מְשַׁלְּמִים עָלָי ("are you seeking a recompense against me?"). The idea behind these questions is for YHWH to incredulously ask whether these nations think that they have standing to call him to account.[19] The key to these questions is the word גְּמוּל ("recompense"). It occurs in this question and then it recurs in participial form and as a noun in YHWH's answer in Joel 4:4c–d[3:4c–d]. Essentially, YHWH appropriates the concept of "recompense," revealing that the nations' supposed grievance against him is illusory. Meanwhile, YHWH enacts his claim against these nations and punishes them as they deserve.[20]

Joel 4:5[3:5] builds off of the foundation of YHWH's promised repayment and delves deeper into the crimes of Tyre, Sidon, and Philistia. Joel 4:5a[3:5a] indicates that they have angered YHWH by taking his treasure in their attacks against Judah. Key to this verse is YHWH's personal stake in what these nations have taken since YHWH describes it as כַּסְפִּי וּזְהָבִי ("my silver and my gold").[21] Joel 4:5b[3:5b] parallels this accusation, using מַחֲמַדַּי ("my precious items") as a synonym for silver and gold (cf. 1 Kgs 20:6; 2 Chr 36:19; Isa 64:10; Lam 1:10; Hos 9:6). YHWH's ownership of the land and its treasures means that the nations' assault draws YHWH into the fray as an injured party.[22] These first-person suffixes make a sharp contrast with where the nations take YHWH's treasures, which is לְהֵיכְלֵיכֶם ("to your temples").[23] The nations are

---

17. Assis, *Book of Joel*, 219–20.
18. Allen, *Joel*, 111. Allen highlights the legal context of these rhetorical questions. He argues that YHWH acts as a plaintiff, before issuing judgment and executing punishment.
19. This use of rhetorical questions fits into what Moshavi calls a "presumptive" form of argumentation. By asking if the nations have a valid claim against him, YHWH asserts that this is not the case and that the burden of proof has shifted to the nations. Of course, the nations do not respond in this passage, which means that YHWH's perspective on the situation is unchallenged. See Adina Moshavi, "Two Types of Argumentation Involving Rhetorical Questions in Biblical Hebrew Dialogue," *Biblica* 90 (2009): 32–46.
20. Crenshaw, *Joel*, 179.
21. Ibid. The claim in this verse extends beyond the treasures found in the temple which the Babylonians captured. The silver and gold probably refer to the plunder of raiding since there is no evidence that a Philistine-Phoenician alliance ever looted the Jerusalem temple.
22. Daniel Timmer, *The Non-Israelite Nations in the Book of the Twelve: Thematic Coherence and the Diachronic-Synchronic Relationship in the Minor Prophets*, BibInt 135 (Leiden: Brill, 2015), 36.
23. This noun refers to both temples (1 Sam 1:9; 2 Kgs 18:16) and palaces (1 Kgs 21:1; 2 Kgs 20:18). Since it is YHWH's treasure that the nations are stealing, it seems likely that they would be placed in the homes of the gods of the plundering nations (cf. 1 Sam 4–6). For extrabiblical descriptions of this practice, see Sa Moon Kang, *Divine War in the Old Testament and in the Ancient Near East*, BZAW 177 (Berlin: de Gruyter, 1989), 71.

charged with taking the precious items that belong to YHWH and using them to honor their gods.

Joel 4:6[3:6] raises the stakes by shifting from inanimate treasure to enslavement of YHWH's people. YHWH accuses Tyre, Sidon, and Philistia of selling the children of Judah and Jerusalem into captivity to the "children of Javan" (בְּנֵי הַיְּוָנִים) or Greeks.[24] Ezekiel 27:13 also mentions the "children of Javan" in conjunction with the slave trade in an oracle against Tyre. Joel 4:6a[3:6a] fronts the grammatical objects וּבְנֵי יְהוּדָה וּבְנֵי יְרוּשָׁלַםִ ("the children of Judah and Jerusalem"), emphasizing the captured peoples' identity. Joel 4:6b[3:6b] begins with a purpose clause introduced by לְמַעַן, stressing the intention of the captors to send the Judahites far away from their borders. This idea of distant captivity proves significant in YHWH's forthcoming announcement of judgment.

Joel 4:7–8[3:7–8] moves from enumerating the crimes of Tyre, Sidon, and Philistia to articulating YHWH's response. YHWH directly addresses these nations while the actual audience of Joel's prophecy hears his words as hopeful promises. Joel 4:7a[3:7a] focuses attention on YHWH's agency through the use of the particle הִנְנִי that acts as the subject of the suffixed participle מְעִירָם ("rousing them").[25] YHWH rouses his people so that they return from the far-off places to which they were sold. This reversal of the injustices continues in 4:7b–8b[3:7b–8b] with punishment for the nations mirroring restoration for his people. The keyword גְּמוּל ("recompense") occurs for a fourth and final time in 4:7b[3:7b], this time with an attached second-person suffix representing the nations (גְּמֻלְכֶם). This use of recompense is the object of the clause וַהֲשִׁבֹתִי גְמֻלְכֶם בְּרֹאשְׁכֶם ("I will return your recompense upon your head"). In other words, YHWH rejects the nations' claims of grievance from 4:4[3:4] and instead judges them according to their mistreatment of his people.

Joel 4:8a–b[3:8a–b] then draws from the principle of *lex talionis* as YHWH reveals that the punishment for enslaving his people is for his people to enslave their captors. This is in keeping with the "poetic justice" that often characterizes prophetic oracles against nations (cf. Ezek 25–32).[26] Essentially, the punishment that YHWH enacts suits the crimes that the nations have committed. The geography found in 4:4–8[3:4–8] furthers the picture of retributive justice. The "seaboard coalition" of Philistia, Tyre, and Sidon sells Judahites into slavery across the sea to the northwest (Greece). In response, YHWH declares that the Judahites will sell their captors into slavery to the Sabeans who control the trade routes to the southeast.[27] YHWH uses the Sabeans to concretize the idea of "off the map," since he refers to them as a גּוֹי רָחוֹק ("far-off nation") in 4:8b[3:8b].

Joel 4:8c[3:8c] concludes this subsection with the declaration כִּי יְהוָה דִּבֵּר ("for YHWH has spoken"). This along with 2:12 are the only places where Joel uses prophetic oracle formulae. This formula usually concludes divine speech (cf. 1 Kgs 14:11; Isa 1:2; 22:25; 24:3; 25:8; Jer 13:16; Obad 18), and here it adds the finishing touch to YHWH's promises that he will judge the specific nations who have mistreated his people.[28] The shift from first-person divine speech to a third-person oracle formula provides a tone of certainty to YHWH's judgment. YHWH has spoken, the nations will see

---

24. Crenshaw, *Joel*, 182; Barton, *Joel*, 101. References to Greeks are infrequent in the Old Testament but they are present in several other prophetic passages (cf. Isa 66:19; Dan 8:21; 10:20; 11:2; Zech 9:13).
25. On the use of forms of הִנֵּה to express the newsworthiness of a change in the situation, see *BHRG* §40.22.4.
26. Raabe, "Transforming," 199.
27. Sweeney, *Twelve*, 180.
28. Crenshaw, *Joel*, 184.

his justice, and his own people will rejoice in their restoration from captivity.

Joel 4:4–8[3:4–8] thus begins to put into practice YHWH's promises to restore his people by judging the nations. This subunit turns the tables on three specific nations, inverting their position with regard to the Judahites. YHWH turns the captors into captives while releasing and restoring the prisoners. Joel's audience hears YHWH's condemnation of Tyre, Sidon, and Philistia and experiences hope that their God is acting on their behalf to rescue them.

3. YHWH's Judgment on the Nations (4:9–17)

Joel 4:9–17[3:9–17] continues to unpack YHWH's commitment to restore the fortunes of his people and to judge the nations. It actualizes YHWH's declarations in 4:1–3[3:1–3] by summoning the nations to come and face the day of YHWH. Tyre, Sidon, and Philistia from 4:4–8[3:4–8] are replaced by the nations as a collective entity. This encounter with the nations ends with promises of YHWH's presence in Zion, protecting his people from the threat posed by the nations. Joel 4:9–12[3:9–12] begins this new subunit with a series of imperative phrases setting up the climactic conflict. The identity of the one issuing these imperatives is not readily apparent since the prophetic oracle formula that ended 4:8[3:8] creates room for a shift in speaker.[29] Possibilities include the prophet, YHWH, or even the nations speaking among themselves.[30] The best approach is to suggest that the voices of YHWH and the prophet as his herald have merged. The rhetorical purpose of the commands remains the same; the nations are summoned to face YHWH's judgment, which provides deliverance for the Judahite community.

Joel 4:9a[3:9a] begins with the command to קִרְאוּ־זֹאת בַּגּוֹיִם ("proclaim this among the nations"). The ensuing clauses unpack the content of what is to be proclaimed. They summon the nations to an encounter with YHWH. The next command is קַדְּשׁוּ מִלְחָמָה ("sanctify a battle") in 4:9b[3:9b]. The imperative קַדְּשׁוּ ("Sanctify") also occurs in 1:14 and 2:15 in the prophet's call to the Judahites to sanctify a fast. There is a further link between 2:15 and 4:9 since both use the imperative קִרְאוּ ("Proclaim"). The effects of these commands are quite different on account of the difference in their intended audience. Whereas 2:15 calls the Judahites to consecrate a fast and to call for a solemn assembly to entreat YHWH, 4:9[3:9] calls for the nations to consecrate a battle in opposition to YHWH. This inverts the idea of holy war where YHWH fights and a priest sanctifies an army to be his agents (cf. Deut 20:1–20).[31] In 4:9[3:9], however, the army being sanctified stands in opposition to YHWH.

Joel 4:9c–e[3:9c–e] continues to summon the nations by focusing on the composition of their forces. In 4:9c, the nations receive the command הָעִירוּ הַגִּבּוֹרִים ("rouse the warriors"), which evokes images of fighters working themselves into a frenzied state. This is followed up in 4:9d–e[3:9d–e] with the volitional prefix verbs יִגְּשׁוּ יַעֲלוּ ("let them draw near, let them go up"), which have כֹּל אַנְשֵׁי הַמִּלְחָמָה ("all men of battle") as their subject. This expression is also parallel to הַגִּבּוֹרִים ("warriors") from 4:9c[3:9c]. Together, these clauses draw the

---

29. Wendland, *Prophetic Rhetoric*, 14.
30. See Sweeney, *Twelve*, 181; Prinsloo, *Theology*, 97, Assis, *Book of Joel*, 228 for each of these respective options.
31. Sweeney, *Twelve*, 181. Prophetic literature also envisions YHWH fighting alongside a supporting army. This army may not explicitly be sanctified by a priest according to the law of war in Deut 20 but it clearly is understood to be doing YHWH's will (Isa 13:2–3; Jer 51:27–28; Mic 4:13). In some cases, the chosen army even attacks YHWH's people (Jer 6:4; 22:7; Hos 5:8).

moment of conflict closer, urging the nations to begin their march toward the sanctified battle with YHWH.

Joel 4:10[3:10] further anticipates conflict between YHWH and the nations by encouraging the nations to go to extreme lengths to assemble their military might. Joel 4:10a–b[3:10a–b] calls the nations to take their agricultural implements and turn them into weapons, devoting all of their energy to the conflict. Specifically, the nations are called to turn plowshares and pruning hooks into swords and spears, adopting a footing of total war.[32] Correspondingly, the nations are called to gather every potential fighter they can, including the weakling (הַחַלָּשׁ), who now proclaims גִּבּוֹר אָנִי ("I am a mighty man") in 4:10c–d[3:10c–d].[33] This verse emphasizes that when challenging YHWH, the nations should spare no effort.

Joel 4:11a–c[3:11a–c] continues the sequences of commands directed at the nations, building to their impending confrontation with YHWH. The first two clauses (4:11a–b[3:11a–b]) contain the imperatives עוּשׁוּ וָבֹאוּ ("hasten and come").[34] Joel draws in the widest collection of nations, identifying כָל־הַגּוֹיִם מִסָּבִיב ("all the nations from all around") as the recipients of these imperatives. The rhetoric of gathering the largest possible collection of nations echoes earlier summons to gather the Judahite community to petition YHWH in 1:5–14 and 2:15–17. In these passages, Joel explicitly summons everyone from youngest to eldest to gather and cry out to YHWH to plead for rescue. Now, all nations are called to gather where they will face YHWH's judgment.[35] Joel 4:11c[3:11c] continues to summon the nations, directing them וְנִקְבָּצוּ שָׁמָּה ("gather yourself there").[36] The verb וְנִקְבָּצוּ is in the suffix conjugation rather than the imperative but it provides the purpose of the preceding commands.[37] After gathering their host, the nations must assemble in opposition to YHWH.

Joel 4:11d[3:11d] provides yet another interpretive challenge for this verse. This clause seems to break the chain of verbs summoning the nations and instead offers a plea from the prophet for YHWH to meet the nations' challenge. The text reads הַנְחַת יְהוָה גִּבּוֹרֶיךָ ("bring down your warriors, o YHWH"), which shifts the addressee of the commands away from the nations. This apparent incongruity informs the readings in the LXX and other versions.[38] However, it also makes sense to suggest that YHWH would assemble his own force to face the challenge of the nations (cf. Isa 13:1–5;

---

32. I will discuss the relationship between this phrase and the opposite image of turning weapons into agricultural implements in section on Canonical and Practical Significance (cf. Isa 2:2–4; Mic 4:1–4).

33. This is the only occasion in Joel where the first-person pronoun does not have YHWH as its antecedent. The "weaklings" of the nations now are proclaiming their strength by claiming a pronoun otherwise used for YHWH's provision for this people (cf. 2:27; 4:17). This verse is frequently stripped out of its context in popular Christian culture where it has become a call for people to acknowledge their own weakness and find their strength through reliance upon God.

34. The first imperative עוּשׁוּ is a *hapax legomenon*. In order to gain greater clarity, some suggest alternatives including "rouse yourselves" (עוֹרוּ) and "hurry" (חוּשׁוּ), even though there is no textual evidence in support. Consequently, commentators typically assign it a meaning synonymous to the second imperative וָבֹאוּ. For a more detailed discussion of the alternatives, see Simkins, *Yahweh's Activity*, 229; Wolff, *Joel and Amos*, 72.

35. Deist, "Parallels and Reinterpretation," 72.

36. This clause division requires ignoring Masoretic accentuation which places the *atnach* (the main verse divider) under the verb וְנִקְבָּצוּ. However, the syntax of the verse is more consistent if "there" (שָׁמָּה) is understood to be the object of that verb. This reading divides v. 11 in four clauses, each beginning with verbs with volitional senses.

37. See *BHRG* §21.5.2.4; Crenshaw, *Joel*, 189. Other commentators follow the LXX and change the verb to the imperative form וְהִקָּבְצוּ (Wolff, *Joel and Amos*, 27; Simkins, *Yahweh's Activity*, 229).

38. The LXX reading is "let the meek become a warrior" (ὁ πραΰς ἔστω μαχητής), which reproduces the sentiments found in Joel 4:10c. The Syriac and Targum change the verb to ויחת, which reflects a *hiphil* volitional prefix form of the verb "to shatter" (חתת). In this reading, the nations gather so

Jer 50:14–16). It is also possible for the voice of the prophet to interrupt the flow of divine speech to insert a personal evaluation of the situation (cf. Zech 3:5).[39] Consequently, reading the text as it stands in the Masoretic tradition is preferable.

Interjecting an appeal to YHWH allows Joel to provide a brief glimpse into the hopes and expectations of the Judahite audience. While the nations have been the referents of the commands in 4:9–11[3:9–11], it is the Judahite audience that reads and hears Joel's prophecy. As the tension builds between YHWH and the nations, Joel now provides the Judahite audience a voice to express their desired outcome. When the nations come to challenge YHWH, the actual audience of the prophecy now has the opportunity to address YHWH and implore him to deliver them from this threat.[40] The appeal for YHWH's warriors to descend provides symmetry with the summons to the nations to ascend in Joel 4:9, 12[3:9, 12]. As the nations go up in response to YHWH's commands, Joel 4:11d[3:11d] suggests that YHWH's host will come down to meet them, setting up a climactic confrontation.

Joel 4:12[3:12] reverts to addressing the nations. Joel 4:12a–b[3:12a–b] mirrors a construction found in Joel 4:9c–d[3:9c–d] by placing two volitional prefix forms side by side, in this case calling the nations to be roused and ascend (יֵעוֹרוּ וְיַעֲלוּ). It again specifies the place where they are to assemble as the Valley of Jehoshaphat, which was first introduced in 4:2[3:2]. Joel 4:12c[3:12c] uses the first-person verb אֵשֵׁב ("I will sit") to indicate that YHWH is now acting. This clause also employs a pun on the name of the valley as YHWH declares his intention to judge (לִשְׁפֹּט) there. YHWH also emphasizes the breadth of this judgment by again using the phrase "all nations from around" that occurred in the summons to the nations found in the previous verse. Now that the nations have gathered, YHWH can respond to their challenge.

The nature of the encounter between YHWH and the nations is fascinating. Joel 4:9–11[3:9–11] calls the nations to marshal for war, to gather their hosts, and to commit every resource. However, 4:12[3:12] does not permit the nations to pose any threat to YHWH. Instead, once they assemble, he announces his intention to judge, which he then describes in greater detail in 4:13–17[3:13–17]. Consequently, 4:9–12[3:9–12] reflects a creative modification of a prophetic call to war that typically consists of (1) a call to arms; (2) the preparation of weapons; and (3) an account of the war itself (Jer 6:4–6; 46:3–5; Mic 4:11–13).[41] The third phase is absent since resistance against YHWH is futile. The nations cannot stop YHWH's judgment. Overall, 4:9–12[3:9–12] heightens the tension for the Judahite audience by taking YHWH's declared intentions to judge the nations and restore Judah and Jerusalem and delaying the full account of YHWH's judgment until after the nations are summoned. Joel then reveals the futility of the nations' challenge by omitting any discussion of the battle and portraying YHWH as the victor who can pronounce the nations' fate.[42]

Joel 4:13–17[3:13–17] reveals what happens when the nations gather according to YHWH's summons. YHWH alone is able to act, and his

---

that YHWH might shatter their warriors. See Wolff, *Joel*, 73; Simkins, *Yahweh's Activity*, 229. This has the advantage of not switching the addressee of the imperatives, but it seems more likely to be an attempt to smooth out a difficult text.

39. Dillard, "Joel," 306–7.

40. While the term גִּבּוֹרֶיךָ ("your warriors") can refer to humans who fight on YHWH's behalf (Josh 10:2; 1 Kgs 1:8, 10; Nah 2:4), it is more likely here that Joel is urging YHWH to confront the nations with his heavenly host (Judg 5:23; Ps 103:20). See Patrick D. Miller, *The Divine Warrior in Early Israel*, HSM 5 (Cambridge: Harvard University Press, 1973), 138.

41. Simkins, *Yahweh's Activity*, 231.

42. Wendland, *Discourse Analysis*, 300.

judgment reverberates through the natural realm. This judgment commences in 4:13[3:13] with imperatives from YHWH to the heavenly host who carry out his will. This interpretation fits with the prophet's appeal in 4:11c[3:11c] for YHWH to bring down his warriors. Now, YHWH's host begins to fulfill its commission. Joel 4:13[3:13] employs two images drawn from the agricultural realm. It consists of imperatives followed by an explanation introduced by כִּי. Joel 4:13a–b[3:13a–b] consists of the command שִׁלְחוּ מַגָּל ("send in the sickle") followed by an explanatory clause כִּי בָשַׁל קָצִיר ("because the harvest is ripe"). Joel 4:13c–e[3:13c–e] directs the heavenly host בֹּאוּ רְדוּ ("come, tread"), followed by an explanatory clause כִּי־מָלְאָה גַת ("because the winepress is full"). These images suggest that the appropriate time for judgment has arrived since grain-harvesting and grape-crushing happen when the crop has reached maturity.[43] The images also overlap with the militaristic tone of this subunit since falling grain and crushed grapes suggest the fall of enemy soldiers and their spilled blood.[44] Isaiah 63:1–6 also uses this imagery, portraying YHWH as the divine warrior whose garments are stained with the blood of enemies whom he has trampled (cf. Rev 14:18–20; 19:15).

Joel 4:13f[3:13f] then provides the rationale for these judgment images. It strengthens the image of the full winepress by declaring that the הֵשִׁיקוּ הַיְקָבִים ("vats overflow"), using a phrase also found in 2:24. This demonstrates the flexibility of prophetic metaphor since Joel uses overflowing vats to suggest unbridled prosperity when YHWH restores his people. Here, the reason for the overflow is the wickedness of the nations in 4:13g[3:13g]. Joel 4:13 thus indicates that the evil of the nations has reached its saturation point.

Joel 4:14[3:14] shifts from declaring that it is time for judgment to describing its occurrence. The verse begins with repetition, identifying הֲמוֹנִים הֲמוֹנִים ("multitudes, multitudes") whom YHWH will judge. This word can refer to a horde gathered for battle (Judg 4:7; 1 Sam 14:16 1 Kgs 20:13; Isa 29:5; Dan 11:10) and repeating it suggests that the nations are bringing an innumerable host. This calls to mind the host that threatened to overrun Zion in 2:11, but the potential outcome is quite different since rather than leading the assault, YHWH is now present in his city (4:16[3:16]). Isaiah 13:4, another day of YHWH passage associated with Joel (cf. Isa 13:6; Joel 1:15), uses this noun to refer to the sound of the nations who have gathered to challenge YHWH. Its use in 4:14a[3:14a] may be onomatopoetic since given its repetition and the rarity with which הָמוֹן occurs in the plural.[45] As the great multitude of nations gather, their voices mix together in a cacophony of sound.

Joel 4:14[3:14] also uses repetition to identify the location of divine judgment, ending both of its constituent clauses with the phrase בְּעֵמֶק הֶחָרוּץ ("in the Valley of Decision").[46] This is synonymous with the Valley of Jehoshaphat mentioned in 4:2, 12[3:2, 12], and the repetition of its new name in this verse marks a progression from YHWH's intention to judge to his verdict. The new name of the valley is also likely a double entendre since חָרוּץ can also refer to an instrument for threshing (Job 41:22; Isa 28:27; 41:15; Amos 1:3). This fits

---

43. See Isa 17:5; Jer 24:2; 48:32; Hos 2:9; Amos 8:1–2 for other passages where metaphors of ripeness reveal that judgment is about to unfold.

44. Sweeney, *Twelve*, 182.

45. Aaron Schart, "Deathly Silence and Apocalyptic Noise: Observations on the Soundscape of the Book of the Twelve," *Verbum et Ecclesia* 31 (2010): paragraphs 30–34.

46. These are the only occurrences where חָרוּץ is thought to have this definition. Coggins connects it to the semantic range of the associated verb חָרַץ ("to determine"), which points to the meaning "decision" in this verse (cf. 1 Kgs 20:40; Isa 10:22–23). Coggins, *Joel*, 60.

with Joel's use of agricultural imagery to describe YHWH's judgment here. By naming the place of judgment the Valley of Decision, Joel also invokes imagery of what YHWH will do to those nations who oppose him.

This verse also invokes the day of YHWH one more time. Joel 4:14b[3:14b] begins by declaring that the day is near, which echoes 1:15 and 2:1. Here, Joel uses the same language to achieve a dramatically different effect. Whereas the nearness of the day in 1:15 and 2:1 urged the Judahite audience to cry out to YHWH as they faced destruction, in 4:14b[3:14b] the proximity of the day is a sign of deliverance. This follows the trajectory established for the day in 3:1–5[2:28–32] where those who call upon the name of YHWH find rescue. Now that YHWH has decreed his intention to restore the fortunes of his people, the imminence of the day of YHWH offers hope against external threats.

Joel 4:15–16[3:15–16] then further describes the nature of the day of YHWH in language suggestive of the Divine Warrior. These verses describe the effects on the heavenly luminaries, echoing descriptions found in 2:10–11 when YHWH thundered at the head of the army that was about to assault Zion. The order of activities changes slightly since in 4:15a–16c[3:15a–16c] the heavenly luminaries darken, YHWH shouts, and the heavens and the earth quake.[47] In 2:10–11, the quaking of the heavens and the earth precedes the other two activities. Although YHWH's effect on the natural world is the same, the implications are dramatically different. When Joel portrays YHWH leading his army against Zion in 2:10–11, the response of the natural realm reinforces the terror of this situation for the Judahite audience, suggesting that there is no escaping YHWH's wrath. In contrast, YHWH is present in Zion, providing security for his people as the cosmos shakes in 4:15–16[3:15–16].

Joel 4:16d–e[3:16d–e] builds upon YHWH's protective presence in Zion by describing him as a shelter for his people and a refuge for the children of Israel. YHWH's presence in Zion reflects Divine Warrior imagery where the deity defeats foes on behalf of his people and then returns to establish his reign in a sacral location. Peace and prosperity then ensue since the presence of the deity offers security from outside threats.[48] Essentially, these clauses reverse the shocking revelation that YHWH would attack his own dwelling place. Now YHWH restores the idea of Zion's inviolability (Pss 46:2–4; 48:5–9; 76:4–10; Isa 4:6; Jer 7:4) and uses it as the place from which he will restore the Judahite community. The day of YHWH announced in 4:14[3:14] thus brings about convulsions in the natural world that now spell doom for YHWH's enemies as his presence in Zion secures deliverance for his people.

Joel 4:17[3:17] concludes this subsection by addressing the Judahite audience and declaring that YHWH's judgment on the nations and his renewed presence in Zion should provide confidence that their relationship is restored. YHWH claims that as a result of these actions וִידַעְתֶּם כִּי אֲנִי יְהוָה אֱלֹהֵיכֶם ("then you will know that I am YHWH your God,"), a phrase also found in Exod 6:7 and 16:12 in contexts of YHWH delivering his people from Egypt and threats in the wilderness. The simpler phrase

---

47. In both Joel 2:10 and 4:16, the verb describing the convulsions of the heavens and the earth is רָעַשׁ. When inanimate objects are the subjects of this verb, they stress the tremendous power of the actor who can cause them to quake. Kessler, "Shaking," 161.

48. On the march of the Divine Warrior and the positive effects upon his people, see Leonard Greenspoon, "The Origin of the Idea of Resurrection," in *Traditions in Transformation: Turning Points in Biblical Faith*, ed. Baruch Halpern and Jon D. Levenson (Winona Lake, IN: Eisenbrauns, 1981), 272. On this pattern within an ancient Near Eastern context, see Tremper Longman III and Daniel G. Reid, *God is a Warrior* (Grand Rapids: Zondervan, 1995), 83–91.

אֲנִי יְהוָה אֱלֹהֵיכֶם ("I am YHWH your God") can also point to this act of divine deliverance (Num 15:41; Deut 29:5; Ezek 20:5, 7). This verse recalls 2:27 and its assurance that YHWH's people will know that he is in their midst and that he alone is their God. These two formulae answer the question "who knows?" the nature of YHWH in 2:14. YHWH's character and his relationship with his people now are rooted in their knowledge of his provision and protection.[49]

Joel 4:17c[3:17c] continues the divine self-identification formula, indicating that YHWH is rooted in Zion, his holy mountain. Joel 2:1b also described Zion as הַר־קָדְשִׁי ("my holy mountain") before threatening its sanctity in the remainder of the passage. Now that YHWH has promised to restore the fortunes of his people, he proclaims his intention to dwell in Zion, securing its holiness from all threats.[50] Joel 4:17d[3:17d] reframes this promise, declaring that Jerusalem will be holy, expanding upon that in 4:17e[3:17e] with the declaration that וְזָרִים ("strangers") will no longer pass through it. Prophetic literature often uses this term pejoratively, here setting up a contrast with the holiness guaranteed by YHWH's residence in Zion (cf. Isa 1:7; 29:5; Jer 5:19; 30:8; 51:51; Ezek 7:21; 28:7, 10; Obad 11). These "strangers" come to violate Zion's sanctity, but they are powerless now that YHWH is present.[51]

Joel 4:17[3:17] also provides a further answer to the plaintive cries of the people in 2:17. In that verse the prophet summoned the people to call out to YHWH and to implore him not to let his inheritance become an object of mockery among the nations who derisively ask, "where is their God?" Joel now responds by announcing that YHWH is present in the midst of his people, which means that the nations cannot mistreat them since they are secure in his protection.[52]

Joel 4:9–17[3:9–17] thus continues to fulfill YHWH's promise to restore the fortunes of Judah and Jerusalem. It reuses day of YHWH imagery and the cries of the people to reveal the drastic shift in the situation. The shaking of the cosmos and the darkening of the heavenly luminaries now provide proof of YHWH's presence in Zion, guaranteeing security for the Judahite audience. This subunit also provides hope for YHWH's people by assuring them of YHWH's supremacy over the nations who are called to challenge YHWH and face his judgment. YHWH's actions alone accomplish this great feat, and as the Judahite audience observes the interactions between YHWH and the nations and hears his promises, they are encouraged to place their trust in the one who calls himself "YHWH your God."

4. YHWH's Restoration of Judah and Jerusalem (4:18–21)

The final subsection explores the implications of the judgment on the nations and YHWH's renewed presence in Zion. It addresses both YHWH's promise to restore Judah's fortunes and to judge the

---

49. Leslie C. Allen, "Some Prophetic Antecedents of Apocalyptic Eschatology and Their Hermeneutical Value," *Ex Auditu* 6 (1990): 21.

50. James L. Crenshaw, "Freeing the Imagination: The Conclusion of the Book of Joel," in *Prophecy and Prophets: The Diversity of Contemporary Issues in Scholarship*, ed. Yehoshua Gitay (Atlanta: Scholars, 1997), 143–44.

51. L. Snijders, "The meaning of זָר in the Old Testament," *OtSt* 10 (1954): 39–40. In keeping with the challenges of iden-

tifying the date of *Joel*, it is hard to point to a specific referent for these "strangers." In a post-exilic setting, it could evoke the memory of the Babylonian conquest, but this is not certain. Given that Joel refers to the nations as a collective throughout 4:9–17 [3:9–17], it is best to understand the "strangers" as any enemy who comes against Zion.

52. Assis, *Book of Joel*, 237. Assis has a useful chart illustrating the connections between Joel 2:17 and 4:17.

nations by weaving together hopeful promises for the Judahite community with further pronouncements of judgment against Egypt and Edom. Joel 4:18a[3:18a] commences with the temporal formula וְהָיָה בַּיּוֹם הַהוּא ("and it will be on that day"), which is found in prophetic literature and marks moments divine action and its consequences (Isa 7:18, 21, 23; 11:10, 11; 24:21; 27:12, 13; Ezek 39:11; Hos 2:23[21]).[53] Its occurrence here recalls the use of the phrase בַּיָּמִים הָהֵמָּה וּבָעֵת הַהִיא ("in those days and at that time") in 4:1[3:1]. Zechariah 14 follows a similar pattern, beginning with the temporal phrase יוֹם־בָּא לַיהוָה ("a day is coming for YHWH") and then using בַּיּוֹם הַהוּא ("on that day") in Zech 14:4, 6, 8, 13, 20 to refocus attention on YHWH's actions.[54] Consequently, Joel 4:18a[3:18a] links this subunit to the broader promises of restoration in this chapter.

The remaining clauses of 4:18[3:18] push this hope of restoration into the realm of the hyperbolic. Whereas 2:18–27 reverses the crises of locusts and drought, 4:18[3:18] uses images of flowing liquid to suggest fertility that goes well beyond the natural state of affairs. Joel 4:18b–c[3:18b–c] provides two parallel clauses declaring יִטְּפוּ הֶהָרִים עָסִיס וְהַגְּבָעוֹת תֵּלַכְנָה חָלָב ("the mountains will drip sweet wine, the hills will flow with milk"). These suggest overwhelming abundance in the grape and grain harvests, with enough fodder for cattle to produce milk unceasingly, which resonates with the promise of Canaan as the land of milk and honey (Exod 3:8, 17; 13:5; Num 14:8; Deut 6:3; 26:15).[55]

The promises of abundant liquid continue in 4:18d[3:18d] as Joel envisions flowing streams of water. This clause declares that the אֲפִיקֵי יְהוּדָה ("streams of Judah") will be filled with water. Taken together with wine and milk flowing from the hills, it creates a geographical *merismus* where the whole landscape, from high to low, experiences this abundance. Full "stream-channels" also reverse the announcement of drought that dominates Joel 1:15–20 and provide tremendous hope in a land dependent upon seasonal rains.

Joel 4:18e–f[3:18e–f] continues to use water imagery that goes even further into the realm of hyperbole. Joel envisions a spring flowing out of the temple in Jerusalem that irrigates the Wadi Shittim.[56] It is probable that this title is symbolic rather than a reference to a specific place since no such location has been conclusively identified.[57] The noun שִׁטִּים refers to acacia trees that grow in an arid environment, so if they are receiving irrigation it suggests that the stream flowing out from the temple is reaching desert-like regions. Significantly, a temple-sourced spring resonates with a number of other texts that use this image to communicate hope rooted in YHWH's presence (Ps 46:5; Ezek 47:1–12; Zech 14:8).[58] It also shares verbal parallels with the rivers flowing out of Eden in Gen 2:10 (שָׁקָה, יָצָא), suggesting here that Joel

---

53. For a study of the functions of this phrase, see Simon De Vries, *Yesterday, Today and Tomorrow* (Grand Rapids: Eerdmans, 1975), 279–323.

54. The full expression וְהָיָה בַּיּוֹם הַהוּא is found in Zech 14:6, 8, 13, while the וְהָיָה is omitted in 14:4, 20.

55. Crenshaw, *Joel*, 199; Strazicich, *Joel's Use of Scripture*, 243.

56. Some have tried to find physical locations for the Wadi Shittim, including somewhere in the Kidron Valley (Crenshaw, *Joel*, 200; Dillard, "Joel," 312; Allen, *Joel*, 124) and the Wadi Qaddûm between the Mount of Olives and Jerusalem (T. Milik, "Notes d'épigraphie et de topographie palestiniennes," *RB* 66 [1959]: 553–55). Other biblical references to Shittim refer to a location somewhere in Moab (Num 25:1; 33:49; Josh 2:1; 3:1). Sweeney suggests that the Moabite location could be in view if Joel is envisioning a restoration to fertility that extends even beyond the borders of the land. See Sweeney, *Twelve*, 184.

57. Ben Zion Luria, "And a Fountain Shall Spring Forth from the House of the Lord," *Dor le Dor* 10 (1981): 49. Luria comments on the futility of trying to find an actual location for the Wadi Shittim.

58. These parallels will be discussed in more detail in "Canonical and Practical Significance."

is connecting YHWH dwelling in the temple with the prospect of paradisiacal restoration.[59] This again reverses the drought imagery of 1:15–20 that mirrored YHWH's apparent absence. The created realm responds to YHWH's presence in the temple with "holy fecundity," symbolized by this flowing stream.[60]

Joel follows up this idyllic picture with promises of judgment against Egypt and Edom that he contrasts with hope for Judah and Jerusalem in 4:19–20[3:19–20]. Joel 4:19a–b[3:19a–b] are nearly identical as each clause begins with the name of the targeted nation and concludes with the same verb in the prefix conjugation (תִּהְיֶה). The nations meet the same fate, with Edom becoming לִשְׁמָמָה ("a desolation") and Egypt לְמִדְבַּר שְׁמָמָה ("a desert of desolation"). Essentially these clauses reflect the same symmetrical approach to justice meted out to Tyre, Sidon, and Philistia in 4:4–8[3:4–8], whom YHWH promised to change from slavers to enslaved. Egypt and Edom face the prospect of desolation that mirrors the situation faced by the Judahites in 2:3. Egypt's punishment is especially striking since it would be a dramatic reversal for Judah to have a divinely-powered source of water that could even outstrip the Nile River.

Joel 4:19c–d[3:19c–d] articulates the reason for punishment, accusing Egypt and Edom of violence against the children of Judah, and the spilling of innocent blood. These are rather generic accusations, but many identify an allusion to the condemnation of Edom in Obad 10a since both clauses accuse Edom מֵחֲמַס ("on account of the violence") they committed against the Judahites.[61] Obadiah further emphasizes Judah and Edom's fraternal connection, suggesting that its crimes against Judah carry special weight. Obadiah has no corresponding allusion that would invoke Egypt but it is possible that Joel is trying to complete a geographical circuit of nations surrounding Judah.[62]

Joel 4:20[3:20] establishes that the fate of Judah and Jerusalem is the mirror opposite of Egypt and Edom. The violence committed by Egypt and Edom will not overcome YHWH's commitment to his people. Joel 4:20a[3:20a] begins with a disjunctive use of *waw*, attaching it to Judah. This marks the switch from condemnation to restoration. The rest of the clause consists of the temporal marker לְעוֹלָם ("forever") and the verb תֵּשֵׁב ("it will be inhabited"), which provide a picture of continuous dwelling.[63] Joel 4:20b[3:20b] restates this basic theme by eliding the verb and using close synonyms for both the name of the city ("Jerusalem") and the duration of the inhabitation ("for generation to generation"). YHWH's presence, which is explicitly guaranteed in Joel 4:21b[3:21b], guarantees that his people can dwell in their city in security.

This hopeful declaration leads into the final

---

59. Assis, *Book of Joel*, 250–51. The connection between the rivers of Eden and Jerusalem is strengthened by the fact that the Gihon, one of the four Edenic rivers, is also a source of water for Jerusalem.

60. This turn of phrase comes from Cook's discussion of Ezek 47:1–12. See Stephen L. Cook, "The Fecundity of Fair Zion: Beauty and Fruitfulness as Spiritual Fulfillment," in *Daughter Zion: Her Portrait, Her Response*, ed. Mark J. Boda, Carol J. Dempsey, and Leanne Snow Flesher, AIL 13 (Atlanta: SBL, 2012), 99.

61. Block, *Obadiah*, 69–70. The presence of a previous allusion to Obad 17 in Joel 3:5 strengthens the probably of this connection. Here, the attached preposition מִן indicates the grounds of Edom's indictment. See *BHRG* §39.15.

62. Tyre, Sidon, and Philistia in Joel 4:4–8 cover the west and northwest. Egypt and Edom cover the south and southeast.

63. Assis, *Book of Joel*, 254. Assis suggests that there is a pun here that connects this verb to the phrase אָשׁוּב אֶת־שְׁבוּת ("I will restore the captivity") in 4:1. He bases this on the grounds of orthographical similarities between the roots יָשַׁב and שׁוּב, which are quite easily confused when adding on preformatives and sufformatives. He also draws attention to several verses where it appears that the author deliberately employs both roots in the same phrase to take advantage of their similar spelling (Jer 32:37; 34:22; Amos 9:14).

verse, which is the subject of significant debate. The Masoretic text of Joel 4:21a[3:21a] is a rather terse clause that reads וְנִקֵּיתִי דָּמָם לֹא־נִקֵּיתִי, typically translated as "I will hold innocent their blood [that] I did not hold innocent." Contextually, the blood most likely refers to the Judahites whom YHWH has just promised to protect. This suggests that YHWH is promising to forgive Judah for a particular offense that incurred bloodguilt. However, there is no mention of such an offense and it does not fit the focus of this chapter on restoring the fortunes of God's people.[64] This reading would also contradict the clear identification of Judah's דָּם־נָקִיא ("innocent blood") in 4:19d[3:19d]. Ahlström speculatively suggests a different gloss of נָקָה, connecting it to an Akkadian root meaning "to pour out."[65] In this proposal, YHWH promises to pour out the blood of Egypt and Edom, which is unlikely since it involves skipping back over the mentions of Judah and Jerusalem in 4:20[3:20] to find the antecedent for the suffix on דָּמָם. It is also possible to read וְנִקֵּיתִי דָּמָם as an unmarked rhetorical question, asking "shall I leave their blood unpunished?" before answering in the negative.[66] In this reading, "their blood" refers to the Judahites and those being punished are the nations who have spilled it. This approach is conceivable, but a rhetorical question is unlikely in the wake of YHWH's overt declaration of punishment on these nations in 4:19.[67]

A stronger option is to consider the LXX reading that appears to read the verb נָקַם ("to avenge") rather than נָקָה ("to hold innocent"). In this case, 4:21a[3:21a] declares YHWH's intention to avenge the shed blood of his people that he has not yet avenged.[68] This reading does provide greater clarity since it turns this clause into a final judgment on the nations, which assures Jerusalem's security.[69] It also links the "innocent blood" of 4:19[3:19] and "their blood" in 4:21[3:21] since both refer to the Judahites. Consequently, Joel 4:21a[3:21a] guarantees Judah's existence by pronouncing final judgment on the nations who shed Judah's innocent blood. YHWH's promise to avenge the blood of his people provides further evidence of his intention to restore their fortunes and judge the nations.

Joel 4:21b[3:21b] then triumphantly asserts the conclusion וַיהוָה שֹׁכֵן בְּצִיּוֹן ("and YHWH dwells in Zion"). This is the final confirmation of YHWH's promises to restore his people and to preserve them from their enemies. The promise of YHWH's dwelling in Zion confirms the progression of Joel's prophetic word. Joel 2:1–11 culminates with the shocking revelation that YHWH leads the army assaulting Zion, which requires the people to gather and cry out to him to turn from judgment. The nations' derisive question "where is their God?" in 2:17 receives its final answer as 4:21b[3:21b] confidently reveals YHWH's presence in Zion, from where he will judge the nations who threaten his people.

---

64. Barton, *Joel*, 109.
65. Ahlström, *Joel*, 95.
66. See especially Allen, *Joel*, 117–26. The NIV 2011 also adopts this approach. Jeremiah 25:29 offers a potential parallel since it uses the same root (נָקָה), although those verbs occur in the *niphal* rather than the *piel*. On the syntax of unmarked rhetorical questions, see *Gesenius' Hebrew Grammar*, 2nd ed., ed. E. Kautzsch, trans. A. E. Cowley (Oxford: Clarendon: 1910) §150a. It suggests that a connection to the preceding sentence marked by וְ might further signal a rhetorical question.
67. Simkins, *Yahweh's Activity*, 237.
68. The NETS of the LXX renders this clause, "I will avenge their blood, and I will not hold it guiltless." The ESV is similar, reading "I will avenge their blood, blood I have not avenged."
69. A selection of those commentators who follow this approach includes Crenshaw, *Joel*, 203; Barton, *Joel*, 109; Garrett, *Hosea, Joel*, 397.

Summary

Joel 4:1–21[3:1–21] is the third passage celebrating Judah's deliverance from despair, following the hinge of 2:12–17. It expands the description of restoration in 2:18 onward by focusing on the threat of foreign nations. Joel 4:1–3[3:1–3] sets the tone for this chapter by declaring YHWH's intention to restore the fortunes of the people and to enter into judgment against other nations. This process plays out in 4:4–8[3:4–8] which dares Tyre, Sidon, and Philistia to bring an accusation against YHWH, who promises to treat them as they have treated YHWH's people. Joel 4:9–17[3:9–17] then adopts a broader perspective, summoning the nations to challenge YHWH where they will face judgment. It also repurposes language surrounding the day of YHWH in 2:1, 11 to make it a day of hope when it targets foreign nations. Finally, 4:18–21[3:18–21] summarizes YHWH's intentions by contrasting Judah's paradisiacal future with a final declaration of judgment on those who shed its innocent blood. YHWH is no longer absent, and his people find hope in the promise of his eternal presence.

Canonical and Practical Significance

Poetic Justice

A key element in this chapter is its use of retributive justice, also known as *lex talionis* (law of retribution), which is exemplified in its discussion of Tyre, Sidon, and Philistia in 4:4–8[3:4–8]. Joel details how YHWH will make their punishment fit the crime, taking those engaged in the slave trade and turning them into slaves themselves. This "eye for an eye" brand of justice resonates throughout the OT. It is developed in legal material in Exod 21:23–25; Lev 24:19–20; Deut 19:18–21, which apply this principle to scenarios ranging from redress when a pregnant woman is harmed to an indictment of false testimony.[70] In narrative contexts, the captured Canaanite King Adoni-Bezek is maimed in a fashion that corresponds to his own treatment of prisoners (Judg 1:7), while Haman is hung on the very gallows he had built for Mordecai (Esth 7:10). The punishment is carefully crafted to match the crime, suggesting that justice has been fulfilled.

Examples also abound of prophets who employ *lex talionis* to confirm the rightness of YHWH's judgment against transgressors, whether Israelite or foreign (Isa 3:9b–11; Jer 5:19; 50:16; Ezek 15:69; 35:1–10; 36:6–7; Hos 4:4–6; 8:1–6; Obad 15–16; Zech 7:13).[71] Obadiah 15–16 provides the closest parallel to Joel 4:4–8[3:4–8] since it is set against the backdrop of the day of YHWH and it also uses the noun גְּמוּל that played a significant role in Joel. Obadiah 17 also covers the same ground as Joel

---

70. Exodus 21:23–25 focuses on injuries to a pregnant woman or her *in utero* children; Lev 24:19–20 applies the principle more broadly to instances of physical harm; while Deut 19:18–21 makes it more abstract and suggests that those who give false witness should suffer the fate intended for the one they accused.

71. Patrick D. Miller, *Sin and Judgment in the Prophets*, SBLMS 27 (Atlanta: Scholars, 1982), 111–15. Miller provides a categorized list of the different ways that the prophets employ *lex talionis*.

3:5[2:32], suggesting that Zion is a refuge for those who escape the day of YHWH. Obadiah 15b announces, "As you have done, it will be done to you; your deeds will return upon your own head." YHWH then promises punishment for Edom suitable to its actions of taking advantage of Judah's desolation, promising that Judah will return to destroy Edom. This subsection of Obadiah (Obad 15–18) then ends in the same fashion as Joel 4:4–8[3:4–8], declaring that YHWH has spoken. Both passages stress YHWH's commitment to restoring his people by punishing their oppressors in a manner worthy of the crime. These promises offer hope that ultimately YHWH will redress the grievances against his people when he comes to "settle accounts" with the nations.

YHWH's agency is essential to understanding the use of *lex talionis* in prophetic literature, especially in 4:4–8[3:4–8] where the Judahite audience observes YHWH's interactions with the nations. The fact that YHWH enacts appropriate judgment makes it possible to comprehend NT discussions of this topic. Jesus declares in Matt 5:38–42 that his followers should not try to hold to "an eye for an eye" judgment, but should acquiesce in humility to different injustices. This teaching is challenging but it takes on greater clarity when considered alongside Paul in Rom 12:17–21. He cites Deut 32:35 while calling on believers not to repay evil for evil, but rather to let YHWH enact vengeance at the appropriate time. Human participation in an "eye for an eye" approach to justice escalates into a tit-for-tat cycle as opposing sides disagree as to when proper retribution has been achieved.[72] Jesus offers a way to break that cycle by commending his followers to love and good deeds while promising to enact appropriate judgment on those who do not submit to his sovereignty. Followers of Christ can take hope in promises of future judgment while resisting the impulse to seek revenge.

Swords and Plowshares

The interaction of 4:10[3:10] with other prophetic literature merits further reflection. In this verse, Joel inverts Isa 2:4 (and Mic 4:3) by calling the nations to take farm implements and turn them into weapons, which is a procedure that occurred in ill-equipped, conscript armies.[73] This sharply contrasts the vision in Isa 2:2–4 of an idyllic future where the nations worship YHWH in Zion. God's presence in Zion

---

72. I experienced a low-stakes version of this while playing in an adult recreational soccer league run by a Christian organization. A member of the opposing team committed a potentially dangerous slide tackle, which prompted my teammate to respond with a similar attempt a few minutes later. Of course, the original offender did not think he had done anything wrong and now considered himself the aggrieved party who needed to even the score. I had to adjust my halftime devotional to an impromptu discussion of "eye for an eye" justice.

73. Most commentators agree that Joel is reworking Isaiah. See Allen, *Joel*, 115; Wendland, *Discourse Analysis*, 247; Nogalski, *Book of the Twelve*, 247. On transforming farm implements into weapons, see H. G. M. Williamson, "Swords into Plowshares: The Development and Implementation of a Vision," in *Isaiah's Vision of Peace in Biblical and Modern International Relations: Swords into Plowshares*, ed. Raymond Cohen and Raymond Westbook (New York: Palgrave Macmillan, 2008), 147.

is beneficial for all nations since they have the opportunity to encounter him and acknowledge his sovereignty. The nations cease striving for dominion, which allows those who dwell in Zion to be at peace. Zechariah 8:22–23 envisions the nations' eagerness as they entreat the Judahites to bring them up to Zion so that they experience for themselves the dwelling place of God. This desire indicates that they no longer need swords and spears but can turn them into plowshares and pruning hooks.

Joel reformulates this picture by invoking a known prophecy only to reverse its expectations. Shared vocabulary reinforces the connections between the passages since the words used for weapons and farm implements are nearly identical, with only the word for "spears" being different.[74] Joel 4:10[3:10] changes the vision for the future from idyllic co-existence to hostile confrontation. The nations do not make a pilgrimage up to Mount Zion to worship, but rather answer the summons to come to the Valley of Jehoshaphat and confront YHWH. The nations do not submit to YHWH's sovereignty willingly, but rather have to be broken when they challenge him. This inversion allows Joel to demonstrate the futility of opposing YHWH. In Isa 2:4, the submission of the nations allows them access into YHWH's holy city where they learn to worship him, whereas in Joel 4:10–14[3:10–14] the call to turn farm implements into weapons leads to pronouncements of judgment and the unleashing of the day of YHWH. The prophetic vision is consistent in asserting that the nations will submit to YHWH, but the manner in which they do may be willingly or unwilling.

The theme of all peoples eventually acknowledging divine authority echoes throughout Scripture, as the NT attributes to Jesus the honor that God is due. Philippians 2:6–11 envisions the day when all creation will bow and confess that Jesus Christ is Lord. Christ's earthly humility actually guarantees his ultimate exaltation, and all must give him his due. Revelation 14:15–20 and 19:11–21 resonate with images of the nations' submission. These passages draw their imagery from Joel 4:13[3:13], describing angels with sickles that reap the harvest of judgment (Rev 14:17–20) and the Messianic rider on the white horse who tramples the nations like grapes in the winepress (Rev 19:15).[75] God's authority over all of creation is found throughout Scripture. Those who submit willingly have the hope of the idyllic vision of Isa 2:4, while those who challenge God and his Messiah will be trampled in the manner of Joel 4:10–14[3:10–14] and its adaptations in Revelation.

The Promise of Presence and Paradise

YHWH's sovereignty over the nations is rooted in the declaration of his dwelling in Zion. This guarantees Joel's promise of restored fortunes described as a vision of renewed paradise for Judah. The Zion tradition is essential to the relationship

---

74. Isa 2:4 uses חֲנִית, while Joel 4:10 uses רְמָחִים. The terms are synonymous.

75. Gregory K. Beale, *The Book of Revelation*, NIGTC (Grand Rapids: Eerdmans, 1999), 774–75.

between YHWH and his people in the OT. Zion is the dwelling place of God (Deut 12:5; 1 Kgs 5:5; 8:16–17), the place where his residence intersects with the earthly realm (Ps 132:7).[76] It is rooted in the idea of divine kingship and the promise of refuge for those who submit to YHWH's sovereignty.[77] The psalms in particular resonate with how Joel uses Zion in this chapter since they focus on YHWH's protection. His divine presence indicates that Zion is an inviolable sanctuary, and the hostile nations addressed throughout this chapter cannot harm it (Pss 46, 48, 76, 122, 132). In 2:1–11, the prophet brings Zion under threat, with YHWH's absence being a key signal that the day of YHWH could have catastrophic consequences. As mentioned previously, this fits into what Poulsen has identified as the "dynamic Zion motif," in which Zion can be threatened and even destroyed, but will be restored and rebuilt.[78] However, 4:1–21[3:1–21] marks a return to the "classical Zion motif" since YHWH's presence indicates that Zion's safety is assured. Essentially, as the people turn to YHWH and because YHWH demonstrates his great mercy, Zion in Joel 4:16[3:16] symbolizes divine deliverance from the hands of oppressors.[79]

In Joel 4:16[3:16], YHWH utters a roar from Zion that shakes the heavens but provides refuge for his people. This roar confirms YHWH's presence and his authority over the created order. The exact same phrase is found in Amos 1:2, which is usually considered to provide the theme of that book.[80] Joel and Amos, however, use the divine roar for different purposes. Amos uses it to set up a geographical *merismus* stretching from "the pastures of the shepherds" to "the top of Carmel." This provides a sense of completeness to YHWH's intention to judge the nations in Amos 1:3–2:16. Amos's oracles spring a rhetorical trap that ultimately identify Israel as YHWH's primary target, indicating that YHWH's divine roar from Zion brings woe to those who should be his people.[81] In Joel, YHWH's roar offers hope for his people that YHWH will defeat foreign oppressors. The divine roar thus conveys a sense of YHWH's power rooted in the place where he chooses to dwell, but it can convey both woe and weal depending on the relationship between YHWH and his people.

YHWH's presence in Zion also offers the promise of boundless blessing. Joel 4:18[3:18] looks to the aftermath of the day of YHWH and sees a land flowing with wine, milk, and water sourced from a fountain rooted in the temple. This image is found several times in Scripture with the closest parallel occurring in Ezek 47:1–12 (cf. Ps 46:5; Zech 14:8–11). Ezekiel provides greater detail than Joel, detailing the depth and directions of the stream (v. 1–6) and describing the life that it sustains (v. 7–12). This stream permits fruit-bearing trees to flourish throughout the year,

---

76. For a detailed examination of Zion imagery throughout the entire Bible see Lois Dow, *Images of Zion: Biblical Antecedents for the New Jerusalem* (Sheffield: Sheffield Phoenix, 2010).

77. Ollenburger, *Zion*, 46.

78. Poulsen, *Representing Zion*, 71.

79. Ibid., 107.

80. Nogalski, *Book of the Twelve*, 249.

81. Judah is also targeted in Amos 2:4–5, again revealing that human obedience is necessary for divine presence to bring blessing and security.

fertilizes desert regions, and even is the house for abundant quantities of fish. Ezekiel 47:1-12 thus shares with Joel 4:18[3:18] a vision of great fruitfulness for the land, rooted in God's presence among his people.

The idea of abundant blessing rooted in a stream flowing from the temple in Joel and Ezekiel intentionally evokes visions of Eden. As mentioned above, Joel 4:18e-f[3:18e-f] uses the same verbs to describe the stream from the temple as Gen 2:10 uses for the rivers flowing out from Eden (שָׁקָה, יָצָא).[82] Jerusalem's actual water supply was much more tenuous, but the Gihon spring that supplied it does take on superlative overtones when it becomes one of the four rivers sourcing the garden of Eden.[83] Eden and its rivers are essential to the Hebrew Bible's conception of sacred geography, comparable to an umbilical cord nurturing all of creation. Eden further operates as a symbol of harmony between God and humanity, marred only by human transgression.[84] By conflating temple and Edenic imagery in the wake of disaster, Joel and Ezekiel envision a return to the pre-fall state with a renewed temple housing God's presence in the midst of his people.

This promise of a return to paradise finds its ultimate manifestation in the hope of the new Jerusalem in Rev 21. God promises to dwell in the midst of his people and provide permanent restoration and healing (Rev 21:3-4). As with the image of a temple-sourced stream, Revelation's vision goes well beyond the bounds of human understanding to describe the space where God and his people can live in harmony. The new Jerusalem has no temple because God's presence cannot be restricted to one location in this restored Eden. It infuses the entirety of creation and provides for every need, even supplanting the necessity of heavenly bodies like the sun and moon.[85] As in the book of Joel, Revelation calls us to look beyond the crises of the current moment and to draw hope from the vision of future restoration between God and his people. The broken nature of the world and the afflictions that we experience should lead us to hold onto the expectation that there is a return to paradise ahead. The vision of God's presence in the temple reflects the church's anticipation of eternal dwelling in his presence, guaranteed by Christ's defeat of all enemies.

---

82. Strazicich, *Joel's Use of Scripture*, 243.

83. Leslie J. Hoppe, *The Holy City: Jerusalem in the Theology of the Old Testament* (Collegeville, MN: Liturgical, 2000), 27-29.

84. Fishbane, *Biblical Interpretation*, 369.

85. Beale, *Book of Revelation*, 1093-94.

Scripture Index

Genesis
1:2 . . . . 84, 134
1:11 124
1:26–28 74
2:5–3:24 74
2:8 84
2:10 . . . . 84, 163, 170
2:15 84
3:23 84
4:16 84
6:6 109
6:12 138
6:13 138
7:12 125
7:21 138
7:23 142
8:2 125
12:6 125
12:8 141
13:4 141
14:8 86
21:33 141
22:22–23 47
24:15 47
24:24 47
24:47 47
24:50 47
26:25 141
28:12–17 138
37:5–11 138
40:8–23 138
41:14–27 138
41:31 137
41:35 126
41:49 126
45:2 102
50:10 102

Exodus
3:8 163
3:17 163
6:7 . . . . 128, 161
7:14–24 140
10:2 128
10:21–29 140
13:5 163
14:3 70
14:6–7 86
16:12 . . . . 128, 161
19:3–6 109
19:5 110
19:16–19 91
19:16 83
20:2 132
20:3–5 132
20:5 119
20:21 83
21:23–25 166
21:34 127
21:36–37 127
22:1–5 127
22:3 127
22:6 127
22:8 127
22:12–13 127
29:46 132
32:12–14 . . . . 103, 109
32:12 108
32:19–25 103
32:30–35 104
33:19 141
34:1–7 103
34:5 141
34:6–7 . . . . 103, 104, 107, 108,
                      109, 110, 114

Leviticus
4:15 52
9:1–2 52
10:4–7 59
19:3 132
19:4 132
19:10 132
19:21 132
19:25 132
19:34 132
19:36 132
21:10–12 59
23:36 63
24:19–20 166
25:9 . . . . 81, 105
26:3–4 126
26:4 . . . . 125, 129
26:18–20 . . . . 126, 129
27:30–33 57

Numbers
11:10–30 143
11:16–30 52
14:8 163
14:13–16 100
14:18 . . . . 103, 108
15:41 162
18:12 57

18:15 138	29:5 162	11:2 107
21:35 142	31:11–13 4	13:5 86
22:16 59	32:10 84	14:16 160
25:1 163	32:22–27 100	14:19 89
29:35 63	32:25 139	24:9[8] 137
33:49 163	32:35 167	25:19 119
	34:8 102	26:12 55
Deuteronomy		28:6 138
2:34 142	**Joshua**	28:8–10 138
4:11 83	2:1 163	
5:6 132	3:1 163	**2 Samuel**
5:7–9 132	6:4 81	2:1 137
5:9 119	7:7 72	6:15 105
5:12–15 139	7:33 52	12:11 119
5:26 138	8:22 142	12:16 . . . . 59, 102
6:1–3 61	10:2 159	12:22 104
6:3 163	23:4 142	13:10 106
8:10–14 130		13:36 102
9:26–28 108	**Judges**	22:10 83
11:13–15 126	1:7 166	24:16 109
11:14 . . . . 125, 129	3:27 81	
11:15 . . . . 125, 130	4:3 86	**1 Kings**
11:30 125	4:7 160	1:8 159
12:5–7 69	5:4 89	1:10 159
12:5 169	5:23 159	4:25 56
14:22–29 57	5:28 86	5:5 169
15:6a 87	6:3–5 53	5:19 119
15:8 87	6:34 81	8:3 52
16:8 63	7:1 125	8:16–17 169
16:11 139	7:8 81	8:35–36 126
16:14 139	7:12 53	8:37–48 101
18:1–8 57	11:35 72	8:53 106
19:18–21 166	13:19 128	11:31 119
20:1–20 157	15:1 106	12:6 52
20:7 106		12:13 52
21:2–20 52	**Ruth**	14:11 156
21:17 127	1:4b 124	17 73
24:5 106	4:9–11 52	17:7 125
24:10 87		18:24 141
26:1–15 57	**1 Samuel**	18:45 125
26:15 163	1:9 155	20:6 155
28:12 129	2:27–36 142	20:13 160
28:22–24 . . . . 73, 126, 129	4–6 155	20:40 160
28:38–44 100	4:2 86	21:1 155
	10:1 106	

21:27 59	9:32 90	58 62
18:39–45 73	13:10–12 120	59:3–4 99

2 Kings

	Esther	60 62
2:9 127	4:3 102	65:10 126
2:11–12 86	4:13 70	65:13 71
3:10 73	4:14 104	68:10 106
4:31 55	7:10 166	69:11 102
6:5 72	**Job**	73:20 55
6:15 72	12:10 138	74 62
6:17 86	22:13 83	74:2 153
18–19 99	26:10–12 91	76 169
18:3 56	29:23 125	76:4–10 161
18:16 155	36:22 125	77:16 89
18:28–29 52	37:22 120	77:18–19 89
18:35 99	38:15 59	79 62
19:28 99	41:22 160	79:1 153
20:3 102	**Psalms**	80 62
20:18 155	2:1–12 81	81:4 . . . . 81, 105
21:14 106	3:6 55	83 62

1 Chronicles

	7:3–5 99	84:7 125
15:28 105	12 62	85 62

2 Chronicles

	18:8 89	86:15 . . . . 103, 109
15:14 81	18:10[9] 83	90 62
20:3 102	19:6 106	90:11 104
20:20–26 153	28:9 153	94 62
20:35 137	30:12 102	97:2 83
36:17 119	33:5 134	98:6 105
36:19 155	33:12 106	103:8 . . . . 103, 108
	35:13 102	103:20 159

Ezra

	35:26–27 122	104:30 134
3:1–7 29	42:2 71	106:5 106
3:13 102	44 62	109:24 102
8:21 102	44:13 154	122 169
	46 . . . . 131, 169	123 62

Nehemiah

	46:2–4 161	126 62
1:5 90	46:5 . . . . 163, 169	126:4 71
4:8 90	47:6 81	129 62
8:18 63	48 . . . . 131, 169	132 169
9:1 102	48:2–7 81	132:7 169
9:17 . . . . 103, 108	48:3 120	145:8 . . . . 103, 108
9:31 108	48:5–9 161	148:12 139
9:31b 103		150:3 81

Proverbs

- 1:8–19 61
- 4:1 52
- 5:13 125
- 7:24 52
- 16:15 125
- 23:35 55
- 30:27 87

Ecclesiastes

- 2:19 104
- 3:21 104
- 6:12 104
- 8:1 104

Song of Solomon

- 1:4 106
- 8:2 56

Isaiah

- 1:1 46
- 1:2 156
- 1:7 162
- 1:10 52
- 1:13 63
- 1:19–20 98
- 1:26 135
- 2:2–4 . . . . 158, 167
- 2:2 137
- 2:4 . . . . 35, 167, 168
- 3:9b–11 166
- 3:26 57
- 4:2 141
- 4:6 161
- 5:30 82
- 6:8–13 39
- 7:18 163
- 7:21 163
- 7:23 163
- 9:7 119
- 10:5–6 81
- 10:5–19 122
- 10:22–23 160
- 10:24–27 123
- 11:10 163
- 11:11 163
- 12:4 141
- 12:6 123
- 13:1–5 158
- 13:1–22 33
- 13:2–3 157
- 13:4 160
- 13:6–13 91
- 13:6 . . . . 33, 35, 72, 92, 160
- 13:6–9 91
- 13:8 86
- 13:9 33
- 13:10 89
- 13:13 89
- 14:13 120
- 17:5 160
- 19:25 106
- 21:3 86
- 22:1–5 153
- 22:1–14 68
- 22:1 153
- 22:6–11 91
- 22:12 102
- 22:25 156
- 24:3 156
- 24:7 35
- 24:18 121
- 24:21 163
- 25:8 156
- 26:17 86
- 27:12 163
- 27:13 163
- 28:27 160
- 29:1–8 81
- 29:5 . . . . 160, 162
- 29:8 55
- 30:20 125
- 32:9–20 134
- 32:15–20 142
- 32:15 . . . . 134, 139
- 34:1–10 91
- 36:16 56
- 41:15 160
- 41:25 120
- 44:1–5 . . . . 139, 143
- 44:10 125
- 45 132
- 45:5 132
- 45:6 132
- 45:14 132
- 45:18 132
- 45:21 132
- 45:22 132
- 49:26 . . . . 56, 138
- 50:3 89
- 51:3 . . . . 84, 93
- 52:1 56
- 52:7–10 123
- 54:1 123
- 54:4 107
- 55:6–7 98
- 55:10 125
- 58:1–12 102
- 63:1–6 160
- 64:10 155
- 66:16 138
- 66:19 156

Jeremiah

- 1:1 46
- 1:13–15 120
- 1:15 119
- 2:35 119
- 3:3 59
- 3:12–13 98
- 3:21 102
- 4:1–2 98
- 4:5–8 81
- 4:5 81
- 4:6 120
- 4:6b 81
- 4:10 73
- 4:14 56
- 4:27–28 89
- 5:19 . . . . 162, 166
- 5:24 125
- 6:1 81

6:4 157	29:8 138	2:22 68
6:4–6 159	30:3 153	3:40 99
6:8 56	30:8 162	3:61 107
6:21 119	30:18 153	
6:22 120	31:16 102	**Ezekiel**
6:23 86	31:23 153	1 86
6:24 86	31:26 55	1:4 120
6:26 102	32:37 164	4:13 121
7:1–8 102	32:44 153	4:16 119
7:1–11 93	33:7 153	5:11 119
7:4 161	33:11 153	6:3 52
7:4–8 131	33:15 152	6:7 .... 128, 132
7:13–15 81	34:11 137	6:13–14 128
8:3 121	34:22 164	7:1–9 91
9:9 71	35:17 119	7:4 128
9:21 88	36:6 102	7:21 162
10:10 89	36:9 102	7:26 .... 52, 142
10:18 53	42:17 142	8:16–18 106
10:22 120	44:14 142	9:8 73
12:4 57	46:1–12 91	10:18–19 131
12:10–11 57	46:2–20 68	11:3 119
12:12 138	46:3–5 159	11:10 128
13:14 119	46:23 53	11:13 73
13:16 156	46:27–28 123	13:1–9 68
16:5 89	47:4 28	13:1–16 91
16:16 137	48:32 160	13:5 .... 33, 140
18:1–10 .... 110, 111	50:4 152	14:6–11 98
18:18 .... 52, 142	50:9 86	15:7 128
22:3–5 98	50:14–16 159	15:69 166
22:7 157	50:16 166	16:22 128
22:23 86	50:20 152	20:5 162
23:10 .... 57, 71	50:43 86	20:7 162
23:15–16 113	51:27–28 157	22:19 119
23:25–26 138	51:27 81	23:22 .... 91, 119
23:40 107	51:51 162	24:14 109
24:2 160		25–32 156
24:9 121	**Lamentations**	25:15–17 155
25:5–6 98	1:2 68	26:10 .... 89, 120
25:29 165	1:4 57	27:13 156
26:4–6 81	1:10 155	27:32 102
26:13 109	2:2 119	28:7 162
26:19 109	2:8 57	28:10 162
27:9 138	2:17 119	28:26 132
28:13–16 113	2:21–24 119	29:6 128

29:9 128	4:4–6 166	1:7 . . . . 54, 56, 58, 124
29:16 128	5:8 157	1:7a–c 55, 56
29:23–24 143	6:3 125	1:8–10 . . . . 55, 56
30:1–4 91	6:6 102	1:8 . . . . 40, 49, 52, 57, 59, 99
30:3 140	8:1–6 166	1:9–10 120
31:9 84	8:1 81	1:9 . . . . 29, 30, 57, 59, 105, 134
31:16 84	9:6 155	1:9b 57, 59
31:18 84	12:11 138	1:10 . . . . 35, 38, 57, 68, 126
32:7–8 89	14:2 98	1:10a–e 57
35:1–10 166		1:11–12 . . . . 55, 58, 60, 70
36:6–7 166	**Joel**	1:11 . . . . 40, 49, 52, 58, 89, 99
36:35 . . . . 84, 93	1 . . . . 21–22, 70, 76	1:11a 58
37:1–14 113	1:1 27	1:12 . . . . 35, 58, 100
37:6 139	1:1–2:27 27	1:12d 58
38–39 153	1:1–3:5[2:32] 31	1:13–14 . . . . . . 29, 55, 58–61, 90, 94
38:6 120	1:1 . . . . 35, 45–47, 65, 78, 95,	1:13 30, 40, 49, 52, 73, 99, 105, 106,
38:15 120	115, 135, 148	134
38:16 91	1:1b 28	1:13f. 69
38:19–20 121	1:2–2:12 . . 30, 39, 40, 41, 53, 94, 95,	1:14–18 32
39:11 . . . . 153, 163	98, 101, 113, 114, 119, 122	1:14 . . . 36, 38, 40, 49, 63, 64, 67, 68,
39:25 119	1:2–2:17 . . 31, 32, 39, 101, 118, 120,	82, 95, 99, 103, 106, 120, 157
39:26 143	124, 126, 128, 129, 131, 147, 154	1:14a–b 105
39:28–29 . . . . 132, 143	1:2–2:27 . . . . 31, 32	1:14e 67
39:29 139	1:2–2:28 114	1:15–16 . . . . . . 40, 42, 45, 48, 49, 52,
47:1–12 . . . . 163, 164, 169, 170	1:2–3 . . . . 38, 52, 53, 54, 83, 89	65, 67
	1:2–3:5[2:32] 146	1:15–20 . . . . . . 64–75, 78, 90, 94, 95,
Daniel	1:2–4 . . . . 42, 49, 61	115, 122, 126, 128, 129,
8:21 156	1:2–14 . . . 40, 42, 45, 48–65, 75–78,	131, 135, 148, 163, 164
9:3 102	83, 90, 94, 95, 115, 122,	1:15 . . . . 27, 31–36, 38, 67–69,
9:4 90	127, 135, 148	147, 160, 161
9:7 121	1:2–20 . . . . 34, 152	1:15a 67
10:20 156	1:2 . . . 30, 36, 40, 49, 52, 60, 83, 106	1:15b 67, 68, 82
11:2 156	1:2a–d 52, 53	1:15c 68
11:10 160	1:3–4 52	1:16–20 124
	1:3 . . . . 49, 53, 83	1:16 . . . . 65, 69, 70, 123
Hosea	1:3a–c 53	1:16a–b 69
1:1 46	1:4 . . . . 38, 53, 54, 127	1:17–18 . . . . 42, 65, 69, 70
2:8 119	1:4a–c 54	1:17 126
2:9 160	1:5–14 . . . . 42, 49, 52, 55, 61, 67, 94,	1:17a–d 69, 70
2:10–11[2:8–9] 130	100, 105, 141, 158	1:18 . . . . 70, 71, 99
2:23–25 34	1:5 . . . . 40, 49, 52, 55, 89, 99	1:18a–d 70
2:23–25[2:21–23] 130	1:5a–d 55, 56	1:19–20 . . . 36, 38, 40, 42, 64, 65, 67,
2:23[21] 163	1:6–7 . . . . 56, 90	69, 70, 71, 73, 75, 124, 134
4:1 . . . . 52, 53	1:6 . . . . 32, 54, 56	1:19 129
	1:6a–d 56	1:19a–b 67, 70, 71
		1:19b–20c 71

1:20a-c 67, 70
2 . . . . 22–23, 98
2b[2:28b] 138
2b[2:29b] 138
2:1 27
2:1-2 90
2:1-11 . . . . 36, 38, 40, 42, 45, 49, 64, 65, 68, 75–95, 97, 98, 107, 115, 118, 120, 121, 122, 127, 128, 135, 141, 142, 148, 165, 169
2:1-2b 78, 83
2:1 . . 31–33, 38, 67, 81, 85, 89, 147, 161, 166
2:1a-2e 42, 81, 82, 162
2:2 . . . . 76, 83, 86, 87, 89, 92
2:2a-b 82
2:2c-5c 42, 78, 83
2:2c-9e 83
2:3-9 87
2:3 . . . . 32, 76, 77, 84, 85, 86, 93, 121, 124, 141
2:3a-e 84, 85
2:4 . . . . 76, 85
2:4a-b 85
2:5 . . . . 76, 85, 86, 87, 89
2:5a 85
2:5b 76, 86
2:5c 86
2:6 . . . . 42, 78, 86, 146
2:6a 86, 87, 89
2:6b 87
2:7-9 . . . . 30, 42, 77, 78, 87, 88, 92, 121
2:7 . . . . 76, 87
2:7a 76
2:7a-d 87
2:7c-8b 87
2:8 88
2:8c-d 88
2:9 . . . . 76, 88
2:9a-d 88
2:10-11 . . . 42, 77, 78, 81, 83, 88–91, 94, 97, 121, 134, 140, 147, 161
2:10 . . . . 32, 77, 90
2:10a-d 89
2:11-4:21[3:21] 31

2:11 . . 27, 31–33, 37, 38, 67, 91, 97, 101, 102, 104, 110, 124, 127, 140, 160, 166
2:11a-e 90
2:11f 90, 93
2:12-17 . . . 30, 33, 37, 39–42, 45, 49, 60, 62, 65, 72, 73, 77, 78, 90, 92, 94–112, 114, 115, 119, 122, 126, 129, 130–135, 142, 148, 166
2:12 . . . . 36, 60, 97, 98, 101, 156
2:12a 97, 101
2:12b 103, 106
2:13 . . . . 98, 99
2:13a-d 102, 103, 104
2:14 . . . . 111, 129, 162
2:14a-e 102, 104, 105
2:15-17 . . . . 38, 42, 45, 97, 99, 103, 104, 141, 158
2:15 . . . . 60, 98, 105, 120, 157
2:15b-c 105
2:16 . . . . 32, 98, 105, 139, 141
2:16a-g 105, 106
2:17 . . . 29, 36, 41, 70, 98, 100, 105, 106, 113, 114, 118, 122, 129, 138, 143, 146, 154, 162, 165
2:17a-f 106, 107, 120
2:18 . . 31, 38, 113, 118, 119, 126, 132
2:18a 119
2:18-4:21[3:21] . . 31, 32, 37, 39, 41, 56, 95, 153
2:18-27 . . . . . . 41, 42, 45, 49, 54, 65, 70, 78, 95, 100, 113–35, 137, 138, 142, 143, 146, 148, 163
2:18-19a 118, 124
2:19 . . . . .38, 100, 126
2:19-20 . . . . 118, 119, 123
2:19a-c 118, 119
2:19e 120
2:20-4:21[3:21] 32
2:20 . . . . 81, 120
2:20b-g 121, 122, 123
2:21-24 . . . . . . 42, 118, 122–26
2:21a-d 122, 123, 123
2:22 123
2:22b-d 122, 123, 124
2:23 . . . . 114, 124, 126
2:23a-e 124, 125

2:24 . . . . .38, 126, 160
2:24a-b 126
2:25-27 . . . . 42, 118, 126–29
2:25 . . 38, 53, 77, 114, 126, 127, 129
2:25a-e 126, 127
2:26-27 . . . . 36, 134
2:26 . . . . 41, 100, 127–30
2:26a-c 127, 128
2:27 . . . . 32, 41, 100, 114, 128, 129, 158
2:27a-e 128
2:28-32 . . . . 27, 144
3[2:28-32] 24
3:1[2:28]-4:21[3:21] 31
3:1-2 43
3:1-2[2:28-29] 37, 138–39
3:1-4[2:28-31] 137
3:1-4[2:28-31] 140
3:1-4:21 114
3:1-4:21[2:28-3:21] 31
3:1-5 . . . . 27, 114, 144
3:1-5[2:28-32] . . . 31, 41, 43, 45, 49, 65, 78, 95, 115, 134–46, 148, 161
3:1-21 27
3:1 138
3:1c-e[2:28c-e] 138
3:1[2:28] . . 31, 36, 137, 139–41, 152
3:1b 138
3:1b[2:28b] 138
3:2[2:29] 139
3:2[2:29] 32, 68
3:2a 139
3:3-4 43
3:3-4[2:30-31] 137, 139–140
3:3 140
3:4[2:31] 27, 32, 33, 38, 41, 67, 135, 140
3:4a-c[2:31a-c] 140
3:5 . . . . 43, 85, 140, 164
3:5[2:28] 31
3:5[2:32] . . 32, 137, 139–42, 166–67
3:5a[2:32a] 140
3:5b[2:32b] 140
3:5c[2:28c] 141

3:5c[2:32c] 141
3:5d[2:28d] 142
3:5e–f[2:28e–f] 142
4[3] 24–25
4:1–3 43
4:1–3[3:1–3] 41, 148, 152–55, 157, 166
4:1–20[3:1–20] 141
4:1–21 . . . . 27, 64
4:1–21[3:1–21] . . . 31, 41, 43, 45, 49, 65, 78, 95, 115, 135, 146–170
4:1 152
4:1[3:1] 36, 68, 137, 146, 163
4:1b[3:1b] 152
4:2–3[3:2–3] 153
4:2[3:2] 37, 148, 153, 159, 160
4:2a–b[3:2a–b] 153
4:2c–3d[3:2c–3d] 153, 154
4:3 152
4:3[3:3] 148
4:3a–d 154
4:4–8[3:4–8] 28, 31, 41, 43, 147, 148, 152–57, 164, 166
4:4 152
4:4[3:4] 156
4:4a–d[3:4a–d] 154, 155
4:5[3:5] 155
4:5a[3:5a] 155
4:5b[3:5b] 155
4:6 152
4:6[3:6] 29, 156
4:6a[3:6a] 156
4:6b[3:6b] 156
4:7–8[3:7–8] 156
4:7 152
4:7[3:7] 32
4:7a[3:7a] 156
4:7b[3:7b] 156
4:7b–8b[3:7b–8b] 156
4:8 152
4:8[3:8] 29, 101, 157
4:8a–c[3:8a–c] 156
4:9–17[3:9–17] . . 37, 38, 41, 43, 147, 148, 152, 157–62, 166
4:9[3:9] 157, 159
4:9a[3:9a] 157
4:9b[3:9b] 157
4:9c–e[3:9c–e] 157, 159
4:10–14[3:10–14] 168
4:10[3:10] 35, 158, 167, 168
4:10a–d[3:10a–d] 158
4:11–12[3:11–12] 37
4:11[3:11] 32
4:11a–d[3:11a–d] . . . 158, 159, 160
4:12[3:12] 12, 32, 159, 160
4:12a–c[3:12a–c] 159
4:13–17[3:13–17] 159
4:13[3:13] 126, 160, 168
4:13a–g[3:13a–g] 160
4:14[3:14] 27, 31–33, 38, 67, 68, 147, 153, 160, 161
4:14a[3:14a] 160
4:14b[3:14b] 161
4:15–16[3:15–16] 147, 161
4:15a–16c[3:15a–16c] 161
4:16[3:16] 32, 90, 160, 169
4:16e[3:16d–e] 161
4:17[3:17] . . . 32, 147, 158, 161, 162
4:17c[3:17c] 162
4:17d[3:17d] 162
4:17e[3:17e] 162
4:18–21[3:18–21] 41, 43, 71, 93, 124, 148, 152, 162–66
4:18[3:18] 31, 68, 163, 169, 170
4:18a[3:18a] 163
4:18d–f[3:18d–f] 163, 170
4:19–20[3:19–20] 164
4:19 165
4:19[3:19] 29
4:19a–d[3:19a–d] 164, 165
4:20[3:20] 164, 165
4:20a[3:20a] 164
4:20b[3:20b] 164
4:21[3:21] 41, 165
4:21a[3:21a] 165
4:21b[3:21b] 164, 165

Amos

1:1 46
1:2 . . . . 57, 169
1:3 160
1:3–2:16 169
1:6–10 155
2:4–5 169
2:6 154
3:1 52
4:1 124
4:4–5 102
4:6–11 130
4:7 125
4:9 34
5:8–10 90
5:16 102
5:18–20 . . . . 33, 82, 91, 92
5:18 . . . . 33, 72
5:20 33
5:21–23 102
5:21 63
6:14 119
7:1–8 138
7:3 109
7:4–6 71
7:6 109
7:7–9 109
7:8 119
8:1–2 160
8:1–3 109
8:5 126
8:6 126
8:11–12 142
9:14 164

Obadiah

1 46
11 . . . . 154, 162
15 . . . . 33, 92
15–16 166
15–17 91
15–18 167
15b 167
17 . . . . 141, 164
18 156

Jonah

3:4 111

3:5 102
3:9 104
4:1–4 110
4:2 . . . . 103, 109, 110

Micah
1:1 46
1:4 89
1:8 102
1:11 102
3:6–7 142
3:11 131
3:12 109
4:1–4 158
4:1 137
4:3 . . . . 35, 167
4:4 56
4:11–13 159
4:13 157
6:1–8 102
6:1 52
7:18–20 . . . . 103, 106, 108

Nahum
1:1 46
1:2–3 108
1:3 103
1:4–6 91
2:4 159
2:11 87
3:10 154
3:15–16 53

Habakkuk
1:1 46
1:6 91
3:8–15 91

Zephaniah
1:1 46
1:7–18 91
1:7 92
1:14–16 81
1:14–18 28
1:14 92

1:15–16 . . . . 82, 90
1:17 33
2:1–3 . . . . 91, 92
2:8 107
3:8 91
3:9 141
3:14–15 123
3:14 57
3:16–18 123
14 33

Haggai
1:4–11 73
1:10–11 34
1:12–15 73
2:9 34

Zechariah
1:14 119
2:9 128
2:10 120
2:14[10] 123
3:5 159
3:10 56
4:9 128
6:15 128
7:13 166
8:9–12 73
8:19 73
8:22–23 168
9:9–10 123
9:13 . . . . 57, 156
10:1 125
10:2 138
10:6 132
11:6 119
12:1–9 91
12:10 . . . . 102, 139
13:9 141
14 153
14:1–21 91
14:1 153
14:2 91
14:4 . . . . 153, 163

14:6 163
14:8–11 169
14:8 163
14:20 163

Malachi
2:13 102
3:1–4 91
3:2 93
3:8–12 73
3:11 73
3:23 . . . . 90, 140
3:23[4:5] 33, 92

Matthew
5:38–42 167

Acts
1:8 144
2 . . . . 142, 144
2:5–21 . . . . 143, 144
8:14–17 144
10:44–48 144
19:6 144

Romans
8:38–39 133
12:17–21 167

Philippians
2:6–11 168

2 Timothy
3:16–17 9

Hebrews
12:4–11 62

Revelation
9:2–11 76
9:3–4 76
9:10 76
14:15–20 . . . . 160, 168
19:11–21 168
19:15 . . . . 160, 168
21 170
21:3–4 170

Subject Index

Book of the Twelve, 33–35, 47, 68, 98, 102

community, calling, 40–41, 48–63

compassion, 23, 41, 99, 103–19, 122–33, 154

creation, care for, 73–74, 131, 170

creation, sovereignty over, 93, 168–69

delay techniques, 38, 53–54

deliverance
    calls to rejoice, 122–26
    canonical significance of, 129–33, 142–45
    in day of YHWH, 13, 27–43, 139–45
    divine deliverance, 23, 28, 113–33, 161–62, 169–70
    from drought, 23, 113–33
    explanation of, 118–29, 138–42
    fertility of land and, 114, 120–30
    hinge for, 40, 94–112, 142, 166
    hope for, 90–91, 98, 108, 120, 141–43
    literary context and, 113–14, 134–35
    literary form and, 115–18, 135–37
    from locusts, 23, 113–33
    outline of, 116–17, 136, 149–51
    potential for, 98
    practical significance of, 129–33, 142–45
    promises of, 28, 45, 91
    sign of, 161
    source of, 132
    summary of, 122, 126, 166
    through divine judgment, 24–25, 146–70
    through spirit, 24, 134–45

despair
    call to repentance, 98–101
    call to return to YHWH, 40, 94–112, 141–42
    canonical significance of, 108–12
    character of YHWH, 94–112
    crying to YHWH, 94–112
    in day of YHWH, 13, 21–22, 27–43, 45–49, 64–66, 75–93, 115, 135, 148
    drought and, 22, 64–74
    explanation of, 98–108
    hinge and, 40, 94–112, 142, 166
    invasion and, 22, 75–93
    locusts and, 21, 48–63
    moving beyond, 90–91, 98
    outline of, 96
    plan of return to YHWH, 105–8
    practical significance of, 108–12
    sense of, 60, 90–91
    summary of, 100–101, 108, 122, 166

divine agency, 38–39

divine authorization, 45–46, 68, 168

divine deliverance, 23, 28, 113–33, 161–62, 169–70. *See also* deliverance

divine judgment
    canonical significance of, 166–70
    deliverance through, 24–25, 146–70
    explanation of, 152–66
    "eye for an eye" justice, 166–67
    literary context and, 146–47
    literary form and, 148–52
    outline of, 149–51
    poetic justice, 29, 121, 156, 166–67
    practical significance of, 166–70
    retributive justice, 156, 166–67

doom, 33, 77–92, 109–11, 121, 152, 161

drought
    calls to rejoice, 122–26
    canonical significance of, 72–74, 129–33
    care for creation and, 73–74, 131
    crisis of, 68–73
    crying to YHWH and, 72–73
    day of YHWH and, 67–72
    deliverance from, 23, 113–33
    despair and, 22, 64–74
    effects of, 69–70
    explanation of, 67–72, 118–29
    fertility of land and, 73–74, 114, 120–30
    literary context and, 64–65, 113–14
    literary form and, 65–67, 115–18
    outline of, 66, 116–17
    practical significance of, 72–74, 129–33
    summary of, 71–72

drunkards, call to, 55–56

Eden, garden of, 22, 76, 84, 93, 163, 170

epistrophe, 40–41, 67, 115–18

"eye for an eye" justice, 166–67

farmers, call to, 58

fast, call to, 59–61, 105

fertility of land, 34–35, 73–74, 93, 114, 120–30, 143, 163

God. *See also* YHWH
    character of, 13, 27, 35, 103, 108–10, 119
    compassion of, 23, 41, 99, 103–19, 122–33, 154
    crying to, 72–73, 94–112
    dwelling place of, 81, 161, 168–69
    image of, 74
    presence of, 29–32, 41, 62, 68, 83, 89–93, 114, 118, 128–32, 135–43, 147, 157–70
    trustworthiness of, 101–2, 111–12, 132–33, 162
    word of, 21–22, 35, 45–47, 98
    zeal of, 41, 126, 129, 131–33

Hebrew text explanation, 12, 27–28
hinge
    call to repentance, 98–101
    call to return to YHWH, 40, 94–112, 141–42, 166
    canonical significance of, 108–10
    character of YHWH, 94–112
    crying to YHWH, 94–112
    for deliverance, 40, 94–112, 142, 166
    despair and, 40, 94–112, 142, 166
    explanation of, 98–108
    literary context and, 94–95
    literary form and, 95–97
    outline of, 96
    plan of return to YHWH, 105–8
    practical significance of, 108–10
    return to YHWH, 23, 40, 94–112
    summary of, 100–101, 108
Holy Spirit, 143–44. *See also* spirit
hope, promise of, 27–33, 41, 54, 103, 163

inclusion technique, 37, 58
invasion
    canonical significance of, 91–93
    despair and, 22, 75–93
    explanation of, 81–91
    literary context and, 75–77
    literary form and, 77
    by locust army, 77–78, 83–90, 114, 121–24, 141–42
    outline of, 79–80
    paradise lost and, 93
    practical significance of, 91–93
    summary of, 91–93
    victims of, 78, 86–87, 121
    Zion and, 75–93

Jesus Christ, 13, 73, 144, 167–68. *See also* YHWH
Joel
    background for, 28–29
    Book of the Twelve and, 33–35, 47, 68, 98, 102
    commentary on, 45–170
    composition of, 28–35, 39–40, 47, 125
    explanations regarding, 9–12, 27–31
    Hebrew text and, 12, 27–28
    historical context of, 28–31, 47
    introduction to, 27–43
    literary context of, 45–49, 64–65, 75–77, 94–95, 113–14, 134–35, 146–47
    literary form of, 49–52, 65–67, 77, 95–97, 115–18, 135–37, 148–52
    literary integrity of, 28, 31–33
    Major Prophets and, 47
    Minor Prophets and, 28, 33–35, 68, 100–101
    outline of, 11, 41–43, 46, 50–51, 66, 79–80, 96, 116–17, 136, 149–51
    as rhetorical discourse, 27–28, 35–41, 53–55, 67, 98, 118, 126, 154
    structure of, 39–41, 49–52, 65–67, 77, 95–97, 115–18, 135–37, 148–52
    superscription, 45–47
    translation of, 21–25
justice, retributive, 156, 166–67. *See also* divine judgment

lament, calls to, 31, 55–62
land, fertility of, 34–35, 73–74, 93, 114, 120–30, 143, 163
law of retribution, 156, 166–67
lex talionis, 156, 166–67
locusts
    call to community, 48–63
    call to drunkards, 55–56
    call to farmers, 58
    call to fast, 59–61, 105
    call to lament, 55–62
    call to priests, 58–61
    call to rejoice, 122–26
    call to wail, 56–58
    canonical significance of, 61–63, 129–33
    community role and, 63
    crisis of, 52–55
    deliverance from, 23, 113–33
    despair and, 21, 48–63
    explanation of, 52–55, 118–29
    generational instruction for, 61–63
    literary context and, 48–49, 113–14
    literary form and, 49–52, 115–18
    locust army invasion, 77–78, 83–90, 114, 121–24, 141–42
    outline of, 50–51, 116–17
    practical significance of, 61–63, 129–33
    summary of, 61
    victims of, 86–87
    voice of lament, 62

Lord. *See also* God; YHWH
    deliverance in day of, 13, 27–43, 139–45
    Jesus Christ as, 168
    terms for, 12

Major Prophets, 47
merismus, 37, 40, 60, 106, 119–21, 125, 139–40, 163, 169
Minor Prophets, 28, 33–35, 68, 100–101
outlines
    of deliverance, 116–17, 136, 149–51
    of despair, 96
    of divine judgment, 149–51
    of drought, 66, 116–17
    of hinge, 96
    of invasion, 79–80
    of *Joel*, 11, 41–43
    of locusts, 50–51, 116–17
    of spirit, 136
    of superscription, 46

paradise
    hope of, 41, 93, 124
    promise of, 168–70
    return to, 124, 168–70
    transformation from, 84–85, 93
plowshares, 24, 158, 167–68
poetic justice, 29, 121, 156, 166–67
priests, call to, 58–61

recursion technique, 38, 41
rejoice, calls to, 122–26
repentance, call to, 34, 98–101, 130
restoration
    calls to rejoice, 122–26
    promises of, 27–41, 45, 48, 54, 61–62, 68–70, 91–93, 98–111, 114–31, 134–57, 162–70
    summary of, 166
retribution, law of, 156, 166–67
rhetorical discourse, 27–28, 35–41, 53–55, 67, 98, 118, 126, 154

spirit
    call to repentance, 130
    canonical significance of, 142–45
    deliverance through, 24, 134–45

Subject Index

explanation of, 138–42
gift of, 120, 126, 130, 138–45
Holy Spirit, 143–44
literary context and, 134–35
literary form and, 135–37
outline of, 136
practical significance of, 142–45
promise of, 138–44
of YHWH, 24, 134–45
superscription
explanation of, 45–47
literary context of, 45–46
literary form of, 46–47
outline of, 46
structure of, 46–47
swords, 24, 158, 167–68

Tetragrammaton, 11–12
theophany, 67, 83, 86, 89, 91
trustworthiness, 101–2, 111–12, 132–33, 162

wail, call to, 56–58
woe, 92, 110–11, 169. *See also* doom
"word of YHWH," 21–22, 35, 45–47, 98

"Yahweh," 12. *See also* YHWH

YHWH. *See also* God
announcement of day of, 22–25, 67–72, 81–83, 89–93, 137, 139–42
appeal to, 40–41, 48–49, 60–67, 70–71, 94–9, 104–9, 114, 159–60
call to return to, 23, 32–34, 40, 94–112, 141–42, 166
character of, 13, 27, 35, 94–112, 119
compassion of, 23, 41, 99, 103–19, 122–33, 154
crying to, 72–73, 94–112
deliverance in day of, 13, 27–43, 139–45
despair in day of, 13, 21–22, 27–43, 45–49, 64–66, 75–93, 115, 135, 148
effects of day of, 69–70
explanation about, 11–12
hinge and, 23, 40, 94–112, 141–42, 166
plan of return to YHWH, 105–8
presence of, 29–32, 41, 62, 68, 83, 89–93, 114, 118, 128–32, 135–43, 147, 157–70
restoration promises, 27–41, 45, 48, 54, 61–62, 68–70, 91–93, 98–111, 114–31, 134–57, 162–70
return to, 23, 32–34, 40, 92–112, 130–31, 141–42, 166
spirit of, 24, 134–45
trustworthiness of, 101–2, 111–12, 132–33, 162
word of, 21–22, 35, 45–47, 98
zeal of, 41, 126, 129, 131–33
Zion and, 22–25, 30–41, 45–48, 75–93, 108–9, 140–42

zeal, 41, 126, 129, 131–33
Zion
assault on, 75–93, 120, 134
children of, 30, 122–26
day of YHWH and, 22–25, 75–93, 140–42
downfall of, 89
existence of, 81–82
gates of, 78
imagery of, 91, 169
inhabitants of, 87–91
invasion and, 75–93
inviolability of, 81–82, 141, 161–62, 169
as sacred mountain, 32, 81, 141, 168
security in, 81–82, 86, 93, 140–42, 161–62, 169
walls of, 30, 86–89
YHWH and, 22–25, 30–41, 45–48, 75–93, 108–9, 140–42

Author Index

Ahlström, Gosta W., 60, 87, 98, 137, 141, 165
Allen, Leslie, 39, 83, 85, 89, 95, 99, 106, 109, 114, 120, 125, 130, 137, 138, 155, 162, 163, 165, 167
Alter, Robert, 83
Anderson, G., 67
Andiñach, Pablo R., 53
Archer, Gleason, 28
Arnold, Bill T., 77
Assis, Elie, 29, 55, 58, 69, 71, 76, 83, 84, 85, 87, 89, 93, 95, 99, 106, 107, 113, 124, 126, 130, 131, 138, 139, 155, 157, 162, 164
Aucker, W. Brian, 30
Augustine, 121
Austin, J. L., 111

Baker, David W., 91, 92, 132
Barker, Joel, 13, 33, 36, 108
Barton, John, 35, 59, 77, 82, 83, 85, 87, 88, 95, 103, 107, 108, 119, 129, 152, 156, 165
Beal, Timothy K., 68
Beale, Gregory K., 168, 170
Bechtel, Lyn M., 99, 100
Beck, Astrid, 99, 147
Bellis, Alice Ogden, 60
Ben Zvi, Ehud, 35
Bendor, Shunya, 139
Bergler, Siegfried, 88, 140
Bergmann, Claudia D., 86
Bitzer, Lloyd F., 36
Black, Matthew, 32
Blenkinsopp, Joseph, 137
Block, Daniel I., 12, 13, 31, 34, 57, 139, 143, 144, 147, 164

Boadt, Lawrence, 125
Boda, Mark J., 33, 57, 70, 101, 103, 104, 123, 148, 164
Bolin, Thomas M., 109
Borowski, Oded, 126
Brueggemann, Walter, 62, 119, 137

Campbell, Ken M., 57
Cazelles, Henri, 120
Chance, John K., 100
Childs, Brevard S., 121
Chisholm, Robert B., 76, 82, 144
Choi, John H., 77
Claasen, W., 32
Clark, Gordon R., 103, 104
Clendenen, E. Ray, 100, 101
Clifford, Richard J., 81, 82
Clines, David J. A., 57
Coats, George W., 46
Coggins, Richard J., 35, 63, 125, 160
Cohen, Raymond, 167
Conrad, Edgar, 123
Cook, Stephen L., 164
Cowley, A. E., 165
Credner, K., 28
Crenshaw, James L., 29, 39, 53, 56, 57, 59, 71, 76, 78, 82, 84, 85, 86, 88, 89, 95, 99, 101, 103, 104, 108, 119, 120, 121, 123, 126, 127, 128, 138, 141, 142, 154, 155, 156, 158, 162, 163, 165
Crüsemann, Frank, 123

De Moor, Johannes C., 62
De Vries, Simon J., 137, 163
DeCaen, Vincent, 85
Deist, Ferdinand, 32, 114, 122, 158

Dempsey, Carol J., 101, 123, 164
Dempster, Stephen, 13
Deutsch, Richard R., 32, 54, 84, 128, 153
Di Giulio, Marco, 67
Dillard, Raymond B., 47, 48, 55, 57, 58, 64, 86, 87, 90, 95, 104, 120, 125, 126, 127, 128, 137, 138, 143, 144, 153, 154, 159, 163
Dille, Sarah J., 86
Dow, Lois, 169
Dozeman, Thomas B., 103
Duhm, Bernard, 29, 31

Everson, A. Joseph, 68

Falk, Daniel K., 57
Fassberg, Steven Ellis, 85
Fields, Weston W., 82
Finley, Thomas J., 95, 137
Firth, David G., 135, 143
Fishbane, Michael, 82, 104, 109, 170
Flesher, Leanne Snow, 123, 164
Floyd, Michael H., 70, 148
Fox, Michael V., 27
Futato, Mark D., 125

Ganzel, Tova, 29
Garr, W. Randall, 85
Garrett, Duane A., 32, 52, 107, 165
Gitin, Seymour, 85
Grabbe, Lester L., 60
Greenspoon, Leonard, 161

Hahn, F., 141
Halpern, Baruch, 161
Haran, Menahem, 60
Hayes, John H., 81

Author Index

Hayes, Katherine M., 57, 58, 73
Hoffman, Yair, 67
Hoftijzer, Jakob, 85
Holladay, William L., 102
Hopfe, Lewis M., 99
Hoppe, Leslie J., 170
Houston, Walter, 111
Humbert, Paul, 119
Hurowitz, Victor, 59
Hurvitz, Avi, 85

Jemielity, Thomas, 55
Jeremias, Jorg, 141
Joosten, Jan, 118, 119
Joüon, Paul, 85, 124, 127

Kang, Sa Moon, 155
Kapelrud, Arvid S., 28, 84, 120, 126
Kaufman, Stephen A., 85
Kautzch, E., 165
Kelly, Joseph, 109
Kessler, John A., 89, 161
Khan, Geoffrey, 53, 67, 84
Klein, Ralph W., 83
Kovacs, Brian W., 120
Kroeze, Jan H., 56, 119

Laato, Antii, 62
Landy, Francis, 35
LeCureux, Jason T., 102, 103
Levenson, Jon D., 161
Lewis, C. S., 111
Lim, Timothy H., 30
Linafelt, Tod, 68
Linville, James R., 30, 60, 76, 90, 106
Loewenstamm, Samuel E., 91
Long, Burke O., 46
Longman, Tremper, III, 161
Luria, Ben Zion, 163
Lyons, Michael A., 147

Magonet, Jonathan, 109
Marcus, David, 138
McComiskey, Thomas E., 47
McConville, J. Gordon, 33

McDowell, Catherine L., 74
Merx, A., 115
Meyers, Carol L., 82
Meyers, Eric M., 82
Middleton, J. Richard, 74
Milik, T., 163
Miller, Patrick D., 159, 166
Möller, Karl, 36
Moo, Douglas J., 131
Moo, Jonathan A., 131
Moore, Erika, 134–35
Moshavi, Adina, 53, 69, 155
Mowinckel, Sigmund, 67
Muraoka, T., 85
Myers, Jacob M., 29

Nash, Kathleen S., 55, 58, 127
Naudé, Jacobus A., 56, 119
Nogalski, James, 29, 31, 32, 33, 34, 35, 39, 45, 68, 73, 92, 93, 98, 109, 118, 130, 148, 167, 169

O'Connor, Michael, 76, 88
Ogden, Graham S., 32, 54, 84, 99, 128, 153
Olbrechts-Tyteca, L., 55
Ollenburger, Ben C., 81, 169

Perdue, Leo, 120
Perelman, Chaim, 55
Petersen, David L., 34
Plöger, Otto, 141
Poulsen, Frederik, 91, 141, 169
Prinsloo, Willem S., 29, 30, 32, 48, 54, 57, 58, 95, 97, 122, 128, 129, 139, 141, 142, 157

Raabe, Paul R., 147, 154, 156
Raitt, Thomas, 98
Redditt, Paul, 33, 98, 141
Reid, Daniel G., 161
Reimer, David James, 35, 120
Rendtorff, Rolf, 68, 72
Rezetko, Robert, 30
Rosenberg, D., 99
Roth, Cecil, 125
Rudman, S., 141

Sandy, D. Brent, 36
Schafer, A. Rahel, 70
Schart, Aaron, 33, 160
Seitz, Christopher R., 57, 69, 76, 83, 84, 101
Sellers, O. R., 54, 125
Sellin, E., 122
Shapiro, H., 99
Simkins, Ronald A., 54, 55, 56, 57, 58, 59, 69, 70, 71, 77, 84, 87, 90, 95, 99, 121, 125, 127, 153, 158–59, 165
Smalley, William A., 32
Smith, Gordon T., 101
Smith, Mark S., 125
Snijders, L., 162
Sokoloff, Michael, 85
Stephenson, F. R., 29
Stiebert, Johanna, 100
Strazicich, John, 30, 47, 81, 88, 101, 113, 138, 139, 140, 141, 143, 153, 163, 170
Stuart, Douglas, 28, 39, 53, 54, 55, 67, 75
Sweeney, Marvin A., 34, 45, 46, 52, 57, 58, 63, 68, 81, 90, 95, 120, 125, 141, 156, 157, 160, 163

Thompson, John A., 32, 54, 129, 138
Thurén, Lauri, 37
Timmer, Daniel, 155
Toffelmire, Colin M., 70, 148, 152
Tooman, William A., 147
Tov, Emanuel, 82
Treier, Daniel J., 144
Treves, Marco, 29
Troxel, Ronald L., 31, 107, 113, 137, 140, 141, 142
Tucker, Gene M., 46

Van Dam, Cornelius, 52
Van der Merwe, Christo H. J., 46, 49, 54, 56, 59, 61, 67, 68, 70, 71, 84, 85, 87, 88, 89, 97, 119, 154
Van Pelt, Miles, 13
VanGemeren, Willem A., 135, 137
Vernes, Maurice, 32
Von Rad, Gerhard, 67

Wagner, S., 140

Waltke, Bruce, 76, 88
Watts, John D. W., 45, 46
Wegner, Paul D., 135, 143
Wendland, Ernst R., 36, 40, 46, 48, 49, 54, 56, 59, 61, 67, 68, 70, 71, 77, 84, 85, 87, 88, 89, 91, 97, 98, 118, 129, 152, 157, 159, 167

Werline, Rodney, 57
Westbook, Raymond, 167
White, Eugene E., 36
Whitley, Charles Francis, 120
Williamson, H. G. M., 167
Wolff, Hans W., 32, 52, 55, 60, 76, 83, 98, 102, 115, 122, 125, 129, 132, 137, 138, 141, 152, 158–59

Yates, Gary E., 98
Youngblood, Kevin J., 110

Zevit, Ziony, 85

Zondervan Exegetical Commentary on the Old Testament

Obadiah

A Discourse Analysis of
the Hebrew Bible

Daniel I. Block

With careful discourse analysis and interpretation of the Hebrew text, the authors of the Zondervan Exegetical Commentary on the Old Testament series trace the flow of argument in each Old Testament book, showing that *how* a biblical author says something is just as important as *what* they say.

Responding to the spiritual and theological crisis created by the disaster of 586 BC, Obadiah sought to rekindle the hope of his countrymen with two principal points. First, *divine justice will prevail* with respect to Israel's kinsmen the Edomites, who had gloated over Judah's fall. Second, *divine fidelity will prevail* with respect to descendants of Jacob themselves, presently dispersed among the nations and divorced from their homeland.

Available in stores and online!

Zondervan Exegetical Commentary on the Old Testament

Jonah

A Discourse Analysis of the Hebrew Bible

Kevin J. Youngblood

With careful discourse analysis and interpretation of the Hebrew text, the authors of the Zondervan Exegetical Commentary on the Old Testament series trace the flow of argument in each Old Testament book, showing that *how* a biblical author says something is just as important as *what* they say.

In the book of Jonah, two problems keep the prophet from fully enjoying and freely sharing divine mercy. The first is Jonah's inability to reconcile YHWH's concern for nations hostile to Israel with his election of Israel. The second is Jonah's inability to reconcile YHWH's justice with his mercy. The narrative's conclusion reveals an even deeper problem: a distorted understanding of both divine election and divine justice.

Available in stores and online!

Zondervan Exegetical Commentary on the Old Testament

Ruth

A Discourse Analysis of the Hebrew Bible

Daniel I. Block

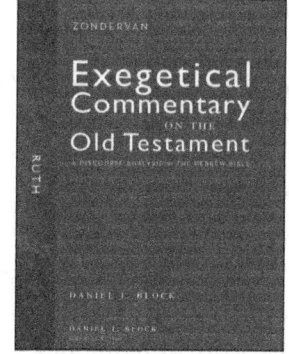

With careful discourse analysis and interpretation of the Hebrew text, the authors of the Zondervan Exegetical Commentary on the Old Testament series trace the flow of argument in each Old Testament book, showing that *how* a biblical author says something is just as important as *what* they say.

Ruth is widely recognized as a superlative literary achievement of ancient Israel. With its sensitive portrayal of women in crisis, its admiration for a righteous man, and its profound theology of providence it offers hearers in every age a window into life in the ancient Near East, inspiration for good and godly living, and reason to wonder at the common roots of Israel's royal and messianic hope. Bridging the historical and theological gap between Judges and Samuel, the book of Ruth explains specifically first how David, the most important character in the Hebrew Bible, could emerge from the spiritual and ethical morass of the premonarchic period, and second to account for the Moabite blood in this king's veins.

Available in stores and online!

Zondervan Exegetical Commentary on the Old Testament

Nahum

A Discourse Analysis of the Hebrew Bible

Daniel C. Timmer

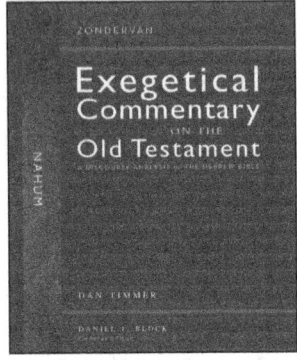

With careful discourse analysis and interpretation of the Hebrew text, the authors of the Zondervan Exegetical Commentary on the Old Testament series trace the flow of argument in each Old Testament book, showing that *how* a biblical author says something is just as important as *what* they say.

The Zondervan Exegetical Commentary on the Old Testament series is the go-to resource for pastors and Bible teachers looking for deep but accessible study that equips them to connect the needs of Christians today with the biblical text.

Available in stores and online!